China's Financial Opening

The twenty-first century has not only seen China become one of the world's largest trading nations, but also its gradual integration into the global financial system. Chinese-sponsored project financing schemes, such as the Belt-and-Road Initiative and the Asian Infrastructure Investment Bank, and the expanding international footprint of the renminbi, have raised the specter of Beijing shaping established market rules and practices with its financial firepower. These dramatic developments beyond the "Great Wall of Money" have overshadowed the equally remarkable opening of China's domestic capital markets. These include initiatives that make cross-border equity trade and investment easier; attempts to internationalize exclusively domestic-oriented equity markets; and creation of the first offshore renminbi hub in Hong Kong, paving the way for the "big bang" of renminbi use worldwide.

Li interrogates the domestic political dynamics underlying the dizzying switches between liberalization and restriction. This book argues that the interplay between the pro-opening coalitions and dissenting parties has been central to the policymaking process. Financial opening has not only been driven by central bureaucratic actors, but also by financial industry interests and the local authorities of financial centers acting in concert as coalitions. The local and financial constituents have shaped policy agendas and priorities, and defined and framed liberalizing initiatives in ways that appealed to bureaucratic entities. They also sought wider political support by capitalizing on connections with top decision-making elites. To allay opposition and maintain political and technical consensus, the coalition constituents have offered concessions to dissenting parties over implementation specifics. This, however, has not always succeeded. Dissenting parties who recognized adverse distributional and policy risk implications inherent in the opening initiatives might decline concessionary offers, leading to policy tendencies other than opening.

As one of the very first political economy contributions to studies of China's financial opening from the 2000s, this book will appeal to researchers of international political economy, East Asia and China specialists, and financial practitioners and policymakers wanting to make sense of the country's liberalizing logic.

Yu-Wai Vic Li is an assistant professor in the Department of Social Sciences at the Education University of Hong Kong. He specializes in international political economy and focuses on China's financial opening and renminbi internationalization, and the East Asian politics of financial regulation since the 2008 crisis.

Routledge Contemporary China Series

For our full list of available titles: www.routledge.com/Routledge-Contemporary-China-Series/book-series/SE0768

China's Financial Opening
Coalition Politics and Policy Changes

Yu-Wai Vic Li

Routledge
Taylor & Francis Group

LONDON AND NEW YORK

First published 2018 by Routledge

2 Park Square, Milton Park, Abingdon, Oxfordshire OX14 4RN

52 Vanderbilt Avenue, New York, NY 10017

Routledge is an imprint of the Taylor & Francis Group, an informa business

First issued in paperback 2019

British Library Cataloguing-in-Publication Data
A catalogue record for this book is available from the British Library

Library of Congress Cataloging-in-Publication Data
Names: Li, Yu-Wai Vic, author.
Title: China's financial opening : coalition politics and policy changes / Yu-Wai Vic Li.
Description: Abingdon, Oxon ; New York, NY : Routledge, 2018. | Series: Routledge contemporary China series | Includes bibliographical references and index.
Identifiers: LCCN 2017055960| ISBN 9781138727540 (hardback) | ISBN 9781315190792 (e-book)
Subjects: LCSH: Finance–Government policy–China. | China–Economic policy–2000– | China–Politics and government–2002–
Classification: LCC HG187.C6 L52725 2018 | DDC 332.0951–dc23
LC record available at https://lccn.loc.gov/2017055960

ISBN: 978-1-138-72754-0 (hbk)
ISBN: 978-0-367-37568-3 (pbk)

Typeset in Galliard
by Wearset Ltd, Boldon, Tyne and Wear

To my parents and Ka Chuen

Contents

Illustrations

Figures

Tables

Acknowledgments

China's capital market developments always seem to be an enigma to many market participants inside and most observers outside the country. The problem goes beyond the challenge of understanding the Chinese language and deciphering the policy rhetoric of Chinese officialdom, and often has to do with the surprising decisions, and the unexpected turns of policy before implementation. This book aspires to disperse the fog that obscures the Great Wall of Money and illuminate the financial policymaking process. It centers on three aspects of China's financial opening, including the liberalization of the outbound equity investment regime, the attempts to internationalize the domestic stock market, and the emergence of an offshore renminbi center in Hong Kong.

The project stems from a pre-global crisis discussion I had in 2007 with my academic colleagues about the financial development of China. On the watchlist were several issues, but none of us had any sense of how they might unfold or how we might piece them together systematically. What happened then in the global capital market changed Chinese capital market development and the world. I hope this book represents a modest effort that contributes to the original dialogue by showing how the myriad developments of China's financial market might be made sense of.

Such a herculean task would not have been possible to complete without the intellectual support of my PhD supervisors, Derek Hall and Eric Helleiner, who have witnessed the project's gestation from the very beginning. They have unremittingly shared with me their deep and extensive knowledge of the literature, and provided me with incisive feedback on my writing. I must also thank the Balsillie School of International Affairs and Wilfrid Laurier University for the generous doctoral fellowships without which I would never have had the chance to savor a great Canadian education experience.

The Early Career Scheme grant (Project number: 28402114) of the Hong Kong Research Grant Council has made possible a more in-depth exploration of the initial project focus, a thorough revision of the writing, and the dissemination of the study to academic and policy audiences in conferences. Colleagues from the social sciences department at the Education University of Hong Kong, including Tweety Cheung, Daniel Wong, Daniel Yeung, Siwei Huang, and Vane Xu, have supplied their invaluable research assistance.

x *Acknowledgments*

As the chapters took (and retook) shape and the project was reformulated and refined, I have benefited from the insightful comments of Anton Malkin, Justin Robertson, Hyoung-kyu Chey, Marcus Chu, Shirley Lin, Harry Harding, Alfred Wu, Kevin Bo Miao, Dennis Hui, Sonny Lo, and Ming Chan. Wanxin Li, Paul Higgins, and Shiru Wang have kindly broadened my exposure to the literature of China studies and policy science. Alfred and Kevin were also instrumental in arranging a marvelous lineup of interviewees in China. I am also grateful for thoughtful suggestions about the project's analytical framework from the panelists and audiences of the International Studies Association conferences (Atlanta 2016 March; Hong Kong 2016 June, 2017 June), and International Asian Dynamics Initiative (ADI) Conference (Copenhagen 2016 June).

My thanks also go to the interviewees, who must stay anonymous due to the ethics of research. The financial regulators and central bank officials as well as local finance officials I have spoken to have been great hosts during my research visits and generously shared their insights on capital market development amid their tight schedules. Researchers at Tsinghua University and The Chinese Academy of Social Sciences, and the journalists of top financial media outlets brought erudite knowledge to every discussion. They represent the cream of an intellectual crop that the country's future could hinge on. They have contributed to my deeper understanding of the empirical contexts and reminded me of the complexities of understanding the country. As the usual caveat lector goes, all errors are mine.

Ka Chuen has flavored my many clueless hours of writing with humor I relished and with unstinting support during the many years since the start of the project. For us, the book represents a handsome end and marks the beginning of a new phase of life. Lastly, I hope this book provides some relief to my parents who have never questioned where their son's life is heading. Without their love and trust, very little could have been possible.

Abbreviations

ADB	Asian Development Bank
ADR	American Depository Receipt
BOC	Bank of China
BOCHK	Bank of China (Hong Kong)
BoCom	Bank of Communication
CAS	Chinese Accounting Standard
CBRC	China Banking Regulatory Commission
CDR	China Depository Receipt
CEPA	Closer Economic Partnership Arrangement
ChinaClear	China Securities Depository and Clearing Corporation
CICC	China International Capital Corporation
CIRC	China Insurance Regulatory Commission
CNH	Offshore renminbi
CNOOC	China National Offshore Oil Corporation
CNY	Onshore renminbi
CSRC	China Securities Regulatory Commission
ETF	Exchange-traded fund
EU	European Union
FDI	Foreign Direct Investment
FSDC	Financial Service Development Council
FTZ	Free Trade Zone
HKD	Hong Kong dollar
HKEx	Hong Kong Exchanges and Clearing Limited
HKMA	Hong Kong Monetary Authority
IFC	International Finance Corporation
IFI	International financial institution
IFRS	International Financial Reporting Standards
IMF	International Monetary Fund
IPE	International political economy
IPO	Initial public offering
ISDA	International Swaps and Derivatives Association
MOF	Ministry of Finance
NAFMII	National Association of Financial Market Institutional Investors

NDF	Non-deliverable forward
NDRC	National Development and Reform Commission
PBOC	People's Bank of China
QDII	Qualified Domestic Institutional Investor
QFII	Qualified Foreign Institutional Investor
OTC	Over-the-counter
OTCBB	Over-the-Counter Bulletin Board
RMB	Renminbi
RQFII	Renminbi Qualified Foreign Institutional Investor
SAFE	State Administration of Foreign Exchange
SEHK	Hong Kong Stock Exchange
SEZ	Special Economic Zone
SFC	Securities and Futures Commission
SHIBOR	Shanghai Interbank Offered Rate
SMEB	Small and Medium Enterprises Board
SOE	State-owned enterprise
SSE	Shanghai Stock Exchange
SZSE	Shenzhen Stock Exchange
TMA	Treasury Market Association
WTO	World Trade Organization

1 Introduction

The analytical puzzle

China's financial opening is one of the few issues that generates unflagging interest from policy communities, academic researchers, and market professionals. The twenty-first century has not only seen China become one of the world's largest trading nations, but also its gradual integration into the global financial system. In recent years, Chinese-sponsored project financing schemes (such as, for example, the Belt-and-Road Initiative and the Asian Infrastructure Investment Bank) and the expanding international footprint of the renminbi have raised the specter of Beijing beginning to reshape established market rules and practices with its recently acquired massive financial firepower (Subramanian 2011a, 2011b; Overholt, Ma, and Law 2016; Subacchi 2016).

These dramatic developments beyond the "Great Wall of Money" have overshadowed the equally remarkable opening-up of China's domestic capital markets.[1] This included, but was not limited to, initiatives to make cross-border equity trade and investment easier, attempts to internationalize exclusively domestic-oriented equity markets (which would transform Shanghai into China's international financial center), and the creation of the first offshore renminbi hub in Hong Kong, which paved the way for the "big bang" of renminbi use worldwide.

Although existing studies have examined these market developments and attempted to unpick the underlying political forces, the research has not adequately explained a paradox that has emerged: despite Beijing's commitment to achieving financial openness, the rhetoric has not always been matched by concrete policy action; supportive signals have been quickly followed by disavowals and resistance by the same government. Seemingly concrete promises have been retracted, delayed, or watered down. Such "on-again" and "off-again" liberalizing trajectories have confused market participants and policy analysts, who have found China's positions inconsistent, if not entirely incomprehensible.

This book interrogates the domestic political dynamics that have lain beneath the dizzying switches between liberalization and restriction. It explains China's financial opening policy changes by revealing the coalition politics and extensive lobbying of policy actors drawn from well beyond the central financial bureaucracy and top decision-making elites. These have included movers from the local authorities of financial centers and financial industry interests, who have peddled policy initiatives and preferences critical to the origination, deliberation, and implementation of central mandates. The book shows the complexity of the interplay between the multitude of domestic constituents and conceptualizes three mechanisms of policy change—agenda-setting politics, leverage politics, and concessionary politics—to examine China's liberalizing trajectory.

These different actors depended on each other and acted in concert as a pro-opening coalition of the liberalizing initiatives. By shaping the policy agenda, capitalizing on connections with decision-making elites, and extending concessionary offers to dissenting parties, the coalition and its constituents sought political support and attempted to drive and sustain opening tendencies.

The findings of this book might surprise scholars that have stressed the domination of central government and party machinery. This book shows that their positions and decisions have not been as impermeable to actors from outside Beijing as was once thought. It reveals that local and financial industry interests often posed as allies of the center and thereby ensured the successful execution of the liberalizing initiatives. These findings might challenge researchers that have previously seen changes of international financial and economic conditions as the direct cause of Chinese policy shifts. This book argues that, while external crisis led to both aversion and openness in some instances, local, central, and industry agents also exploited circumstances to further their own political economic agendas.

The following sections review different clusters of scholarship on financial opening and surveys their underlying political economic determinants, together with the historical context of China's financial opening before the mid-2000s. A synopsis of the argument and analytical framework of the book follows. The chapter finishes with a discussion of theoretical and policy significance, research design, and methodological considerations.

Financial liberalization and opening: a note on terms

Financial liberalization, in a general sense, refers to a "transition away from a financial system characterized by state intervention and ownership and toward a more market-oriented system" (Rancière, Tornell, and Westermann 2008). It consists of two main dimensions: deregulation of domestic capital market and capital account liberalization. The former is often known as internal liberalization, where the state loosens its reins governing the domestic financial market, especially controls over economic parameters such as interest rates. International, or external financial liberalization, reduces the state's control of capital flows between the domestic economy and global capital market, and often involves exchange rate reform toward market-based pricing together with an increase in the presence of foreign financial actors (Auerbach 2009).

Financial liberalization, however, has sometimes been used interchangeably with "financial internationalization," for which there remains no uniform definition. Some have defined it synonymously with liberalization (Haggard and

Maxfield 1996), while others have focused on the internationalization of financial services and an increasing presence and involvement of foreign financial institutions within a domestic economy, excluding the dismantling of capital control and restrictions on currency convertibility (Schlichting 2008).

Financial globalization, on the other hand, has been seen as a term bracketing these multiple processes and stressing the transnational and interconnected nature of the global financial market, particularly the integration of a country's local financial system with international markets and institutions, and different asset markets (Prasad, Rogoff, and Wei 2009: 9). Accordingly, the idea has come to incorporate elements of external liberalization and the internationalization of capital markets. These shifting interpretations have generated confusion within the literature, and their meanings have largely depended on research focus and context.

This study concerns developments more specific than hazy notions of globalization or internationalization. To ensure consistency and clarity, references to "financial liberalization" in this book refer to both internal and external aspects, and the terms "financial opening" and "capital market opening" are used to characterize the latter dimension, specifically capital transactions that involve inbound and outbound capital flows in the financial market. This includes the purchase, sale, and issuance of capital and money market instruments by both residents and non-residents.[2] Internationalization, by contrast, denotes both increasing capital mobility and the presence of foreign financial institutions and capital in China.

The political origins of China's financial opening in perspective

Several strands of scholarship of international political economy (IPE) and China studies have analyzed factors important to the driving of China's financial opening and the aspects that led to policy changes. Although the literature generates insights useful to the addressing of this research puzzle, it falls short of offering a complete understanding of the policy changes surrounding China's financial opening. Relevant works have tended to focus on particular policy outcomes, envisioning either a gradual opening driven by market forces, the perpetuation of financial repression, or a selective opening driven by "financial security" and the considerations of national competitiveness.

China specialists have also been confined by conceptions of financial repression, and have failed to appreciate the different policy possibilities beyond maintenance of the status quo. Attention to bureaucratic politics and financial industry interests makes room for expositions of policy changes previously under-appreciated in the literature. So, although existing studies do provide a useful starting point for analyzing domestic agents of change, accounts of China's financial opening are not complete without reference to the local authorities of domestic financial hubs. Rarely an integral part of the IPE literature, the omission engenders an incomplete understanding of the political dynamics.

External leverage as opening catalyst?

Many contributions to the study of capital account opening and regional political economy have highlighted the importance of market forces, politically powerful states, international financial institutions (IFIs), and neoliberal norms to the driving of financial openness (Goodman and Pauly 1993; Andrews 1994; Helleiner 1994; Laurence 2001; Woods 2006; Abdelal 2007). External crises have also been seen as catalysts of domestic financial reforms (MacIntyre, Pempel, and Ravenhill 2008; Martinez-Diaz 2009; Pepinsky 2012). However, these findings have not entirely proved the negligibility of the role of state authorities and domestic political economic dynamics, or successfully downplayed the importance of domestic institutional settings as a mediator for structural pressure toward market opening. The emphasis on external factors has also led to an overstatement of the degree of national policy convergence as countries have retained residual capital control and have unevenly adopted the international financial standards and practices expected by the IFIs and market players (Mosley 2003; Walter 2008).

In the Chinese context, although IFIs such as the World Bank were regarded by state authorities as important teachers during the early years of reform, their influence steadily declined and became confined to "selected technical" issues that fitted the country's development agenda (Bottelier 2007; Helleiner and Momani 2014). Despite the heightened anticipation for financial opening after WTO accession, barriers to foreign financiers and capital were maintained in the face of pressure from leading economies and IFIs (Calomiris 2007; Allen et al. 2013). The leverage of foreign actors has been uneven at best and dependent on their interplay with domestic firms and government agencies (Schlichting 2008). Unlike in its regional neighbors, financial crises have not galvanized much change in China's policy outlook. While it has embraced capitalist methods as drivers of growth and legitimacy, it has also sought insulation from financial reforms in defiance of neoliberal prescriptions (Wang 1999; Yang 2011, 2015).

The state as analytical focus

A different body of literature considers the state to be the main analytical focus, and has seen financial opening as an endogenous political choice at the nation-state level. Although external economic conditions and leverages might explain the "basic style" of financial opening, they have not been seen to adequately account for the timing and pace of reform or for residual capital controls left after opening, which have been primarily driven by key government and societal interests and their relative bargaining power toward foreign financiers, and have resulted in divergent styles of financial opening (Lukauskas and Minushkin 2000; Thurbon 2001).

China's gradualist (or experimentalist) approach to financial opening has justified its extensive capital control measures, which have been seen as shielding the country from the direct blows of external crises; moves toward full liberalization are expected only when domestic conditions mature. However, references relying on Beijing's choice of strategy overlook the interruptions and policy fluctuations that have not been unusual in the country's liberalizing trajectory. They have been by no means apolitical and cannot be fully understood without considering the domestic dynamics.

Other studies have related China's seemingly grudging opening to the central government's preoccupation with "financial security" (Yeung 2008). In the Chinese context, contingencies like large-scale financial crisis have carried significant political implications and have been weighed heavily by policymakers, particularly since the 1990s when reform-minded leaders witnessed the affliction of Asian economies. These considerations arguably motivated China's return to interventionism and the reversal of some of its liberalizing commitments after the subprime crisis, especially since that crisis has demonstrated the enormous risks associated with financial innovation (Wang 1999; Lo 2010: 148–53; Yang 2015). Financial security, however, has been at best an ill-defined concept, and has served to legitimize the state's unwillingness to reform by recasting finance as a national security issue (Yeung 2008).

By contrast, some analysts have seen China's financial integration as a political project driven by a party-state breaking ideological dogmas. In this view, through economic gains made by integrating with the global economy, the state has hoped to maintain legitimacy and political grip (Ploberger 2009). This, however, overlooks the domestic dynamics and the underlying choices of policy actors. Recent analyses of global and regional financial centers have similarly tended to see capital market opening as a means of enhancing the international competitiveness of the state and domestic financiers' interests (Jarvis 2011). While this assumption is sometimes true across national contexts, it views the quest for competitiveness as the predominant factor pushing financial opening and sees liberalization of different market domains as driven by a single motivation, overlooking domestic unravelings that involve different constellations of power.

The political logic of financial repression and selective opening

A different strand of literature explores the political logic behind the Chinese choice to maintain financial repression and pursue a selective opening. It can be said that China's control over interest rates and credit allocation has depressed growth in household incomes because it has deprived individuals of productive investment opportunities (Riedel, Jin, and Gao 2007: 71). Capital control also becomes necessary in regulating credit supply and growth and avoiding financial crises (Li 2001; Lardy 2008; Lo 2010).

This all suggests that financial liberalization is both economically and politically difficult, and opening can be at best incomplete. This also echoes the view that China's gradualist liberalizing policy has veiled the political survival concerns of the ruling elites who have sought to protect and distribute rents in "critical economic sectors." Reforms that strive for efficiency alone have not been viable because they might infringe the elites' interests. Consequently, reforms have been "bound to be partial, compromised, and ultimately ineffective" and the beneficiaries have had great incentive to maximize their own gains before the rent is dissipated (Goldstein 1995; Pei 2006: 96).

Other studies have turned to China's selective financial opening since the 2000s and argued that Beijing's deliberate control of its financial sector is intended to cushion the potential loss of the comparative advantage enjoyed by domestic interests during liberalization. Perhaps more importantly, the authorities have also striven to defend the high strategic value of the financial sector seen as crucial to national security. This has led to reinforcement of the state's authority, where the Chinese state exercises pervasive and thorough control of ownership and restriction of the business scope of foreign firms (Chan and Unger 1999; Hsueh 2011: chapter 8). These insights go some way to explaining the tension between China's quest for "reform and openness" and the state's intent to maintain the competitiveness of its domestic financial industry.

However, such an analysis of Beijing's regulatory approach to finance primarily examines the state's responses to foreign entry into the sector. Although it constitutes an important aspect of financial opening, it leaves the "endogenous" liberalizing choice pursued by domestic policy actors unaddressed. While China's financial opening may remain incomplete, "superficial," and constrained by the demands of constituents, the different liberalizing initiatives in equity markets and currency internationalization, not to mention the policy rhetoric, have indicated the state's intention to pursue financial opening. To fully make sense of these developments, the agents of change should all be considered.

Bureaucratic actors and financial interests as change agents

Among the different domestic change agents that have driven policy change and achieved occasional breakthroughs, bureaucratic and financial industry interests have drawn particular attention. IPE research has tended to see policy elites as the primary movers of banking sector opening and the adoption of international financial standards (Pauly 1988; Singer 2007; Walter 2008; Helleiner and Pagliari 2011: 177–81).

Studies of China's domestic financial reforms have delved into disagreements between bureaucratic actors. Green (2004) and Walter and Howie (2006) have seen reform of China's equity market as a political process driven by competing bureaucratic actors to create regulatory institutions and enact policies. Recent literature on renminbi internationalization has also considered the bureaucratic dynamics of the central authorities (e.g., Bell and Feng 2009; Pettis 2012; Yang 2014), and postulated that the process was driven by the pro-opening central bank to ward off opposition to reform from within the government while facilitating an "exit" from mercantilist policies. Likewise, Mallaby and Wethington (2012) have focused on the tension between reform-minded actors and conservatives, and argued that the cacophony from within the state has diminished political support for renminbi internationalization and resulted in policy incoherence.

More generally, Shih (2005, 2007) has extended public choice theories and proposed a political survival perspective of bureaucratic behavior. Officials who lead government agencies do not always avoid risks and uncertainties that might compromise their career stability. These officials are sometimes motivated to demonstrate policymaking competence to ensure their chances of staying in office and avoid any political competition. Policy change unfolds in a quasi-market setting, in which "producers" of policy initiatives (bureaucratic actors) compete for attention and the support of policy "consumers" (top decision-making elites including leaders of the State Council and Politburo – the top party organ). If policy producers find sponsors from consumers who believe that the policy initiatives are practicable fixes for pressing problems, the official and agency leading the effort gain attention from the top elites and have their political status heightened. Such dynamics within the bureaucracy result in occasional self-serving policy innovation and policy change pioneered by ministries or regulators.

Beyond government agencies, financial industry interests constitute another set of change agents that shape the course and outcomes of financial liberalization. Although industrialists and financiers were sometimes obstacles to capital market opening (Calder 1997; Woo-Cumings 1997), financial elites have employed liberalizing rhetoric to advance their parochial interests during financial opening (Perez 1997). Lobbying of New York based financiers was also critical to the establishment of the Federal Reserve that laid the foundation of the US dollar internationalization (Broz 1999).

This contrasts with the Chinese context, where the majority of money banks and concentrated financial institutions might have been better served by the financially repressed system. They were slated to gain disproportionately in a shielded, rather than an open, marketplace because of state control of interest rates and the political backing they relied on (Helleiner and Malkin 2012; Otero-Iglesias and Vermeiren 2015; Germain and Schwartz 2017). In other financial domains such as equity market opening, China's securities industry and exchange have not yet received the same level of attention as they have in the IPE literature (Sobel 1994; Lavelle 2001; Mosley and Singer 2008).

Authorities beyond the center: subnational governments

The trend toward examining the role of financiers' interests in the literature suggests the relevance of interest groups in policymaking even in an authoritarian setting like China. However, one important party that found access to policymaking is still curiously missing—the subnational authorities, who were particularly important in the context of financial opening that concerned the local governments of mainland financial hubs such as Shanghai, Tianjin, Shenzhen, and Beijing.

Indeed, the IPE scholarship of financial liberalization barely goes beyond the central level when looking at local and intergovernmental dynamics. This is partly understandable because of the dearth of connections between the IPE literature and studies of regional development (except Freire and Petersen 2004; Paul 2005). By contrast, Chinese specialists usually incorporate interaction between Beijing and local governments as an integral part of their analyses. The literature, however, is understandably inclined toward domestic policy issues like tax and fiscal reforms, and budget allocations between levels of government (Tsui and Wang 1994; Montinola, Qian and Weingast 1995; Ahlers and Schubert 2015), and it usually privileges the central government as the source of the political economic controls suffered by the lower authorities in the policymaking process (Chung 2015, 2016).

Nonetheless, the autonomy and maneuverability of local authorities remains controversial. Heilmann (2008, 2017a, 2017b) affirmed the role of localities as sites of policy experimentation that hosted new market practices, actors, and institutions. In this view, the specific forms of experiments depended on two major factors: the level of policy risk and the involvement of new actors in policymaking (Heilmann 2008). However, such a framework does not explain why a particular policy option was chosen over others when the feasible choices were all informed by a similar perception of risk. The framework also sees policy experiments as top-down processes in which lower-level governments have little control.

Indeed, most studies continue to assume central authorities played important roles in determining "the timing, pace and economic and spatial configuration" of domestic market development. Shanghai's ambition to become China's top financial center, for example, was derivative of the central government's development strategy at the local level. The city's financial ascent created tensions between national objectives and local needs and between market requirements and the practicalities of financial sector governance (Jarvis 2011: 73). However, such assessments privilege the central authorities and appear to circumscribe the influence of the subnational entities on policymaking.

This contrasts with contributions that examine the discretionary behavior of local authorities in the pursuit of investment liberalization in the early reform years. Even though the center has been seen as predominant in decision making, the local authorities still retained considerable discretion and maneuverability when dealing with the central authorities in the policymaking process (Yang 1997; Li 1998: 42–5; Zweig 2002; Chung 2016, 2017). To influence the policy agenda or seek support for their initiatives, local governments engaged in extensive bargaining throughout policy formation and deliberation before each policy was officially introduced. Local authorities also sought deviations in implementation that might give them leeway when interpreting and implementing central policies, especially when the details and particulars were vague or flexible (Li 1998: 42–3).

In other words, they could be the principals of their own interest, rather than just agents of the central authorities and representatives of the local public (Chung 2016). More importantly, as China has come to integrate with the global economy, the "ever-growing levels of global-local nexus have also expanded the realm where the local state could perform as a principal with its own strategic and entrepreneurial agenda, often bypassing the central state" (Chung 2016: 60). The policy initiatives and choices of the local states within China have had global echoes and ramifications (Antholis 2014).

It should be unsurprising to find similar dynamics in financial development and liberalization. As Xu (2009: 1) remarks,

> the central-local games determine the operation of the financial system. These games deeply affect the finance of most projects. Subnational governments' influences were prevalent and are not negligible in lending decisions of local branches of major banks; and they are important players of financial market regulation.

Indeed, since the early days of reform, local officials took the lead in fostering capital markets (e.g., local stock exchanges and derivative trading) for local economic interests before Beijing had a clear sense of how to regulate market activities. Local officials also pioneered various financial reforms in equity markets on a largely decentralized basis (Green 2004; Walter and Howie 2006).[3]

Once the regulatory strictures consolidated and local authorities could no longer pursue initiatives freely and were more dependent on the center's imprimatur, they turned to other channels of influence and employed strategies like creating local finance offices and calling on the influence of foreign financiers operating in the local markets. These locally initiated policy innovations were important in shaping the course of the larger financial reforms.

The decentralized policy tinkering, however, was not just a "freewheeling trial and error or spontaneous policy diffusion." Guided by purposeful local authorities, it generated policy solutions that were often incorporated into the national policy agenda and deliberations at the central level and were sometimes extended (Heilmann 2009: 458). This is best evidenced in the offshore renminbi product development which Chapter 5 examines. While the local authorities often sought to remove government restrictions and create a healthy environment for financial innovation, the center always insisted that such efforts should "not over-innovate in an irresponsible or excessive way" that might compromise the mainland's interests, even though the central authorities had continuously encouraged and supported the offshore community to get the renminbi "program to critical mass, circulation, liquidity and velocity" (Ramos, Fung and Buchanan 2010: 2). Analyses of the domestic politics of financial opening, therefore, are incomplete without considering the roles and effects of local players consequential to shaping the policy tendency and outcomes.

The dynamics of policy changes

In addition to discussion of the policy change agents, examination of the financial opening trajectories necessitates some examination of the various policymaking models set forth by China specialists. While none have examined financial opening specifically, they do provide frameworks for understanding the policy process and useful insights into the political context in which the different domestic constituents have interacted.

The early years of economic reform drew the attention of researchers to the central bureaucracy as the primary locus of political contention. The "fragmented authoritarianism" model argues that the advent of economic reform made the center's policymaking process more "malleable" to parochial organizations, various vertical agencies, and the regions in charge of enforcing that policy. Each possessed different kinds of resources (for instance factors of production, and market and technical information and know-how) essential to policy input and implementation (Lieberthal and Oksenberg 1988; Lampton and Lieberthal 1992). As the center no longer enjoyed an exclusive say, willingly or not it ceded political authority to lower-level governments; policy outcomes were formed by aggregating the interests of the implementation agencies into the policy process. This diffusion of power resulted in increasingly incoherent and disjointed policy formation and implementation (Shirk 1993: 116–7).

Accordingly, inter-unit bargaining between bureaucratic actors and central-local relations are both crucial to the understanding of policy outcomes (Shirk 1993: 116–7; Mertha 2009). This is especially the case for policy questions related to economic reforms that involved complex tradeoffs and that demanded mastery of technical information and expertise beyond that of the central government (Zhao 1995: 238–40; Heilmann 2017a: 41–3). However, though the model rightly emphasizes the importance of concession, compromise, and consensus building, it does not offer specific descriptions of motivations for pushing forward or resisting certain policy initiatives.

By contrast, the quasi-market model of policymaking, consisting of the policy-producing bureaucratic actors introduced earlier, generates important findings on policy changes (Shih 2005, 2007). A faction-based model centering on power struggles between the "generalist" and "specialist" has been advanced to make sense of the changing macroeconomic policies. In this model, while generalists have tended to favor credit expansion (given their relative power over local development), economic and financial specialists have sought to rein in inflation and maintain economic stability as evidence of their technocratic competence (Shih 2008). Although the dynamics between factions explains nicely the alternations of macroeconomic policy in the 1980s and 1990s, the model inevitably groups together financial policymakers of different bureaucratic portfolios as specialists, overlooking internecine rivalry and battles for the attention and support of the top-level decision makers.

More importantly, the model downplays the extensive input of financial industry interests and local authorities who found increasing access to and influence on the policymaking process. For example, they constituted important sources of policy advocacy, with central-level agendas increasingly originating from sources beyond the small decision-making circles, including think tanks, industry associations, and the general public (Wang 2008). Industry's preferences were also incorporated into the decision making of China's financial bureaucracy on important subjects such as exchange rates and monetary policies (Steinberg and Shih 2012; Bell and Feng 2013; Steinberg 2015). Overall, these studies have provided the insight and analytical underpinning to incorporate the different domestic change agents into a single picture, and made possible a better delineation of their preferences, collective pursuits, and their effect on policy tendencies and opening outcomes.

China's financial liberalization in retrospect

The three financial opening episodes on which this study centers are inseparable from a wider transition that took place over a three-decade period. A brief survey of China's twentieth-century experience of financial liberalization suggests a checkered and uneven process in which most of the efforts concentrated on refurbishing the domestic financial system and devising fixes to the many inherent problems. Despite China's subsequent integration into the global economy, notably marked by its accession to the WTO in 2001, the country is still far from being exposed to and shaped by external and market forces. Domestic actors have continued to retain considerable policy autonomy in shaping the trajectories and outcomes of China's financial liberalization.

The genesis of financial liberalization

The late 1970s marked the birth of the modern financial architecture of China, concurrent with the larger economic reforms unleashed by Deng Xiaoping. Open-door policies became the new hallmark of the country's development. Yet, in the beginning, the domestic capital market was virtually non-existent and access to capital markets and cross-border fund transfers was largely impossible. Despite the preponderance of Deng within the party-state, his agenda continued to meet the opposition of hardliners who had dramatically different views about the scope, pace, and goals of reform, and sought to perpetuate the planned economic system. To maintain the support of moderates and allay the conservatives, Deng unleashed a campaign in the early 1980s that targeted "bourgeois liberalism" and purported to defend the country's socialist ideology (Fewsmith 2008: 21–40).

Notwithstanding this ideological flux, the larger economic reform continued to be pushed through as Deng and his deputies outmaneuvered the conservatives by carefully navigating a middle course. The domestic capital market took off in the mid-1980s, kick-starting internal financial liberalization. Non-bank institutions like trust and investment companies blossomed, breaking the monopoly of the banking industry. Advocated by government economists, the privatization of state-owned enterprises (SOE) took off slowly (Pei 1998: 329–30).

Young professionals within the central bank (many of whom ascended to senior positions in the late 1990s) also publicly called for capital market development, including the establishment of a stock market and the public trading of shares (Branstetter 2007: 43–4). This encouraged the growth of unsanctioned, over-the-counter (OTC) exchanges of shares of joint-stock companies in dozens of cities like Shanghai and Shenzhen. In a complete absence of any regulatory framework, local governments competed to create local bourses to take advantage of the expansive financial gains derived from SOEs' shareholding reforms, in which they could cash out their holdings to investors (Walter and Howie 2001). In Shenzhen, the local government sanctioned the initial public offerings (IPO) of five SOEs in 1987. This ushered the country toward a first "stock fever." Hot money crept in from Hong Kong, often making handsome profits from the stock mania.

Policy reversal and a return to pragmatism

This local activism, however, soon met with significant challenges as the country went through political upheaval. The June 4th incident of 1989 stirred intense political debate within the party about capital market development. As in the early 1980s, conservative hardliners attempted to push back reforms, seeing the practices of capitalist economies as threats to the Communist orthodoxy, and thereby making the regime susceptible to the democratizing wave of the times (Huang 2008: chapters 2–3). To assuage these concerns, the government stepped up efforts to regulate capital market development. Decentralized local ventures were curbed and brought under the control of the central government. Stock exchanges were either incorporated into the party-state machinery like other financial institutions, or shut down. China's financial liberalization experienced retrenchment for the first time (Quintyn et al. 1996: 13).

The swing to conservativism at the center, however, frustrated Deng, who saw his open-door policy as in the best interests of China. Even though he had repeatedly spoken of the imperative of reform to the maintenance of the party's legitimacy, his advice was not heeded. To counteract the conservative backlash, Deng stepped in personally, bringing in reform-minded leaders with a track record of promoting financial reforms, like Zhu Rongji, into the top echelon of the government. (Vogel 2011: 665–7). He emphasized the core importance of finance to a modern economy and accordingly made it an important pillar of China's modernization. In a visit to Shanghai in February 1991, Deng (1993: 366–7) stressed that the city "was once a top financial hub where currency was freely convertible, and so would it be again in the future. China's international financial status would primarily depend on it."

This catalyzed the development of the Pudong District of Shanghai, where the financial industry is now concentrated, and paved the way for the city to become the country's leading financial center. The Shenzhen and Shanghai stock exchanges also began trading in November 1990 and February 1991, respectively. Deng's subsequent tour to Shenzhen and other southern cities in 1992 further consolidated the liberalizing outlook of the government. Deng warned that the country should "maintain vigilance against the right (i.e., capitalist practices), but primarily against the left" (Vogel 2011: 672–3). This charted and defined a middle course of economic and financial reforms for the country. Instead of lingering on ideological struggles, China would pursue a pragmatic outlook over policy experimentation.

This rekindled the stalled shareholding reforms and legitimized equity financing for companies (Zhao 1993). Outreach to the global capital market was made possible as overseas listing was approved. Thousands of Chinese companies raised capital in all the major financial centers worldwide after the first China-concept stock landed on the New York Stock Exchange in 1992. At the subnational level, local governments and budding financial industry interests in Shanghai and Shenzhen jockeyed to strengthen their niche as the financial centers of the country.

Most liberalizing efforts of the decade, however, concentrated on reforming the domestic banking system—still the mainstay of China's financial system. An extensive overhaul of the banking industry took place under Zhu's stewardship, cleaning up debt-stricken balance sheets (Pei 1998; Zweig 2001). To prepare for WTO accession, the 1990s saw gradual moves toward current account convertibility. Restrictions on trade-related transactions and foreign direct investment (FDI), which amounted to most of the capital inflow at the time, were abolished. The Jiang Zemin administration saw the bid for WTO membership as an important boost to the country's international status, a consolidation of Jiang's legitimacy within the party, and a cementing of his legacy as a great statesman (Liang 2002; Fewsmith 2008: 209–10). All this raised expectations that financial opening would be the centerpiece of his next stage of reforms.

Stagnant domestic financial liberalization

The Asian Financial Crisis of the late 1990s, however, dashed such hopes. While Beijing did recognize the imperative of accelerating financial reform, it also saw the virtue in maintaining a strict capital control regime. Dramatic capital outflow in expectation of currency devaluation during the crisis heightened the state's concerns about capital reversal and led to the enhanced screening of outgoing transactions (Steinfeld 2008; Naughton 1999; Wang 1999). This deepened the divisions within the government about the importance of financial opening and the wider WTO negotiations.

Unlike the previous decade that had witnessed the ideological divide between the left and right, the authorities confronted a split between the nationalists and new leftists, who strove to defend China's "economic sovereignty" and "financial security" and cautioned against financial opening, and reform-oriented pragmatists, who downplayed these concerns and sought to pursue domestic reform through tying the country to global market pressures (Fewsmith 2008: 212–23; Freeman III and Wen 2012).

Faced with strong opposition from the bureaucracy, there were few relaxations of capital controls imposed to shield China from the crisis. All foreign financial entities were barred from accessing the capital market. They could not issue, buy, or sell any bonds or shares. Beijing also appeared to feel reassured by the fact that important domestic banking reforms had been successfully achieved without much concomitant advance in financial opening. The disposal of non-performing loans through asset stripping had given rise to banks "investable" to foreign capital and ready for public listing without any easing of capital controls or the state's majority ownership (McGuinness and Keasey 2010).

Indeed, the new administration of Hu Jintao and Wen Jiabao did little to carry forward their predecessors' legacy of reform as they faced resistance from domestic financiers and industrialists. Even though China's entry to the WTO raised hopes of liberalizing the financial system, internal opening stagnated and the state's control over domestic capital markets remained tight (Fewsmith 2008: 258–67). For example, interest rate liberalization has been on the government's agenda since the early 2000s, but owing to the dissent of state-owned banks, little progress has been made throughout the decade (Feyzioğlu et al. 2009: 16). Domestic capital market development similarly suffered.

Repeated calls to expand financing channels for private enterprises were not entertained by the government, which regarded the banking industry and credit provision to state-owned sectors as its primary concerns. Capital access was improved slightly only after two specialized platforms for small and medium enterprises and high-tech firms were founded on the Shenzhen stock exchange in 2004 and 2009 (Allen et al. 2013: 98–100). As a result, informal finance proliferated in the face of a larger financial system unable to meet the capital demand of the non-state economic sector (Tsai 2002; Li and Hsu 2009). Some companies sought exits through overseas listings. Among them were China's internet startups, who found their places on global platforms like NASDAQ (Zhang and King 2010).

Painstaking attempts at financial opening

In contrast to the internal opening, the 2000s saw uneven advances made in the external aspect of financial liberalization. Entry and ownership restrictions imposed on foreign financial institutions were gradually lifted. Overseas banks, securities, and insurance firms were able to establish a presence in China by setting up subsidiaries and joint ventures (Langlois 2001). China's commitment to financial services opening, however, did not translate into the substantial easing of capital controls that many longed for.

Indeed, although central bank officials spoke of achieving full convertibility of the renminbi within five years of joining the WTO,[4] others within the bureaucracy remained wary of the entry and exit of capital for both individuals and institutional investors, and the expected timeframe for achieving currency convertibility was not realized. Equity markets were selectively opened to foreign investors through the Qualified Foreign Institutional Investors (QFII) scheme for designated overseas investors in 2002. However, as China's securities regulators explained, the country's promises to open the industry to foreign firms, a kind of service trade governed by the agreement with the WTO, had no connection to the securities market opening that entailed capital flows under the IMF's purview.[5] Such differences arguably help explain why the country has been able to withstand and deflect the pressures from foreign financiers and IFIs, and to introduce liberalizing moves under its own will and at its own pace.

Beyond the selectively open equity market, other domains of the financial market were largely inaccessible to non-local participants for most of the 2000s. The large bond and derivatives market kept foreign firms at bay with prolonged licensing processes and provisos that restricted the scope of business activities. The onshore currency market, given the inconvertibility of the renminbi, was largely segregated from the rapidly growing offshore market anchored in Hong Kong, and its development was closely guided by the state authorities. Further, investors within and without China continued to be segregated as they traded on separate platforms and experienced the different political economies of the two markets (Allen et al. 2013).

The three cases of financial opening

This book centers on three distinct but related episodes of financial opening that unfolded in the early twenty-first century. Two cases are related to equity market liberalization and one is related to currency internationalization. Their policy trajectories have had a checkered journey, and the processes were not solely a product of power plays at the central level. Constituents at financial industry and local levels also found access to, and interacted with, central bureaucratic actors at different stages of the policymaking.

The first two episodes involve the evolution of the outbound equity investment regime and initiatives that promoted the internationalization of China's securities market. They illustrate the dramatic vicissitudes of China's policymaking. Liberalizing initiatives were announced but subsequently experienced protracted delays or were even overturned. Commitments to dismantle regulatory controls appeared weak and considerable policy barriers remained. The arrangements finally arrived at barely resemble the initial plans of the policy advocates, let alone serve the needs of investors. Investors once lured by promising market opportunities have been frustrated by competing policy signals and analysts have been puzzled by a seemingly indecipherable Chinese policy logic.

Liberalization of the outbound investment regime began in the early 2000s, championed by the offshore community in Hong Kong. An institutional channel, the Qualified Domestic Institutional Investors (QDII) program, was created in 2006 and allowed for domestic financial institutions to invest abroad. This galvanized the premature "Through Train" scheme in 2007 that would have permitted direct individual investment in overseas equity markets (primarily Hong Kong). Pioneered by the offshore community in conjunction with Tianjin, a leading state-owned bank, and the country's foreign reserve manager, the State Administration of Foreign Exchange (SAFE), the world anticipated a prompt launch soon after the initiative was officially announced.

To the surprise of many, the Through Train never departed and was canceled within months as China faced looming domestic and external credit crises. The Through Train idea was then scrapped and taken over by a tightly regulated scheme of overseas Exchange Trade Funds (ETF) that tracked foreign securities made available in the domestic market. The liberalizing tendency that eased outbound investment resumed its pace only after late 2014, when the much expected "Stock Connects" between Hong Kong and the Shanghai and Shenzhen stock markets were introduced.

In the mid-2000s, Shanghai-based interests proactively reasserted their international status and centered on the pursuit of an "international board" to promote the internationalization of their local stock exchange. It was hoped the listing of foreign firms, especially prominent multinationals, would burnish the city's global standing. The idea was backed by China's securities regulator that recognized the virtues of broadening the equity market to foreign companies, including the overseas-listed Chinese firms, and offering domestic investors wider (and supposedly better) choices of products beyond domestic companies. Multiple signals and announcements from the local authorities and central financial officials boded well for the board's launch. The top decision-making elites also endorsed the initiative and promoted it abroad. But, after 2011, the policy was reversed, as had happened to the Through Train, as bureaucratic support waned. As a result, Shanghai's initiatives to internationalize the equity market lost their momentum entirely.

In contrast to the miscarried efforts to open equity markets, the development of an offshore renminbi market in Hong Kong integral to renminbi internationalization was arguably the most notable twenty-first century Chinese financial opening project. The trajectory of the initiative exhibits a punctuated pattern in which the policy pilot of the early 2000s was overtaken by the rapid expansion of offshore renminbi activities in the middle of the decade. Following the launch of individual renminbi businesses in Hong Kong in 2003, offshore renminbi fixed income (i.e., bond) market and trade settlement schemes were introduced, bringing an exponential growth of international renminbi use in just a few years.

Offshore equity and derivatives markets with renminbi-associated financial products and transactions emerged; investment channels that connect the two renminbi markets have also recently been put in place. Whereas these developments might suggest the great success of renminbi internationalization, shifts of policy orientation and uneven progress across different market segments have often been overlooked. Trade settlements and bond markets have stood out, dwarfing the belated and mixed development of offshore renminbi financial products and the connectivity between the onshore and offshore markets.

The argument in brief

To make sense of the shifting policy tendencies and outcomes of China's financial opening underlying the three liberalizing cases introduced above, this book theorizes a model of coalition politics featuring the political interplay between pro-opening coalitions and dissenting parties.

Financial opening was not only driven by central decision-making elites and bureaucratic actors, but also by the local authorities of financial centers and financial industry interests. These pro-opening policy actors (or "opening advocates") did not operate in isolation, but advanced the liberalizing initiatives by working together as policy coalitions, shaping policy tendencies and opening outcomes through agenda-setting politics, leverage politics, and concessionary politics in the different stages of policymaking: from formation and deliberation to implementation.[6] The positions of policy actors over specific opening initiatives, however, were far from immutable and entirely informed by their political and economic standings. Rather, they were shaped by distributional implications and policy risks. All actors were affected by distributional concerns, but central bureaucratic actors also confronted policy risks. Therefore, the three cases of opening had different (and shifting) coalitional compositions and exhibited changing dynamics within the coalition and with parties that dissented from the liberalizing initiatives.

Motivated by the anticipated material gain and political interests, local and financial constituents often acted as the originators of the liberalizing initiatives. They shaped policy agendas and priorities by defining and framing liberalizing initiatives in ways that appealed to bureaucratic actors ("agenda-setting politics"). They also sought wider political support by capitalizing on connections with top decision-making elites and financial bureaucratic actors. Those elites, in turn, became the patrons of local and financial industry interests ("leverage politics") if they anticipated their political interests or standing being promoted by the liberalizing initiative. As pro-opening coalitions were formed and gained strength, they promoted liberalizing initiatives and engaged in bargaining with other stakeholders to build up a political and technical consensus, and to mollify opposition that might act to derail the initiatives ("concessionary politics"). This often involved concessions to dissenting parties over implementation specifics like scope, pace, location, and technical standards and arrangements.

Yet, such moves did not always succeed. Dissenting parties that recognized adverse implications for their own interests, or registered serious policy risk concerns, might resist or simply turn down concessionary offers from the pro-opening coalition. In other instances, the pro-opening coalition failed to offer compromises necessary to gain the support of dissenting parties. This led to a lack of political consensus within the government. Depending on the extent and nature of resistance, policy tendencies other than opening might ensue, including the reversal of previous commitments, or adherence to the status quo.

Together the three cases examined in the book show that the evolution of China's financial system evolved in a highly politicized *but* pluralistic fashion, with a policymaking process not as centralized and smooth as many studies have assumed. Central financial ministries and regulators did not monopolize and dominate the different stages of policymaking; their preferences around the financial opening were shaped by the input and lobbying of local financial hubs like Shanghai, Shenzhen, and Hong Kong, and financial institutions like banks, securities brokers, and stock exchanges. The interplay among coalition constituents and with the resisting forces within the Chinese political economy shaped the direction, scale, and outlook of the financial opening.

The perspective also suggests that the sheer financial virtue of taking down capital barriers seldom constitutes the principal driving force behind the quests of local authorities, the financial industry, or bureaucratic players. While the hurdles of China's financial opening are widely acknowledged, political imperatives underlying capital decontrol are equally, if not more, important to the understanding of the logic of financial reform. As will be demonstrated in the empirical chapters, policy actors get together and act only when they identify political and economic gains to be made through financial opening; market efficiency appears only to be a virtuous, ancillary by-product.

Significance of the study

As China's financial policies occupy news headlines and increasingly entail global ramifications (notably a pursuit of renminbi internationalization and grandiose economic schemes like the Belt-and-Road Initiative), an explication of the country's trajectory of financial opening, arguably the last frontier of China's integration with the world, helps complete our understanding of its ascent to the global capital market and the political economy of reform and transition in general.

The study contributes to the literature of IPE and Chinese political economy in three major ways. First, it presents a systematic exposition of an empirically significant national case of financial opening with multiple liberalizing episodes. Indeed, apart from the growth of the offshore currency market in Hong Kong often seen as a major pillar of China's quest for currency internationalization, other important aspects of capital market opening have largely evaded the attention of researchers (Wang, Yen, and Lai 2014; Overholt, Ma, and Law 2016). This book incorporates the liberalization of outbound equity investment, the internationalization of a domestic equity market, and currency internationalization—topics that are usually examined in isolation—and presents a holistic inquiry.

Second, the book affirms the importance of local authorities and financial industry interests and demonstrates the increasingly pluralistic nature of financial policymaking in China. Studies of renminbi internationalization, for instance, have tended to focus on the initiatives of central authorities, insufficiently addressing the financial industry and local contestations which lie behind developments (Bell and Feng 2013; Prasad 2016; Subacchi 2016). In disaggregating these dimensions that underpinned the market opening, this study sheds light on the domestic dynamics within which local authorities and financial industry interests played an important part in shaping the calculus of financial opening. Policy responses have rarely been prefabricated or originated from a single political source. Rather, they have been the summation of the influences of domestic actors at central, financial industry, and local levels.

Although this perspective inevitably adds complexity, it gains empirical richness by going beyond the central-level decision-making process involving the top decision-making elites and explicates interactions between different kinds of actors and their political pursuits, opening up some possibility of understanding financial policy change—a realm often seen to be shrouded in much secrecy. Last, by showing the extent to which China's financial opening has been tied to a multitude of domestic political concerns that often contravened the liberalization and internationalization rhetoric, the book sheds light on recent debates about China's international financial outreach and power.

Although China's modern financial architecture does perform some important market functions, such as raising capital, price discovery, and risk sharing, the evolution of the system remains highly political as policymakers are preoccupied with domestic priorities and driven by the tug of war involving forces underappreciated by analysts of China's political economy. As Loriaux (1997: 229) reminds us:

> It is common to confuse the idea of liberalization with the idea of "liberation" from arbitrary and inefficient state interference.... But as we examine the dismantling of the decades-old capacity of states to influence and direct productive investment, we see not the contestation of power but the exercise of power. And as interventionist institutions are brought down by powerful actors, we are reminded of the Hegelian claim that human freedom flourishes not outside the realm of the state but within it....

This study, then, seeks to tell how the Chinese state exercises its power from within, and argues that, unlike other regional economies, China's financial opening is essentially driven and shaped by competing domestic political economic interests that range from local financial hubs like Shanghai, Shenzhen, and Hong Kong to the different industries in the financial sector and their patrons in the bureaucracy. In extending its financial reach overseas and facilitating capital mobility, it has been the interests of domestic constituents at the local level and within the financial industry and bureaucracy that have assumed considerable weight. This implies that further projection of China's financial power could ultimately be bounded by political economic dynamics and constraints at home, as some recent studies have concluded (e.g., Chin and Helleiner 2008; Drezner 2009; Cohen 2015; Hung 2016). The suggestion that the Western open economies will be substantially challenged should be viewed with caution.

Research design and approach

This book extends the analyses of comparative and international political economy to the Chinese context, which is curiously missing given the country's significance in both policy and theoretical terms, and features three attempts at financial opening from the last decade. The focus on China is a justifiable one, since the Chinese liberalizing trajectory has been primarily driven by domestic contestations involving a diversity of local, financial industry, and central bureaucratic interests. This can be contrasted with other regional cases like

Taiwan, South Korea, or Japan, who liberalized their capital markets from the 1980s under the influence of a host of different factors.

This does not imply that examining China's cases alone would yield no insights relevant to other contexts. As Scott Kennedy (2011: 19) remarks:

> [the country] is not unique in having internal variation ... other large countries have tremendous variation, and so do even smaller countries.... The Chinese case and its subnational units can provide inspiration (and data) for scholars to analyze more carefully similarities and differences in patterns of variation within countries more generally.

By exploring the internal dynamics of three episodes of financial opening in China after the 2000s, this book prepares the ground for such comparative exercises in IPE and the China studies field (Odell 2001; Reny 2011).

The three episodes—the evolution of the outbound equity investment regime, the internationalization of domestic stock markets, and the emergence of the offshore renminbi market in Hong Kong—are representative of recent attempts by the Chinese government to promote capital mobility by relaxing state control. The first two are instances of equity market liberalization and the last one is a case of currency internationalization. The trajectories and outcomes of these episodes are markedly different, sometimes running contrary to, or diverging from, expectations derived from the literature.

In fact, even though China's unfastening of the capital market has principally concentrated on the equity market, in the two cases related to the loosening of control of securities investment, policy choices toward opening have not been realized as expected. Given its implications for monetary policy and exchange rate regimes, instances of the liberalization of the currency market should be hard to come by. However, since the mid-2000s, gradual moves to develop (and eventually the exponential growth of) the offshore currency center occurred under the auspices of Beijing and proceeded in ways that outpaced the other two episodes of equity market liberalization.

Besides their divergence with theoretical expectations, the three cases are distinctive from other liberalization episodes due to extensive input from actors drawn from beyond the central authorities. This distinguishes them from liberalizing efforts initiated and driven by the center, like interest rate liberalization or bond market reform. They represent an interesting class of cases involving dynamics largely untapped by China or political economy specialists. Moreover, the three cases demonstrate an extensive within-case variation of preferences of various actors at the central and local levels of China over time that resulted in shifts of policy tendencies and opening outcomes—a case selection approach which most China specialists adopt (Hurst 2010).

Indeed, domestic actors have shown preferences and interests in ways conventional understanding would not suggest. For example, although the distinctions between onshore and offshore interests, and the economic planning bodies and financial regulators, provide some insights as to their general inclinations toward financial opening, they do not offer a definitive prediction of actors' positions during specific liberalizing initiatives. Indeed, those positions have been far from immutable or determined solely by the standing of the actors in China's political economy.

More interestingly, the three cases illustrate the different roles of Hong Kong as an offshore financial hub. While the city faces the rising challenge of financial hubs like Singapore and Shanghai in the regional "race for money," and has become highly (and increasingly) dependent on the mainland's development, the onshore authorities have capitalized on Hong Kong's special niche in a painstaking effort to open the financial sector and develop the capital market. In all the instances examined in this book, Hong Kong advocated opening initiatives and opportunities that were later seized on by central bureaucratic actors, onshore local authorities, and financiers.

The analyses span the years preceding the opening initiatives up to the latest developments, with the timeframe of empirical coverage ending in early 2017. This enables an examination of the domestic debates leading up to the liberalization attempts, and maximizes the possibility of sorting out the variations in policy tendencies and the positions of the domestic policy actors. Notwithstanding the relatively recent and ongoing nature of the cases, in which direct access to senior policymakers (through interviews, for example) is largely infeasible, the analytical turn to local authorities and financial industry interests broaches new possibilities of accessing empirical information previously overlooked by scholars seeking an understanding of the liberalization dynamics of China.

To establish strong support for the analysis, an extensive review of primary and secondary sources in both Chinese and English was conducted, including official reports and announcements of central bureaucratic agencies, as well as those of local governments (notably the Financial Services Office and stock exchanges) and the domestic financial community. This gave valuable perspectives on their agendas and interactions with central bureaucratic actors. These complemented insider accounts from the "gray literature," such as the central-level research reports by think tanks affiliated with government agencies (like the Development Research Center of the State Council, and Research Bureau of the People's Bank of China), which provided rare glimpses of the views that informed the senior decision makers. These sources also feature policy assessments and perspectives sometimes denied to the researcher in more open sources, adding credence to the views of secondary sources. To corroborate the information gleaned from documentary materials—an approach Thogersen (2006) advises—15 interviews were also conducted with central financial officials and regulators, their local counterparts, researchers, and financial market practitioners in Beijing and local financial hubs. This enables the book to give an insider view of the way these enormously far-reaching policy decisions were arrived at.

The chapters ahead

Following this introductory chapter, Chapter 2 builds the analytical framework that integrates the insights of the IPE and Chinese political economy literature. It teases out the motivations of the local authorities of financial centers, financial industry interests, and central bureaucratic actors—the three kinds of domestic policy player that have been important to the evolution of the financial opening—as well as the determinants shaping their preferences. This lays the basis for an examination of the formation of policy coalitions, and the political maneuvering of those coalitions that spurred the opening agendas.

Chapters 3 to 5 focus on aspects of the financial opening that unfolded during the last decade. Chapters 3 and 4 examine equity market liberalization, and Chapter 5 inspects currency internationalization. In contrast to studies assuming the primacy of market forces and investors, and those that have focused on bureaucratic politics at the central level, these chapters unravel the domestic dynamics and attest to the relevance of local authorities and financial industry interests to China's careful attempts to open its capital market.

Chapter 3 investigates the evolution of the outbound equity investment regime and illustrates the changing policy tendencies and outcomes. It begins with the initial policy stasis and gradual opening, in which channels for institutional investors were put in place, and a schedule announced for a Through Train scheme for individual investors that might have removed most of the restrictions on individual investors. The chapter examines how all of this culminated in a dramatic policy reversal, and the continuation of the extant institutional investment channels, before discussing how the late 2000s came to witness smaller scale opening attempts in the form of ETFs on the mainland exchanges, and the belated Stock Connects between the Shanghai, Shenzhen and Hong Kong's exchanges.

Chapter 4 addresses a different aspect of equity market opening—the internationalizing of the domestic equity market through securities issuance by international firms on the mainland stock exchanges. It centers on Shanghai's quest to internationalize its local exchange and China's securities market by way of repeated pushes to create a separate exchange for foreign firms (or an international board as it was known), from the mid-2000s. The chapter discusses why it was thought the international board would enhance local and financiers' interests by consolidating Shanghai's position as China's leading financial hub, and how it was also seen as being in line with the political agendas of some central government ministries and top decision-making elites that were trying to promote China's capital market internationalization. The chapter also examines how the highly anticipated opening initiative was derailed and fell off the policy agenda completely in 2011, and why the policy has still not regained traction.

Chapter 5 traces the politics underlying the creation of Hong Kong as an offshore currency center—the foundation of the offshore renminbi market that was the first step to the renminbi expanding its footprint to almost every other continent. The chapter examines how Hong Kong-based interests played a critical part throughout the policymaking process, leading to the exponential growth of the offshore renminbi market in the 2000s. The introduction of individual renminbi businesses in the early years of the decade was augmented by fixed income products and trade settlement schemes that now enjoy worldwide appeal. These followed some advances in the equity and derivatives markets and increasing connectivity between the offshore and onshore currency markets that significantly expanded the investment uses of the renminbi. All of this would not have been possible without the successful political maneuvering of the pro-opening coalition. The chapter reveals the manifold aspects of renminbi internationalization and its uneven progress.

The final chapter concludes and summarizes the important findings of the book. It appraises the roles of local authorities, financial industry interests, and bureaucratic agencies in the different stages of policy process and the mechanisms of policy change. It discusses the theoretical implications for the wider literature of IPE and China studies, the policy relevance to the country's liberalizing trajectory, and raises some possibilities for further research.

Notes

1 This catchy phrase borrows from Helleiner and Kirshner (2014).
2 These regulations and activities are compiled under "capital transactions" of the International Monetary Fund's *Annual Report on Exchange Arrangements and Exchange Restrictions*. See International Monetary Fund (2016), pp. 45–55 for the complete and latest discussion.
3 Examples include the stock craze of the 1980s that involved multiple unsanctioned local stock exchanges, and the recent proliferation of hundreds of "rogue exchanges" that sell over-the-counter shares, commodities futures, and artworks.
4 Tom Holland, "The Day of the Renminbi," *Far Eastern Economic Review* 163, no. 48, November 30, 2000, pp. 76–80.
5 "Zhengjianhui gongbu zhengquan ye dui WTO chengnuo neirong" (CSRC announced China's WTO commitments on securities industry opening), *Xinhua News*, December 11, 2001.
6 The notion of "coalition," however, is adopted in this study with implications slightly different from Western contexts, where organizational arrangements are relatively formal and have enduring memberships and channels of transactions institutionalized between members of the coalition. In that sense, the term has a closer meaning to "grouping," characterizing its informal nature, fluid structure (if any), and an "adhocness" of membership composition. For analytical convenience, however, the two terms are used interchangeably in this research. See Chapter 2 for a more in-depth discussion.

2 The political coalitional perspective of financial policy change

This chapter sketches the coalitional politics that explain the policy trajectories of the three cases of financial opening pursued by the Chinese authorities since the 2000s. It introduces the interests and preferences of the local authorities, financial interests, and central bureaucratic actors, allowing an examination of their policy preferences and alignments—either as part of the pro-opening policy coalition or one of the dissenting parties. The three political mechanisms that unfold at different stages of policymaking—agenda-setting politics, leverage politics, and concessionary politics—are discussed together with how they engendered different policy tendencies and outcomes.

Changing policy tendencies of financial opening

As Chapter 1 demonstrated, China's experience of financial liberalization reveals that, although "reform and openness" had long been the policy watchwords, its praxis was far less clearly defined and consensual. An overhaul of the domestic banking sector dominated the domestic agenda of the time, but equity and bond market innovation and other essential initiatives had lagged. Although foreign firms found an increasing presence in mainland China, capital could only cross the border by way of the state's sanctioned channels and mechanisms.

The three liberalizing episodes this study examines also demonstrate that China's financial opening has been a checkered journey, sometimes interrupted by policy reversal and long periods of stasis before regaining momentum. This pattern defies simplistic labeling and is often seen as a "disorderly" or "guerrilla" policy style that is beyond comprehension (Heilmann and Perry 2011; Heilmann 2017b). As we will see, this is not the case and a complete account must appreciate the multiplicity of actors, including local financial hubs, different financial industry interests, and central bureaucratic actors.

Financial opening, by its nature, unfastens a state's control of its capital markets. This is manifested in increasing financial breadth and depth, a lowering of entry and exit barriers, and the provision of a wider range of products and services to market participants. But openings are rarely introduced uniformly and this gives rise to uneven "residual controls" (Lukauskas and Minushkin 2000). When a reversal of the opening tendency prevails, liberalizing commitments that have been made public are downplayed, renounced, or reneged upon. The Chinese government would appear "imprudent" when assuming changing and contradictory stances, and one should expect an about-face of policy position in this circumstance; consequently, ongoing preparations or initiatives would be halted and rolled back.

Unlike opening or reversal when policy is advanced or is retrenched, stasis does not bring a marked change of state control. In the absence of any previously instituted opening moves, stasis implies that no new measures are introduced and the state errs on the side of capital restriction. However, policy stasis also occurs when some opening initiatives have already been put in place. In such cases, the state usually sticks to the status quo and the established opening channels. Instead of a dramatic policy turnabout, as happens with reversals, one can expect general confusion about the position of the state as neither the existing measure is rescinded nor a new one is introduced.

However, different policy tendencies and outcomes are not static during cases of financial opening. They change and evolve over time. To enable a within-case analysis of policy trajectory and comparisons between different junctures, different policy tendencies are understood with reference to the particular aspects of market development they are related to. For example, the opening tendency in renminbi internationalization is conceived of in relation to the larger institutional framework governing cross-border renminbi flows and uses. Similarly, reversal of the evolution of outbound equity investment regimes denotes a dramatic change of policy tendency within that particular facet of financial opening.

The following sections lay out the building blocks of the explanatory framework. They bring together examinations of domestic change agents and the policymaking models introduced in Chapter 1, notably the fragmented authoritarianism and political survival and quasi-market views, and develop the coalition perspectives that account for the shifts of policy tendencies in China's course of financial opening. This arguably represents a more productive approach in analyzing the country's policy and decision making than seeing the different models in mutually exclusive terms (Harding 1985).

The coalition perspective on policy change

The different models of China's policymaking process—which include the fragmented authoritarianism, factionalist, and political survival and quasi-market models reviewed in Chapter 1—have separately provided analytical ingredients important to understanding the policy trajectories of China's financial opening. While each has its own explanatory focus and inevitable analytical limits, together they form the analytical framework of this study.

Fragmented authoritarianism models point to the diffusion of central power and the increasing diversity of actors with access to policymaking processes, but they lack the clear specification of the actors' motivations. Political survival and quasi-market perspectives fill the analytical void and realistically portray the preferences and inter-elite dynamics at the central level. However, this inevitably downplays the importance of subnational and financial interests. A synthesis of these two models helps build the general policymaking context, but is still inadequate when the combined efforts of different domestic pro-opening actors to promote policy change, and their counterpart dissenting parties, are considered.

To make up for these shortfalls, this study advances a policy coalition framework to explain the shifts in policy tendencies and outcomes during the three empirical cases. Despite the different use of terms like "coalition," "opinion group," and "grouping" that might cause confusion, this study takes the terms "coalition" and "grouping" as synonymous in the same way as Cheng and Chou (2000), and Dittmer (2000). This also echoes the policy studies scholarship of the "advocacy coalition framework" and policy entrepreneurs, which has looked into how policy actors might bring about policy change by articulating and advocating policy ideas, and defining and framing problems, to solicit larger political support (Sabatier and Jenkins-Smith 1993; Weible et al. 2009).[1]

Although a focus on coalitional politics involving multiple domestic actors inevitably introduces complexity, it adds richness by shedding light on the roles and interplays of different actors. As Heilmann and Perry (2011: 11) have written:

> [Understanding] the policy process holds special importance for explaining not only political interaction and rule-making, but also economic markets and social trends that in China are in no way independent of state interference. The policy process is a key mechanism connecting (both empirically and analytically) formal hierarchies, informal networks, market transactions, and social interactions.

No study, including this one, could cover every aspect of any policy process, but empirical analysis will reveal how the larger trends of Chinese financial opening intertwined with political forces, and how the established formal institutions intersected with informal political entities like policy coalitions. These connections present an integrated political economic analysis that takes an actor-oriented perspective and examines how actors' motivations and interplays engendered financial opening policy change (Heilmann 2017a: 43). Before discussing the concept, however, it should be noted that the public policy literature has no consensual view about disaggregating the policymaking process.

Authors adhering to the stage model of policymaking have generally broken down the process according to their research agendas and foci, but a few essential building blocks are commonly used. These include information input, deliberation of policy alternatives, decision making, implementation, and feedback. In the Chinese context, Chang (1978: 3) enumerates five stages of policymaking: problem identification, initiation, consensus building, authorization, and implementation. Shih (2005) describes four stages of China's financial policymaking: input from policy producers, decision making by elite consumers, the "conveyance" of decisions to financial institutions, and local leaders being tasked with implementation.

This study conceives three stages in the policy process: formation, deliberation, and implementation based on the common elements encountered in different mappings of policy stages. Although in practice the stages are inter-related and sometimes overlap, the distinction is made possible and, indeed, supported by the long time span of the three empirical episodes. Each of the three stages assumes predominant salience at different points of time. This allows for analysis of the various effects of domestic actors and coalitions on policy tendencies and outcomes. Formation involves the actors' initiation of policy initiatives and their attempts to define *and* frame the issue. It describes how the policy agenda is shaped and the way the issues are interpreted by decision makers (Dery 2000). Deliberation concerns the process of actors seeking political support, their building of consensus, and the decision making of the central authorities. Implementation describes the way the decision is translated into specifics.

In the Chinese context, driving and shaping the policy process have been policy coalitions with constituents variously made up of local authorities, financial industry interests, and central bureaucratic actors. Analytically, *coalition* is a less formal construct than *faction*—a leader-oriented group based on patron-client networks characterized by "dyadic relations between a patron and several clients, who in turn may be lesser patrons with their own clients" (Cheng and Chou 2000: 43–4). A faction's members also share common attributes like regional origin, educational background, and industrial or organizational experience, and they are commonly motivated by "the search for career security and the protection of power" (Domes 1984: 27–8).[2] While a patron must protect and sometimes reward their protégé to ensure support and foster dependency, the protégé also acts in the interests of their master. This strengthens a member's power within the party hierarchy and protects against rivals and opposition. Interfactional relations are therefore competitive, with periodic struggles that result in changes of political and policy orientation (Pye 1981: 6–7; Huang 2000).

A faction-based account, however, would have difficulty making sense of policy shifts even in the pre-reform eras. As the pioneering study of Chang demonstrated, what underlay the divisions between central elites during the Great Leap Forward could hardly be attributed solely to factional affiliations. Rather, "different policy perspectives, visions, and 'constituents' [were] translated into disputes and shifting coalitions of opinion groups" (Chang 1969: 4). This in turn led to policy shifts and alternations in the ways nationwide political campaigns like agricultural collectivization and the commune system were strategized and implemented. Reardon (2002) has extended Chang's insights into an investigation of the "cycling" of foreign economic policies between inward and outward-oriented strategies in the decades before the opening of the late 1970s. The alternations of strategies were best explained with reference to dynamics between contending opinion groups capitalizing on economic crises to reinforce their political power, rather than by any conventional factional account.

As such, a focus on policy coalitions, where elites are seen as forming "issue-based coalitions which are limited to the very issue at stake and short-term cooperation," provides a far more useful analytical leverage in understanding relevant policy changes (Domes 1984: 28–9; Goodman 1984: 1–7). In contrast with traditional descriptions of factions, policy coalitions rarely have a permanent and constant composition, as sizes and memberships change depending on the issues concerned. As Cheng and Chou (2000: 43) describe, coalitions are "temporary alliances on pre-agreed upon and well-specified issues," in which members rarely surrender their autonomy to the leading unit as happens in factional ties, and inter-elite conflicts often center on "practical issues" related to policy design and implementation. Moreover, disputes within and between coalitions are mostly confined to details pertinent to policy design and implementation, not the larger political procedures that affect "claims for political power and overall control" of the party and state as with factional struggles (Domes 1984: 29).

This provides possibilities to study group politics in realms beyond the state and look at how interest groups matter in the policymaking process (Falkenheim 1987). It should be noted, however, that coalition and faction are not mutually exclusive categories in reality. It is possible that some of the connections maintained within policy coalitions are derivative of existing factional ties, providing a ready basis for the linking up of actors on specific issues and offering mutual support in policymaking. Envisaged this way, the two-faction model of Shih (2008), in which generalists and specialists were seen to assume alternating influences over macroeconomic policy, would appear to be a misnomer. Instead, as the studies of Chang (1969) and Reardon (2002) have shown, changing policy orientations could more appropriately be seen as the political products of competing groups in disagreement over the means and ends of a national economic policy.

To understand the politics of financial opening, this study conceives pro-opening coalitions as the primary movers of policy changes in specific liberalizing episodes. The coalitions and their constituents push the opening agenda, seek political support, and offer concessionary offers to allay dissent. However, given the issue-specific nature of coalitions, the composition of each coalition and dissenting parties cannot be seen as permanent or fixed. In fact, classification attempts based on political economic niches provide few clues about the three cases examined in the study. Local authorities and financial industry interests were also integral and indeed indispensable constituents of the coalitions, as they played important parts in originating the opening initiatives and seeking political support. If it found patronage from bureaucratic actors, the coalition was strengthened and its initiatives were propelled toward deliberation at the central level.

Hence, the subnational and financial industry players were not only the target of central actions, but also the "potential bases of support of leadership coalition," a reserve of policy-related resources and the originators of policy moves as Harding (1985: 79) and the proponents of the fragmented authoritarianism perspective have reminded us (Lampton and Lieberthal 1992, Lieberthal and Oksenberg 1988). The next section teases out actors' preferences and their relevance to the three episodes of financial opening which this study examines, and is followed by a discussion of the two determinants—distributional implication and policy risk—that prompted the formation of pro-opening coalitions and dissenting parties.

Domestic actors in China's financial opening

The local governments of domestic financial hubs, financial industry players, and central bureaucratic actors have been the primary policy stakeholders during China's financial opening. Understanding their preferences and motivations provides an underpinning essential to understanding the alignments of the pro-opening coalitions and dissenting parties.

Local authorities of financial centers

Although the capital market is in theory free from the constraints of geographic locations, the market architecture and supporting infrastructure are not. A functional and well-developed capital market is not location-independent, but is by necessity anchored somewhere. Economic historians and geographers have drawn parallels between the rise and fall of financial centers and the "transformation question" of the global economic order (Cassis 2010; Kindleberger 1974), but largely under-emphasized in their discussions have been the subnational aspects, in particular with respect to countries like China where there are multiple "centers" in which a capital market might take root.

Therefore, consideration of the local governments of financial centers is essential to any analysis of policy change in China's financial opening. The notion of "local" refers to authorities of both mainland financial centers—especially Shanghai, Shenzhen and Tianjin—and Hong Kong, which operates a distinct political economy offshore while simultaneously being part of China. Since these cities enjoy special administrative status, either as municipalities (Shanghai and Tianjin), established special economic zones (Shenzhen SEZ), or special administrative regions (Hong Kong), the effects of the intermediate level of subnational authorities between them and the central government are considered minimal. Due to its unique status, Shenzhen enjoys considerable policy and political autonomy on a par with other domestic financial hubs, even though it is formally under the oversight of the Guangdong provincial government.[3] Accordingly, all the cities carry significant weight in the three episodes and are the loci of the subnational politics.

In general, local authorities seek to enhance their competitiveness vis-à-vis others by promoting the growth and scale of their local financial industry. This benefits the locality with both material and intangible gains that range from increases in fiscal income (tax levies, for example), credits available to local industry, and investment in job creation and financial talent. A booming financial industry also burnishes the local reputation, status, and image both at home and abroad. Local officials appointed by the party state in the mainland financial hubs count their political scorecards as essential to career advancement. Officials in Hong Kong, by contrast, are relatively insulated from these careerist concerns as their territory is independent of, and segregated from, the mainland's personnel system. Promotion from Hong Kong to a senior administrative position in the mainland financial bureaucracy has occurred only once when the Hong Kong securities regulator was headhunted to work as a vice chairperson of the China Securities Regulatory Commission (CSRC).[4]

Across the three episodes of financial opening, the local authorities can be seen to have capitalized on their political and economic influence acting as important constituents of pro-opening coalitions or as dissenting parties. They proposed liberalizing initiatives, aligned with financial industry interests, and lobbied central bureaucratic actors. Hong Kong played a special role in the early 2000s, floating several ideas that would eventually gain momentum. Indeed, it saw itself as the best gateway that might allow the linking of the domestic and global capital market, and sought China's continuing support of its status as a global financial hub. It called for institutional channels and "free walks" of capital that would facilitate the introduction of domestic capital to overseas equity markets in the evolution of the outbound portfolio investment regime. On the other hand, Tianjin was eager to make itself the financial center of China's north by pioneering bold initiatives along the same lines as Hong Kong's proposals.

Similarly, Shanghai's quest to internationalize its local stock exchange through red-chip homecoming and the establishment of an international board from the mid-2000s was driven by its wish to consolidate its role as the leading onshore financial hub—one that would surpass Hong Kong in the longer term. It also strived to consolidate its "designated" status as China's international financial center which it was slated to achieve by 2020. The evolution of the offshore renminbi center in Hong Kong began with the city's initiative of the late 1990s that aimed for Hong Kong to manage a renminbi fund residing offshore and to expand the city's financial services sector. This soon met a challenge from Shanghai, which regarded itself to be a better candidate for launching offshore renminbi business. By contrast, other mainland financial hubs, notably Shenzhen and Tianjin, recognized both a symbolic and economic significance to building closer links with Hong Kong and its offshore renminbi activities. They sought to capitalize on their closer ties with the city and to distinguish themselves as domestic niche markets for new financial products and services offshore and, in doing so, strengthen their local financial industries.

Financial industry interests

The different industries within the financial sector constitute a second group of policy actors. Similarly to the local authorities, financial industry interests have been motivated by material gain. Although the country's financial system remained dominated by the few state-owned banks, the securities industry and local exchanges emerged as important actors when capital market opening progressed in the 1990s and broke the banks' monopoly. As a result, banking institutions sought to ensure that their political economic privileges remained intact by retaining a leading market position and introducing new products and services.

This inevitably put the banks at odds with the fledgling securities sector, which also intended to expand its market share by enhancing its competitiveness vis-à-vis counterparts at home and overseas. Stock exchanges in Shanghai, Shenzhen, and Hong Kong similarly hoped for greater market capitalization and revenues through IPOs and post-listing activities. Even though the mainland bourses have been managed and governed differently from Hong Kong's (the mainland bourses being part of the government structure and Hong Kong's bourse being a demutualized and listed company), all maintained mutualistic relations with local financiers and governments and sought to enhance their market positions (Heilmann 2005). More importantly, financial industry interests have complemented local efforts and contributed market influence and financial expertise. In this regard, their roles were comparable to foreign counterparts driving financial opening. In the US experience, for example, Wall Street financiers lobbied strongly for the creation of the Federal Reserve System not entirely for the sake of the public interest, but also for material gains concomitant with the internationalization of the US dollar. Similarly, Tokyo's brokerages benefited enormously from market opening that boosted their global footprint (Broz 1999; Laurence 2001).

In the three episodes of financial opening examined here, financial industries responded to the initiatives of local authorities and took positions dependent on the distributional implications of the liberalizing moves. Evolution of the outbound equity investment regimes might, in theory, decrease the influence of banks over individual investments, but the institution-based scheme was tilted in favor of banks that introduced and managed most of the funds. Subsequent Through Train arrangements planned to remove the banks' intermediary role and therefore elicited strong opposition from the industry. The listing of ETFs and Stock Connects was made possible in part due to the consent of all onshore bourses and major brokerage centers.

During attempts to internationalize China's stock market, Shanghai's bourse has acted as a strong partner to local authorities in pushing ahead with the agenda and negotiating with the securities regulator. The opening tendency was halted in part due to dissent from other stock exchanges and financiers offshore. The takeoff of the offshore currency market would not have been possible without the support of Hong Kong-based financial industry interests that informed the government of the range of feasible policy options and provided the requisite financial expertise in market development.

Central bureaucratic actors

Bureaucratic actors at the central government level are the last set of important players to be mentioned with regard to China's financial opening. Members of the financial bureaucracy were not entirely "insulated" from the larger political system. As the political survival perspective suggests, they faced intra-elite competition from time to time and officials leading these agencies had to accumulate sufficiently strong political capital to survive and cope with constant uncertainties surrounding their careers (Shih 2007: 1244–6). This was especially true for senior appointees leading ministerial departments or agencies. Like their local counterparts, their advancement to more senior positions of the state and party would in large part depend on their administrative capacity to handle policy problems and whether they had the political skills to convince the policy "consumers" of their competence (Shih 2005).

Regulators of specific financial industries and bureaucratic actors with encompassing portfolios of duties have slightly dissimilar concerns and policy emphases. The CSRC and China Banking Regulatory Commission (CBRC), China Insurance Regulatory Commission (CIRC) oversee the mainland securities, banking, and insurance industries, respectively, and regulate the corresponding market activities. In addition to maintaining market stability and the health of the financial institutions they supervise, the regulators also seek to perpetuate clientelist connections with the leading firms of the financial industries, of which many are state-owned or -affiliated by way of "deliberate control" or active government intervention (Pearson 2005; Ma, Song, and Yang 2010; Hsueh 2011). This close regulator-industry relation also implied that regulators have always been protagonists and defenders of financial industry interests at the center. This not only expanded the regulatory outreach and power of the agency (and the officials), it also afforded considerable rent-seeking opportunities for officials (Ngo and Wu 2009; Khwaja and Mian 2011).

By contrast, actors with encompassing portfolios like the National Development and Reform Commission (NDRC), the Ministry of Finance (MOF), the People's Bank of China (PBOC), and the SAFE—the last two being China's central bank and foreign exchange administrator—have interests beyond any specific industry. They have been the custodians of government stakes in financial institutions and ensured credit access to the state-owned sector, the core economic constituent in China's political economy. They also take on macroeconomic policy objectives like controlling inflation, price stability, and the fiscal health of government and the corporate sector that contributes to economic growth and financial stability at home. Yet this does not mean that these agencies were disinterested guardians of public interest. Officials of these agencies were also career-minded. Politically pressing problems would draw most of their attention, but short-term solutions would often be instituted without much regard to long-term policy consequences and there would be limited effort to fix structural problems. Officials also sought to present themselves (and their agencies) as effective and competent problem solvers while avoiding taking undue risks that accrued failure.

As a result, policy solutions tended to be incomplete and partial; sometimes advocated and initiated in the name of addressing the country's concerns, but also serving the interests of the officials and agencies. Such a conception of financial bureaucracy challenges the insulated technocratic perspective that has an affinity with the developmental state literature, and implies that understanding the political incentives of bureaucratic actors during China's financial opening is equally important to mapping the institutional constraints that are commonly seen to discourage bureaucratic actors from making changes (Shih 2004, 2007).

The easing of China's outbound investment regime was championed by the NDRC after the mid-2000s. The NDRC had become receptive to Hong Kong's initiative to deregulate channels used for committing to overseas investment to cool down an overheated economy that posed significant challenges to the agency and the country's leadership. But the policy process failed to thoroughly consider the effect on the larger financial system and generated fierce resistance from financial regulators and other ministries. Shanghai's attempt to internationalize its stock market was backed by the securities regulator, which had been supportive of efforts by the local authorities and bourse to groom Shanghai's stock exchange into a truly global platform and promote the local securities industry. Hong Kong's venture into offshore currency business, on the other hand, found the support of the central bank after the early 2000s, which defined currency internationalization as a political project under its tutelage with the aim of affirming China's rising global status.

This suggests that, although central bureaucratic actors were important "policy producers" that put forward ideas to "consumers"—the top decision-making elites of the State Council (and Politburo)—they were not the whole story. Subnational and financial industry actors also carried significant weight. They articulated their perspectives and capitalized on local economic resources, market influence, and financial expertise as they sought support at the central level. Seen this way, pro-opening financial policymakers at the central level have been "co-producers" of policy initiatives, aligned with local authorities and financial interests and forming a policy coalition. The following sections delineate the factors shaping policy positions in the formation of coalitions, and the dynamics of different policymaking stages.

Two determinants of actors' positions

Understanding the dynamics between the pro-opening coalition and dissenting parties is crucial to understanding the changing positions of actors within China's financial opening, but the composition of the two camps was not permanent and cannot be inferred simply from respective standings within the political economic hierarchy. Mainland financial centers and economic planning bodies like the NDRC did not necessarily hold negative views; sometimes they were patrons of opening initiatives (see for example, Shih 2008; Yang 2014). Similarly, Hong Kong-based financiers and government have been vocal protagonists of China's financial opening, but only when their interests were served.

To analytically map out the actors' stances during different liberalizing episodes, this section discusses the two factors that determined the actors' positions prior to aligning as a pro-opening coalition or becoming dissenting parties: distributional implications and policy risks. Distributional implications shaped the positions of all three kinds of actors; but policy risks specifically affected the calculus of central bureaucratic actors. The preferences of domestic policy actors therefore evolved in a "deeply political process" in which actors interpreted "their interests in response to an unfolding set of experiences and interactions with others" (Peter Hall, cited in Woll 2008: 23). While the two determinants informed the actors' policy stances, they did not engender the collective pursuits of actors as policy coalitions or galvanize policy tendencies and changes in a spontaneous fashion. This necessitates setting out some explication of the dynamics among constituents within and without coalitions in different policymaking stages.

Distributional implications

As a whole, China reaped significant gains from its financial opening. In addition to significantly expanding its access to global capital and market connections that benefited investors and financial institutions, the government also found enormous opportunities. Levies on a range of market activities generated increasing sources of fiscal revenue; banking sector reforms and the expansion of financial markets beyond the bank-centered system presented new rent-seeking opportunities to officials at both the central and local levels. However, as with trade liberalization that generated distributional problems among domestic groups (Milner 1999; Fewsmith 2001), capital market opening affected the interests of domestic constituents differently, with some made more powerful than others (Perez 1997; Broz 1999; Verdier 2002).

At the subnational level, financial opening empowered some regions over others and complicated the balance of power between the central and local authorities (Verdier 2002). Mainland financial hubs and Hong Kong had been competing since the 2000s over their status in global finance and had engaged in regulatory competition as they tried to promote their own competitiveness when compared to other financial hubs (Zhao 2003; Wang 2009; Lai 2012). Driven by developmental and careerist concerns, local governments often acted in tandem with financiers in calling for opening within their jurisdiction. Those that successfully obtained the center's blessing would clearly stand out relative to their local counterparts as policy forerunners and make a leap in political economic status within the country. Being the host to an opening move was a significant boost to the local cadres' careers and made sure their political achievements would be known nationwide. It also raised the domestic and international reputation of the financial hubs, not to mention the enormous windfall to the local economy it ensured.

Thus, initiatives of capital market opening pioneered by a locality often kicked off competitive subnational dynamics like trade and investment liberalization. Interested financial hubs jumped in and jostled for similar treatment; others that thought their own political agenda and market niches compatible with the proposed move extended their support to the pro-opening coalitions. The positions of interested local authorities, however, also hinged on the responses of the opening advocates. If they agreed to involve the interested parties, the basis of political support at the subnational level might expand. In the contrary case, when the quests of interested parties failed and they were not provided with concessionary offers such as political side-payments, they naturally took an oppositional stance.

In a similar vein, capital market opening posed distributional problems to different financial industry interests. The process often changed the balance of power between different classes of asset holders, fixed or mobile, in which the "exit" power of mobile holders empowered them with political leverage over state authorities (Frieden 1991; Winters 1996). In other instances, financial opening boosted those foreign firms with better expertise and international experience over their domestic counterparts (Singer 2007: 22–3). These uneven and mixed effects depended not only on the international competitive position of domestic firms but also on the dynamics within the financial sector. Some might experience a loss of market monopoly because of domestic competition within the financial industry or the entry of foreign firms. Others might be strengthened with easier access to credit, bigger pools of clients, and booming business opportunities as financial intermediaries, or they might benefit simply because of the government's support.

In Mexico, for example, domestic firms gained far more than their foreign counterparts because of privileged access to new financing opportunities (Mityakov 2011). Private banks in Spain and France close to the governing elites were the exclusive beneficiaries of financial liberalization (Loriaux et al. 1997; Perez 1997). In the Chinese context, while the influence of tradable and non-tradable sectors in exchange rate policy has been a subject of much interest to scholars (Steinberg and Shih 2012; Steinberg 2015), the constellation of financial interests in policymaking continued to evade the attention of researchers until relatively recently. For example, Otero-Iglesias and Vermeiren (2015) focus on the state-owned banks' resistance to renminbi internationalization, whereas Helleiner and Malkin (2012) probe the impacts of currency internationalization on China's financiers.

These works, however, do not explicitly differentiate important industrial constituents, including the banks, securities firms or local exchanges that played a part in the different aspects of renminbi internationalization. In studies of equity market opening, the domestic securities industry is most often the natural focus, but the process also involved local bourses and was entwined with the reduced roles of banks and financial intermediaries (Sobel 1994; Laurence 2001: chapters 4–5). The distributional implications for, and the policy preferences of, financiers, however, have barely been explored.

In China's financial opening, financial interests that found compatibility and anticipated material gains with the local initiatives would side with the pro-opening coalition and opening advocates, whereas those that foresaw the opposite would be reserved and opposed to the liberalizing move. This was especially the case for local bourses, whose business operations depended to a great degree on the policy and political support of the local financial hubs. Financial institutions with a considerable presence in particular localities, or which derived revenues from particular areas, would also position themselves in similar fashion.

Financial opening also altered the political and economic stakes within the financial bureaucracy. In general, China's internal financial opening made the regulatory authorities more powerful over time, posing challenges to the preponderance of the traditional economic planning bodies like the NDRC and MOF and diluting their decision-making influence. The involvement of new and foreign players in the domestic market also helped boost the status and leverage of the financial regulators, who arguably enjoyed more expertise and resources than the planning bodies (Walter and Fraser 2001; Green 2004; Bell and Feng 2009). Thus, the promotion of securities and currency markets beyond the banking industry not only affected the interests of various industries within the financial system, but also their patrons within the bureaucracy that represented and defended industrial interests.

Consider, for example, the financial disintermediation of the domestic market that was pursued with extreme caution. Even though it was clearly in the public interest to reallocate capital to investments with higher yields, the authorities had to address resistance not only from the banking industry but also from the regulator, who limited the scope of services available through securities firms and introduced the provision of "level playing fields" for banks with licenses, so that they could offer comparable products and services to investors.

All this suggests that the distributional implications of the opening initiatives played an important part in galvanizing the emergence of a pro-opening coalition. It prompted the alignment of local authorities and financial industry interests, and brought the central bureaucratic actors into policy coalitions. It also turned those who found their stakes adversely affected into dissenting parties. Thus, it is only partly right to see China's financial liberalization as a process that mostly altered the "existing equilibrium of interests in favor of a depoliticized resource allocation, [fostered] domestic financial market reform and [allowed] for the emergence of independent (domestic and transnational) industry players" (Schlichting 2008: 27). The liberalizing course remains highly politicized in parallel with the depoliticized market.

The policy risk of financial opening

Besides distributional implications, the position of central bureaucratic actors was also informed by policy risk. This study distinguishes two kinds of policy risk for analytical purposes—political risk resulting in adverse consequences specific to a certain bureaucratic agency, and systemic risk with ramifications for the larger domestic economic and financial system. These are not shorthand that reflects objective and unbiased assessments of the potential policy impacts of financial opening, like market volatilities or financial instabilities; instead, they represent the inherently subjective readings of the policy and political implications of capital market development in the view of bureaucratic actors.

Nonetheless, the literature developing the notion of policy risk is sometimes less explicit about usage, in part because of the intractable difficulties of appraising the severity of risk in numerical and relatively objective terms. Singer (2007: 22–3) adopts a firm-centered treatment and looks at the policy choices of regulators and legislatures triggered by incidences of financial instability, including firm failure, asset price volatility, and general crises of confidence. Especially important to the policymakers was "the probability that a firm will collapse as a function of the current regulatory environment". Others have analyzed how the control over the economy of state authorities might be weakened by the ancillary risks of financial liberalization (Kaminsky and Schmukler 2008; Pepinsky 2012). As Brooks (2004) describes, the process might constrain a state's ability to attain policy objectives like the maintenance of stable growth or employment, or to defend its governing legitimacy, and might particularly affect developing countries facing the "high initial cost of deep capital account liberalization."

Latin America stands as a case of when the short-term policy risks outweighed the benefits that financial opening promised when countries "liberalize capital flows in the context of weak or repressed domestic financial sectors or if their governments possess inadequate resources with which to defend their currency, rescue banks, or alleviate the social costs of liberalization" (Brooks 2004: 391). China is no exception to this rule, as economic hardship and financial instability were inextricably linked to the political risk the regime confronted. Even though China exercised foreign financial power through liberalizing the capital market and broadening the use of its currency, the central authorities have been preoccupied with the domestic political economic imperatives. Easing capital mobility made possible by financial opening might divert cheap capital away from the banking sector and toward high return investments, undermining the profits of the state-owned financial sector and compromising the stability of the larger financial system. Not only might this affect the core constituent of the economy, it would also unsettle the political stakes of bureaucratic actors and decision makers with intractable policy risk (Miller 2010).

However, these analyses of policy risk have largely concentrated on the overall perception of state authorities when assessing and responding to policy risk, and have left unexplored a plausible variation of risk perception within the government. To account for the divergent policy positions of bureaucratic actors, policy risk is distinguished into two strands depending on the scale of the impacts on central bureaucratic actors. By centering on the perception of different magnitudes of risk by policy actors, this formulation refines the incident-based typology of policy risk and the existing categories of the different levels of policy risk the Chinese authorities confronted (Jarvis and Griffiths 2007; Heilmann 2008; Toksoz 2014)

Political risk refers to plausible events or scenarios recognized by bureaucratic actor(s) that might only affect their own interests and impact non-vital parts of the larger economy. These include, for example, stock market adjustment or the introduction of financial products and technical standards novel to the Chinese market. These instances might incur market confusion, challenge investors' confidence or cause financial losses, as well as political liabilities to the regulators and agencies concerned, but they do not compromise the stability of the larger financial system centered on state-owned banks and capital control regimes. Accordingly, they are specific to certain bureaucratic actors.

Systemic risk, by contrast, affects the core interests of the Chinese state or undermines its ability to attain important policy objectives and outputs. This includes the stability of the leading banking institutions tasked to supply credit to the state-owned economic sectors, stimulating economic growth and job creation that ultimately helps the state maintain political legitimacy, or the survival of the regime's rule itself (Heilmann 2008). As economists have extensively stated, contingencies like capital flight or speculative attack often result in large-scale capital drain or exchange rate volatility (Demirguc-Kunt and Detragiache 2001). These in turn drastically weaken the levers available to the central government and entail risk beyond the confines of specific bureaucratic actors, bringing sweeping effects to the functioning of the economic system, and posing significant challenges to the interests of the central state (and party) authorities (Yang 2011, 2015).

Indeed, as China witnessed external crises unfolding, Beijing strengthened its grip on the economy. Together with local governments, the central government became the source of investment made possible by the artificially depressed interest rates offered by banks. Capital controls and the currency inconvertibility of the renminbi also kept the capital at home crucial to keeping intact the interests of the state-owned financial institutions and industries (Hsueh 2011; Breslin 2012; Yang 2015). Hence, any initiative heightening concerns about systemic risk among central bureaucratic actors and the decision-making elites has invariably elicited strong reservation and resistance from them.

By contrast, when only political risks were associated with an opening initiative, central bureaucratic actors' preferences were conditioned by distributional implications. In cases where the opening effort was seen to heighten the policy risk experienced by certain bureaucratic actors and adversely affect their political stakes, the call for opening was opposed. The reverse situation occurred when government actors recognized that a liberalizing initiative was helpful and offered remedies for pressing and outstanding policy problems, alleviating the policy risk the agencies experienced. Career-minded bureaucrats would capitalize on such opportunities even if they were incomplete and partial fixes. These opportunities afforded them the chance to demonstrate policy competence and boost their political standing. Accordingly, central actors would be supportive of such a liberalizing initiative, and side with local authorities and financiers.

A slightly different case was when bureaucratic actors foresaw a higher political risk but expected potential gains from the liberalizing move. This led to an ambivalent policy position and calls for postponement as actors tried to achieve two seemingly incompatible objectives. In an even rarer scenario, a liberalizing initiative might be seen as lowering policy risks but entailing unfavorable distributional implications. As in the previous situation, this made bureaucrats hesitant to back the liberalizing initiative.

Mechanisms of policy change

Local authorities, financial industry interests, and bureaucratic actors aligned in response to distributional implications and policy risks and this led to the emergence of pro-opening policy coalitions and dissenting parties. To explain changes of policy tendencies and opening outcomes, this section expands on the mechanisms driven by policy coalitions and their constituents, including agenda-setting politics, leverage politics, and concessionary politics, each exhibiting varying salience at different stages of policymaking.

Agenda-setting politics matters not only during the formation or "incubation" stages of policymaking, in which local and financial industry players solicit the interest of central bureaucratic actors and seek to convince them of the soundness of their policy ideas. As pro-opening actors converge on a shared position and subsequently ally themselves as a policy coalition, the policy process enters the deliberation stage in which leverage and concessionary politics assume critical importance. The constituents of the coalition seek to build political support, making use of their connections with the governing elites. They also offer concessions and side-payments to allay dissent and to maintain the political and technical consensus essential to pushing the initiative forward. These concessionary moves are also essential to sustaining the opening tendency during policy implementation. At the same time, dissenting parties seek to undercut the opening move in policy deliberations by introducing competing policy agendas and capitalizing on their connections with top decision-making elites to prompt their intervention.

Agenda-setting and leverage politics

As the very first stage of policymaking, policy formation involves agenda-setting politics that translate real-life problems into agendas understood and defined by actors prior to any efforts to devise solutions. The process is by no means apolitical given that decision makers rarely recognize and act on the problems without bias or in the best interests of the public. Studies of China's policymaking have pointed to multiple actors competing for the attention of decision makers on issues they consider significant to their interests. While Shih's political survival model reveals the motivations behind the "selling" of policy initiatives by bureaucratic producers, the importance of information inputs from subnational and non-state constituents has also been widely appreciated by scholars subscribing to the fragmented authoritarianism perspective (Halpern 1992). Wang (2008) also enumerates six ways policy agendas have been introduced in China, many of which involve endeavors from below and outside the central authorities.

Agenda setting and problem definition and framing, however, are two distinct but related activities. The former draws the attention of decision makers to particular issues, whereas the latter details efforts to organize "a set of facts, beliefs, and perception—how people think about circumstances" (Dery 2000: 37). This implies that not all issues raised to the policy agenda lead to a response or solution. Change agents often try "presenting evidence in ways that suggest a crisis is at hand, finding ways to highlight failure of current policy settings and drawing support from actors beyond the immediate scope of the problem" (Mintrom and Norman 2009: 652). Others also shape "the contours of political discourse and thus mobilize allies toward the goal of policy change by 'organizing information in a manner that conforms to the structure of a good story' " (Mertha 2008: 12). Indeed, China's local officials have frequently employed careful issue framing strategies to galvanize popular support for reform packages they have devised and lobbied higher authorities in that vein (Zhu 2012).

With respect to financial opening, while the issue stayed on the agenda of central authorities after China's accession to the WTO, specific details like the scope, pace, location, and sequencing of the different possible opening initiatives mostly evaded the center's attention. Much was left open and policy priorities were (and remain) far from agreed within the government except for important issues like the access of foreign financial institutions to the domestic market (Hsueh 2011; Schlichting 2008). This presented considerable opportunities for domestic financial hubs and industry interests to define and articulate their own visions for the future of China's financial opening as the "proactive principal" of their own agenda (Chung 2016). Vested with market resources and infrastructure, the local authorities of financial hubs played a particularly important role. Their efforts were often complemented by financiers, including stock exchanges, and those with a considerable business presence in the localities that provided them with political and financial support.

This often happened when two parties viewed themselves as qualified candidates to host a liberalizing initiative—striving to get ahead of other localities and the center's policy signals. In doing so, they sought to ensure first-mover advantages, since financial opening brought the promise of new services, products, and an expansion of market scales to both localities and financiers. In other instances, local and financial interests responded to gestures of those central government actors with which they maintained close political connection in the belief that the locally-originated efforts would be patronized. This always involved the informal ties cultivated between local and central cadres over years in previous appointments or shared political experiences. In other words, if informal connections existed and served as better conduits through which to foster reciprocal interests, the formal institutional frameworks governing the intergovernmental relation assumed a secondary importance during policy formation.

One could, of course, construe scenarios in which certain financial industry interests or local government acted on their own to hawk their liberalizing initiative to the center. This, however, was far from a politically sound strategy. An effort led only by local authorities was susceptible to challenge from other financial hubs and bureaucratic actors and seen as self-serving. Similarly, a financier-driven venture devoid of any backing from local authorities raised questions about its feasibility and compatibility with the existing market and regulatory infrastructure concentrated in the financial hubs. The different resource endowments which the local and financial actors possessed were therefore complementary. They furnished the local initiative with technicalities and policy options that might lie beyond the center's purview. This enabled the local and financial interests to advance the liberalizing initiative to the financial bureaucracy and draw attention to a particular aspect that had yet to enter the decision or institutional agenda (Cairney 2012: 182–3).

These partnerships between local authorities and financial interests galvanized the emergence of the pro-opening coalitions that would play an important part in policy deliberation and implementation. They solicited support from central bureaucratic actors and sought to maintain at least the acquiescence of concerned others. This was equally important to the local authorities already blessed with some patrons at a central level, as disagreement and resistance within the bureaucracy might delay or doom any liberalizing quest. A successful attempt, however, required more than the putting forward of an opening intent. Liberalizing moves had the best chance of obtaining political backing if they were deemed relevant to the concerns of bureaucratic actors whose positions were shaped by distributional implications and policy risk considerations.

Therefore, local and financial interests would construct "good stories" that might have the greatest appeal to central actors. One common strategy involved relating the liberalizing initiative to pressing policy challenges lacking satisfactory remedies, or to issues that nurtured political stakes. The liberalizing initiative might thereby aim to provide a new solution to an old problem, and would often build on the failure and insufficiency of existing policies, as well as events like crises that forced a consideration of possibilities beyond any repertoires already to hand. This is not to suggest that technical feasibility or investors' interests were of no importance, but seldom did they constitute the primary rationale underlying bureaucratic support.

Yet, as the pro-opening coalitions emerged and their quest entered the decision agenda, local and financial players who found little or no room to play, or were excluded, might find it in their best interests to block, or slow down, the move. Dissenting parties could pursue similar agenda-setting strategies to the pro-opening coalitions, defining and framing a liberalizing move as deleterious to the interests of domestic constituents and the larger economy. Through drumming up adverse distributional and risk implications, they could present a starkly different story of the opening initiative championed by the pro-opening coalition, breaking its agenda-setting monopoly. Like the framing attempt of the opening advocates, such efforts were often facilitated by signs of market instability and looming crises that called the opening initiative into question and alerted cautious bureaucratic actors.

Bureaucratic actors wary of the incidences of policy risk could also make use of connections with the central elites of the state (and party) to solicit their intervention. Such efforts were frequently joined by resisting local and industrial players with interests or agendas irreconcilable with the pro-opening coalition. This could amplify discord within the central bureaucracy and present a stalemate to the decision-making elites.

Concessionary politics and policy tendencies/outcomes

As pro-opening local and financial industry interests obtained bureaucratic patronage and aligned as a policy coalition, they carried the opening initiative forward from policy formation to deliberation. The liberalizing move, however, was seldom introduced in the way it was originally conceived. To address challenges from dissenting parties, concessionary politics was indispensable to policy deliberation and implementation—failure to act invariably meant the defeat of an initiative.

Studies of the fragmented authoritarianism lineage have highlighted the importance of bargaining and accommodation between reform advocates and policy stakeholders whose non-objection is crucial for an agenda to gain momentum as economic and financial policy issues become increasingly complex (Duckett 2003). Lampton (1992: 34), for instance, argues that bargaining has been the defining character of China's policymaking process because no single party, be they a bureaucratic or local entity, can "carry out an undertaking without the cooperation of other(s), but which cannot compel the cooperation of the others(s) and cannot persuade a senior authoritative leader or institution to compel the other(s) to cooperate." Relatedly, Shirk (1993: 118–19) stresses that consensus building serves an important "price discovery" function. Through "delegation by consensus," lower level ministries are delegated by the top decision-making authority to reach consensus among themselves prior to the approval and endorsement of the top decision-making elites. This not only saves the valuable time and energy of the decision makers, it also carries an important signaling function since policy initiatives that travel up to the apex of the political system should in theory be the ones endorsed by the most stakeholders; whereas those that do not have likely faced dissent and resistance (Shirk 1993: 117).

As a result, policy advocates within the bureaucracy have an incentive to engage in bargaining and accommodation, to maximize the extent of agreement with others (and to minimize resistance) during policy deliberation. These insights on the imperative of offering concessions during the bargaining process provide an important analytical tool with which to make sense of otherwise complex interactions between central and local authorities across a range of different policy issue areas (Lampton and Lieberthal 1992). Financial opening pursuits that involve a multiplicity of domestic stakeholders bargaining over issues of a technical and complex nature are no exception.

During policy deliberation, besides setting and framing the opening agenda and obtaining patronage from the financial bureaucracy, constituents of the pro-opening coalition also need to build political and technical consensus before implementation, and consider dissenting voices. Although the outcome of such a process is often understood in binary terms (i.e., with or without consensus), in the process of consensus building this is rarely the case. Since policy actors face inevitable trade-offs when hammering out policy specifics, the process also provides opportunities for them to reach agreement by offering concessions or side-payments (Shirk 1993; Heilmann 2017a: 41–3). In fact, policy advocates must stay open and flexible over details related to particulars, or otherwise mutual accommodation becomes impossible. The different "price levels," strategies, and mechanisms of consensus building essential to moving bargaining forward, however, have rarely been differentiated.

Actors who are initially not part of the pro-opening coalition might be neutral or inclined to extend their support, but the fact that financial opening often introduced new policy or institutional arrangements that impinged on distributional and risk positions sometimes discouraged them from doing so. Other local authorities and financial interests might be eager to take part in the liberalizing move, yet the inability of the pro-opening coalition and its opening advocates to respond to their demands or heed their concerns invites dissent even when the actor might be a potential source of support. Similarly, some bureaucratic actors might be attracted to an opening initiative, but be aware of technical concerns like the unready nature of existing market regulations, infrastructure, or pertinent financial standards—causing reservation and hesitancy and the fear of generating policy risks that might adversely affect an agency's interests and standing.

This analysis suggests how agreement was maintained (and how dissent evolved) within and without the coalitions, and sheds light on the various ways concessionary offers might be extended by opening advocates. One might find partners with a shared a policy outlook and belief that an initiative was worth pursuing and to the benefit of the larger domestic economy. Consensus also arose from agreement surrounding the political and policy objectives of an opening move, including instrumental ends like resolving policy problems and fostering certain local, financial industry, and bureaucratic interests. Actors might also converge on the same position when they acknowledged the policy priority of a pro-opening coalition but saw little stake in its pursuit. Still, this was better than the situation in which consensus was maintained through the non-objection and neutrality of other parties.[5] On the other hand, agreements on technical aspects like the readiness of market infrastructure, financial regulations, and standards for any products and services concerned were equally important in turning an opening endeavor into practice.

These ingredients of consensus were by no means mutually exclusive. Actors might be drawn together by one or more of these elements. Although they appear to imply varying levels of strength of agreement, they might be better viewed in categorical terms analogous to the components underlying an index.

The more of these that were present, the more robust was the consensus; and the fewer that were present, the stronger the dissent. Shared policy objectives, for instance, were no substitute for a lack of technical consensus if the latter emerged as a pressing concern. Similarly, conflicting priorities with other bureaucratic actors might weaken a pro-opening coalition, even if other merits of advancing the initiative were acknowledged. In other words, disagreements among actors could stem from divergent policy outlooks, conflicting objectives and priorities, as well as from the technical arrangements not being ready.

In addition to securing endorsement from within the financial bureaucracy and among senior decision makers, opening advocates had to factor in these different sources of dissent in policy deliberation and implementation. In some cases, these could be foreseen, as actors' stances were informed by distributional and policy risk concerns. In other instances, they emerged in policy deliberations, spurred by the changing calculus of the policy actors. To sustain the opening momentum, concessionary politics played an indispensable part in preempting or allaying dissenting views, and expanding the sources of political support the pro-opening coalition might count on.

More importantly, the different bases of consent (and dissent) suggest that several concessionary strategies are possible. To cope with disagreement over policy objectives, priorities, and technical arrangements, opening advocates might adjust implementation specifics like the scope, pace, location, and technical particularities of the intended liberalizing initiative. These general dimensions are significant as they were crucial to defining the content and spatial scale of economic and financial opening, and illustrate the importance of timing of the opening quests (Nelson 1990; Thurbon 2001; Gallagher 2002: 356–9). By restricting the scale, slowing down the pace, or making adjustments to technical matters, pro-opening coalitions could calibrate and fine-tune certain aspects of their original sketches in the hope of muting dissent (and soliciting new support).

But what if they did not see these as in their interests because they wished to maintain control over the liberalizing initiative? Since financial opening involved multiple dimensions and was inextricably linked with other policy issues, the provision of political and policy side-payments in the form of the exchange of support across different issues to dissenting parties was possible to allay concerns and obtain acquiescence. This took place beyond the central level in China during policy deliberations—just like the logrolling activities in legislatures and among policymakers in other contexts (Lampton, 1992; Shirk 1993: 118–19).

Steinberg and Shih (2012), for example, reveal that the lobbying behavior of tradable and non-tradable industrial groups over the exchange rate level of the renminbi was contingent upon policy compensation being made available. When offered compensation, dissenters withheld their opposition at least temporarily. In pushing forward the opening agenda, pro-opening coalitions and their constituents could offer policy support on varying issues to their dissenting counterparts. To enhance the credibility of an offer, political side-payments like these could be promised by a bureaucratic patron of the coalition.

While concessionary politics was important to bargaining between opening advocates and dissenting parties, it was also critical within policy coalitions because the constituents had to agree on common ground and the range of acceptable results of bargaining well before they reached out to others. This ensured that they stood on the same policy position and acted in a concerted manner when in policy deliberations with the government. Failing to do so would expose the coalition to easy challenges from dissenting policy actors.

If concessionary strategies succeeded, opening tendencies would come to fruition and various opening forms would be possible. Opening outcomes are the products of accommodations extended by pro-opening coalitions to dissenting parties through the adjustment of policy implementation specifics. In cases when the pro-opening coalition and opening advocates extended the liberalizing initiative to other interested local and financial industry interests, the scope and location of the original opening quest championed by the pro-opening coalition was expanded. Multiple financial centers and industries would introduce the similar programs, build market share, and strengthen their niches in offering products and services. This has usually been associated with retrenchment of the center's direct control of market development and an increasing level of policy discretion available to localities and financiers.

In the opposite cases, when pro-opening coalitions agreed to scale down their pursuit, either by restricting the scope and location, slowing down the pace of implementation, or imposing additional regulatory requirements to allay the concerns of dissenting parties, little flexibility remained for localities and financiers in implementation, since deviation from the arrangement might compromise the consensus of the opening quest. In the scenario where political side-payments were provided by the pro-opening coalition, or when there was no dissent in policy deliberation, the pro-opening coalition and its constituents retained policy monopoly, and the liberalizing move retained its original shape.

Yet these concessionary strategies did not always work. They failed when dissenting parties turned down the offered concessions, when promises by the opening advocates to reciprocate through policy side-payments appeared unappealing, or when bureaucratic actors (and sometimes central decision-making elites above them) registered concerns about systemic risks beyond those which the concessionary acts addressed. In other instances, concessionary strategies were not pursued by the pro-opening coalition and its constituents, either because of disagreements over the extent of accommodation, or because making compromises would entail a significant loss of the constituents' initial interests, or for the very simple reason that there was no imperative to do so. In these situations, the coalitions were unable to ward off dissent or to maintain a political and technical consensus.

Depending on the basis and strength of dissent, two other policy tendencies other than opening could result. If the dissent to liberalizing initiatives persisted not only because of conflicting policy priority or political economic interests, but due to systemic risk concerns that alerted the financial bureaucracy and top decision-making elites, the liberalizing initiative was paused and rolled back.

This resulted in policy reversal as previous liberalizing commitments and programs were reneged upon and central actors sought protection through isolation. Continuing calls from opening advocates pushing the agenda ceased to be effective as the dissenting voices dominated and found sympathy with decision-making elites. Although there was a slight chance that such an aborted quest could be revived when policy tendencies changed course, it took considerable time and political maneuvering from an opening coalition to muster sufficient political support to revive a shelved program.

In cases where there were only political risk concerns, it was unusual to expect intervention from the top elites, as bureaucratic actors confronted scenarios with limited implications for the country's core political economic stakes. However, in the face of resistance from local, financial industry, or bureaucratic interests, any opening move would be blocked if the presence of dissenting parties broke the requisite political and technical consensus. Financial liberalization and opening was foiled, just as the blocking coalition prevented the concentration of local capital within the national financial system (Verdier 2002). Initiatives cherished by pro-opening coalitions and opening advocates were sidetracked. Although the central authorities might have appeared neutral toward the issue, conflicting positions within the bureaucracy and among domestic constituents generally resulted in a stalemate.

This formulation of different policy tendencies transcends conventional discussions of the styles of financial opening. Instead of seeing China's experience as gradualist, experimental, or "erratic," trajectories of different aspects of financial opening defy these generic labels and in fact display elements of each. Sometimes the episodes adhere to a gradualist logic, while at other times a "big bang" narrative is more appropriate. The shifts were driven by political and economic dynamics at home involving multiple domestic constituents. This study fills a gap in the literature concerning what drove changes during the financial opening, and how they occurred, with a political explanation illustrated through three recent episodes.

Conclusion

This chapter has established the analytical framework of the study that synthesizes the insights derived from prevailing models of China's policymaking. While the fragmented authoritarianism perspective rightly suggests a multiplicity of actors and the imperative of bargaining and tradeoffs, and the political survival and quasi-market models lay the basis for understanding the bureaucratic dynamics, they each miss the possibility of collective and concerted efforts among domestic constituents at central, local and industrial levels.

This study argues that policy coalition—a relatively informal and impermanent form of association over a certain issue area—and the dynamics with dissenting parties constitute the political sources of the changing policy trajectories and outcomes of China's financial opening. Memberships of the coalitions were not permanent and varied between cases because the interests and preferences of the three kinds of domestic actors were not predisposed by their political standings or market niches. Rather, they were conditioned by the prospective distributional implications and policy risks of the individual opening initiatives. The two conditions have shaped the positions of actors and, in turn, prompted alignments as part of pro-opening coalitions or dissenting parties.

The local authorities of domestic financial hubs and financial industry interests were the primary constituents of the coalitions. Motivated by material interests, they originated opening initiatives through agenda setting and issue framing, and capitalized on connections with policymakers and central decision-making elites to solicit their support. If successful, this strengthened their coalitions and drove policymaking from formation to deliberation, in which bartering with dissenting parties and among opening advocates became inevitable. Especially important were implementation specifics like scope, pace, and location, as well as the technical standards underlying the opening initiative. This helped expand the bases of political support and allayed dissent to ensure that the political and technical consensus was maintained.

Coalition dynamics in turn shaped the policy tendencies and outcomes. The policy tendency of opening was to be expected in the absence of any dissent, or in more realistic cases in the event of successful concessionary offers from the pro-opening coalition and its constituents. This could be achieved in different ways depending on specific contexts. If coalitions reduced the scale of opening moves to ward off dissent, this resulted in an opening with constrained scope and pace. Opposite cases saw the liberalizing scale expanded to other interested localities and financial industry interests which in turn shared the spoils of opening more widely, helping to consolidate support for the opening advocates and preempt opposition. When the coalition and its constituents retained policy monopoly and pursued its achievement in the way it aspired to, it was either because there was no dissent, or because dissenting or interested parties had been compensated by side-payments or promised future political support for other policy quests.

Concessionary attempts, however, did not always work. This happened when coalitions did not appeal to dissenting local authorities and financiers, or when bureaucratic actors were deterred by serious risk implications. Two other policy tendencies—reversal or stasis—then ensue. Reversal from committed opening efforts would see the opening commitment retracted and renounced by the authorities. This happened when systemic risk concerns raised serious concerns in central bureaucratic actors, in addition to political risk and the reservations of domestic constituents. Stasis, with little or no deviation from the existing status quo, was contributed to by political risk affecting specific bureaucratic actors, and by dissenting parties which did not accept concessionary offers.

The next chapter examines the evolution of China's outbound equity investment regime. It originated with Hong Kong's effort to bring forth institutional channels for mainland investment to the city's market in the early 2000s. The slow takeoff in its early years was followed by a significant expansion and culminated in the Through Train investment scheme of 2007. However, the opening initiative experienced policy reversal within months, putting a halt to the quest of the pro-opening coalition. Subsequent efforts by multiple local financial hubs after the global financial crisis brought few breakthroughs. It was not until the turn of the decade that opening of limited scope resumed momentum, making possible a restricted and slow easing after 2011, marked by the launch of ETFs and Stock Connects.

The attempts to internationalize China's stock market examined in Chapter 4 show a different trajectory. Instead of alternating policy tendencies, the pro-opening coalition, consisting of Shanghai-based interests, gained strong support from the CSRC and top decision-making elites as it looked for red-chip homecoming and an international board from the mid-2000s onwards. Yet this did not usher in implementation of the opening initiative as the opening advocates had intended because of their failure to reach consensus with dissenting bureaucratic parties over essential technical matters and because of a breakdown of political and technical consensus within the financial bureaucracy. Escalating financial risk at home ultimately sidetracked the opening tendency and resulted in policy reversal. No foreign firms have issued shares in China's domestic market.

Chapter 5 delves into Hong Kong's transformation into China's first offshore renminbi center—a development integral to renminbi internationalization. It displays fewer twists of fate as the liberalizing initiatives of the offshore authorities and financiers found strong backing from financial industry interests and the bureaucracy. The opening tendency largely stayed on course from the 2000s, as onshore constituents benefited from offshore renminbi activities, or were given concessionary offers. Small-scale individual renminbi businesses in the early 2000s were followed by the dramatic growth of offshore renminbi bond markets and renminbi trade settlement after a few years. Advances in financial products beyond the fixed income species, however, have been slowed and complicated by disagreements between the opening advocates over financial standards and the resurgent challenge from onshore financial hubs. It was only after the initiatives of 2012 that strengthened connections between the onshore and offshore renminbi markets took off, despite domestic economic uncertainties.

Notes

1 Even though policy studies has obviously paid great attention to policy change, the subject began to draw attention from scholars only after the mid-1980s, when the notion of advocacy coalition was conceived. Since then, it has been applied in about 100 studies of different policy domains ranging from environmental protection and social development to economics and foreign relations. To the author's knowledge, however, no existing work has applied the concept to finance or fiscal-policy. The literature surrounding policy entrepreneurs, while finding larger applications in policy studies, represents a related but separate body of work. See Mintrom and Norman (2009).

2 Factions are not peculiar to China, and have been a common political dynamic in East Asian states like Taiwan, Japan, South Korea, and Vietnam, albeit within the diversity of contexts, bases, and effects that grouping implies. For simplicity and to stay focused,

the discussion here is intended to be illustrative and in no way an exhaustive account as it does not touch on the subtle disagreements among China specialists on various aspects of the concept. A good synthesis of the debate and competing perspectives in the voluminous literature can be found in Nathan and Tsai (1995) and Unger (2002).

3 Shenzhen's formal administrative ranking is only half a notch below the provincial government as a "deputy-provincial" city, in which its mayor has political standing equivalent to the vice provincial governor of Guangdong. For details, see Chung (2010).

4 Subsequent appointments saw Hong Kong officials taking up advisory positions with onshore financial regulatory bodies, government-affiliated think tanks, and senior executive positions within domestic financial firms.

5 These varying bases underlying the consensus-building process is like the distinction of the different types of policy beliefs in the advocacy coalition framework. Sabatier and Jenkins-Smith distinguish "deep core belief" (the normative and philosophical bases of policy choices), "policy core belief" (fundamental policy positions) and "secondary aspects" (the operational aspects in policy implementation) in a descending order of strength. Deep core belief provides the strongest glue binding members of the coalition and encourages coordinated activities. See Sabatier and Jenkins-Smith (1993), pp. 203–5.

3 Let the money go abroad
The checkered journey of outbound equity investment

Introduction

This chapter, together with the next, examines the political dynamics of an aspect of financial opening often overlooked in the IPE literature: equity market liberalization (except for Sobel 1994; Lavelle 2001; Green 2004). While the securities market opening was not entirely a novel issue at the time, and was significant to the financial community and investors, treatments by political scientists and China specialists have been conspicuously uncommon. The work that has been completed has tended to focus on the evolution of the regulatory structure, the effects of crisis, the entry of foreign firms into market institutions and practices, and competition between financial hubs (Bell and Feng 2009; Hsueh 2011; Jarvis 2011; Lai 2012). Very little work has been done that examines the liberalizing initiatives pursued by the Chinese authorities and the associated political economic interplays.

This chapter looks at the evolution of the outbound equity investment regime whereas Chapter 4 centers on the internationalization of the domestic stock market. Since these aspects enhanced the capital market opening and the innovation of financial products, mostly technical in nature, the liberalizing initiatives should crystallize more readily than other aspects of financial opening (like the currency internationalization discussed in Chapter 5 that touches upon China's capital control regime and monetary policy). However, this is not the case.

The path of the outbound equity investment regime witnessed remarkable policy twists and turns. Policy stasis was overtaken by opening initiatives of varying forms after the mid-2000s: from the creation of institutional channels to the Through Train scheme (*zhitong che*) that never departed and was canceled within months even after a huge initial fanfare. This false start was followed by belated opening endeavors with indirect forms of access to offshore markets, like the overseas ETFs and the closed-end "Stock Connects" that aimed to link up the Hong Kong and mainland stock markets. These shifting policy tendencies, however, cannot satisfactorily be explained with reference only to changing market contexts and the demands of investors that the market be prized open. If they were sound explanations, we should be able to trace a drastically different policy trajectory with the opening tendency maintained over time and the implementation of initiatives that truly served the interests of mainland investors and allowed for direct and legal exit from the domestic securities market.

The Chinese experience of the time, however, was otherwise. Domestic coalitional politics assumed a far more significant role than other factors. The pro-opening coalition, composed of local financial hubs, financiers and supportive central bureaucratic actors, constituted a major driving force of policy change. It shaped the policy agenda, framed opening initiatives to its advantage, sought additional support from local, industry and bureaucratic counterparts, and offered concessions when possible to allay dissent.

Throughout the evolution of China's outbound equity investment regime, Hong Kong's financial officials and industry interests were the principal constituents of the pro-opening coalition, successfully eliciting support from different central bureaucratic actors in the quest for varying opening initiatives after the early 2000s. Early calls originating from Hong Kong for the Qualified Domestic Institutional Investor (QDII) scheme, the institution-based investment channel, however, failed to be heeded. It was only after the coalition re-framed the initiative in ways that appealed to bureaucratic actors searching for remedies to domestic macroeconomic challenges that the opening gained momentum and made it onto the central political agenda. This buttressed the coalition with central political support and resulted in the launch of the QDII in 2006.

Soon after, the offshore community pioneered the Through Train scheme that would largely circumvent onshore financial institutions in outbound equity investment—a dramatic easing of capital mobility for individual investors. The offshore opening advocates conceived it as a liberalizing attempt that helped cool down an overheating economy, and it found a strong echo from several bureaucratic heavyweights less than two years after QDII was in place. This quickly lifted the Through Train to the top of the government's agenda and its deliberation was fast-tracked.

Unlike QDII, the Through Train was first launched with the northern city of Tianjin and one of the state-owned banks taking the lead, and was soon expanded to other financial hubs and banks to cement local and industry support gained from beyond the initial advocates of the pro-opening coalition. Despite the lack of political consensus from other bureaucratic actors, the coalition precociously announced the Through Train initiative in August 2007, and promised to simultaneously keep the scope extensible and moderate the pace of implementation if necessary to allay dissent. These concessionary efforts were largely ineffectual because the risk implications of the Through Train spurred dissent within the financial industry and bureaucracy, and the unanticipated scale of capital outflow following the Through Train announcement shook the financial system. This weakened political support for the Through Train, undermined the larger opening agenda, and prompted intervention from top decision-making elites that reversed the opening tendency.

As such, despite several local calls to resurrect the Through Train agenda, attempts to solicit industrial, bureaucratic and financiers' support failed. QDII

Table 3.1 Major developments in the evolution of the outbound equity investment regime

2001–2003	Hong Kong's financial opening proposal is submitted to the State Council (July 2001).
	Central bureaucratic entities are divided. Onshore financiers and financial hubs are opposed to the offshore liberalizing initiative.
	QFII takes precedence and is introduced in November 2002.
2004–2006	Central authorities begin to unfasten outbound investment regulations for the government pension fund.
	QDII is introduced (April 2006) for domestic banks and subsequently expanded to onshore securities firms, mutual funds, and insurance companies.
2006–2007	HKMA calls for the Through Train investment scheme and finds support from NDRC, SAFE and PBOC (early 2007).
	Through Train is made public and scheduled to be phased in as a pilot in Tianjin, in partnership with the Bank of China (August 2007). Scheme is scheduled to be expanded to other localities.
Second half of 2007	The central financial bureaucracy splits and there is strong dissent from onshore financiers and local financial hubs, causing delays.
	Top decision-making elites intervene, and the initiative is suspended. Formal policy reversal follows (October 2007). QDII continues as the only legal channel for outbound equity investment.
2008–2010	Attempts are made by onshore financial hubs to resuscitate the Through Train, but they are unable to obtain any support from financiers or central bureaucratic actors.
	Hong Kong turns to overseas ETFs that offer indirect exposure to overseas markets as an alternative to the Through Train. This is met with interest at the PBOC.
2011	Backed by the Shanghai and Shenzhen authorities and exchanges, overseas ETFs gain policy momentum.
	Overseas ETFs are endorsed by the CSRC (August 2011).
2013–2016	The PBOC and CSRC signal the launch of QDII2 (early 2013), eliciting strong interest from both onshore and offshore financial hubs. However, the scheme is postponed and then derailed by concerns of systemic risk (2014/15).
	The offshore community and onshore bourses achieve Mutual Market Access through the Stock Connect scheme. The Shanghai-Hong Kong Stock Connect commences trading (November 2014). The Shenzhen-Hong Kong Stock Connect follows (December 2016).

remained the only legal channel of outbound equity investment. It was not until the late 2000s that a different opening initiative originating in the offshore community, the overseas ETFs with Hong Kong equity underlying, found appeal among mainland financial hubs and won the PBOC's support as it was linked together with the offshore renminbi market development. After concessionary attempts by the pro-opening coalition to restrict its scale and eligibility requirements, the CSRC sanctioned the initiative in 2011.

Nonetheless, direct individual access to offshore equity markets remained improbable despite the backing of central financial policymakers. Highly anticipated initiatives such as the second Qualified Domestic Individual Investor (QDII2) scheme were retracted due to the associated policy risks and disagreements over the opening scale. It was only in late 2014 that the Stock Connect scheme had its debut, bridging the Shanghai (and subsequently Shenzhen) and Hong Kong stock exchanges and providing mutual and partial access to equities for both institutional and individual investors in the onshore and offshore markets. Although this significantly eased outbound equity investment and represented the only legally sanctioned channel for mainland individual investors to purchase stocks offshore, the sealed investment conduits afforded the Chinese regulatory authorities considerable discretion to moderate cross-border capital traffic and contain the policy risks of financial opening.

Local origin of the outbound equity investment regime

The Hong Kong government and financial community were integral constituents of the pro-opening coalition of the outbound equity investment regime. As a gateway connecting China to the rest of the world, Hong Kong has also been the financial hub where mainland capital has found exits and investment opportunities unavailable on the mainland. These players were instrumental in shaping the policy agenda and advancing options available to the central authorities, lobbying central bureaucratic actors, and seeking support from onshore financiers and other local authorities

Agenda setting and concessionary attempts from offshore

As early as 2000, the Hong Kong Monetary Authority (HKMA) and Securities and Futures Commission (SFC), the city's de facto central bank and securities regulator, had examined the competitive edge the city's financial industry held moving into the new century. Together with the city's leading international banks, the offshore authorities envisioned that China would press on with financial liberalization after WTO accession and, as part of China, Hong Kong would be in the best position to help China's capital market dovetail with international practices and standards. This would not only consolidate the status of Hong Kong as an international financial center; the local financial industry, armed with leading financial expertise, would also benefit enormously by providing professional services to mainland companies and investors.[1]

The resultant analysis was submitted to the State Council in July 2001, and included recommendations such as introducing a closed-end fund for mainland individuals making overseas investments, creating ETFs with underlying shares of Chinese companies listed in Hong Kong, and promoting the listing of overseas firms in China in the form of the China Depository Receipt (CDR). It was hoped that Beijing would eventually endorse some of the measures and further China's capital opening.[2] Indeed, the local brainchild was so far-reaching it would also define the range of policy options of China's financial opening in the 2000s. ETF, for example, gained much appeal after the aborting of the Through Train scheme in the late 2000s; CDR listing also constituted an alternative to the initial public offering (IPO) of foreign firms (see Chapter 4).

Regarding outbound equity investment, the closed-end fund proposal laid the technical basis of QDII that allowed for an orderly outflow of mainland capital by institutional investors. However, these recommendations emanating from Hong Kong were not enough to bring forth policy change. Since they foresaw the exclusive participation of foreign financial institutions, they were of little appeal to mainland financial industry interests that would be indispensable to the effective selling of the funds to mainland investors. To entice support from the onshore financial community and its central patrons, Hong Kong modified its plan and proposed that onshore fund providers could play pivotal roles to bridge the mainland investors and overseas markets. Andrew Sheng, the then SFC Chairman, also explained to the central authorities that QDII would be limited in scope and contain built-in regulatory safeguards.[3]

Under the plan, asset management companies on the mainland would raise funds from individual investors before committing to any offshore investment. While no new capital would be accepted after operation (hence *closed*-end), investors could sell their shares on a secondary market and the fund managers would close the fund after a defined period, such that the sum would be remitted entirely onshore. This arrangement hoped to entice the support of onshore financial industry interests and from mainland financial regulators who saw little room for easing capital control at the time.[4] Hong Kong's gesture met with partial success as the CSRC did appear interested in QDII. Vice Chairman Wang Jiangxi acknowledged early on that QDII was on the agency's policy agenda, alongside the Qualified Foreign Institutional Investor (QFII) scheme that permitted foreign portfolio investment in China.[5]

Dissenting central patrons and onshore constituents

Despite Hong Kong's concessionary attempts, most actors in the mainland financial bureaucracy remained noncommittal. Zhou Xiaochuan, the top securities regulator at the time, declined to extend further support to the proposal as policy deliberation continued. Contrary to his deputy's position, Zhou suggested that QDII simply fell beyond his agency's policy purview. Wu Xiaoling, the then PBOC Vice Governor, also viewed QDII as an inchoate idea that had not been scrutinized by the central bank and the SAFE, both of which had a significant say in the future nature of capital account opening.[6] They saw little imperative to ease outbound investment at the time and were sensitized to earlier policy failures in equity market opening. These reservations resulted in a policy stasis out of which the QDII, championed by the Hong Kong government and offshore financiers, could not make further headway.

Indeed, outbound investment was not high on the policy agendas of the CSRC, PBOC or the mainland financial community because they were preoccupied with inbound investment liberalization. The CSRC and PBOC had been examining Taiwan's and South Korea's financial opening experiences since the late 1990s and had recognized the need to introduce channels that facilitated portfolio investment into China after WTO accession in 2001.[7] The CSRC hoped that foreign investors could play an important part in galvanizing securities market reform, balancing the skewed domestic investor base (mostly comprised of individual domestic investors) and smoothing out market volatility as financial institutions usually had a long investment horizon.

The CSRC and PBOC were also sensitive to the political and systemic risks associated with capital outflows, in large part due to earlier policy setbacks originating from similar liberalizing initiatives. The CSRC had the fresh experience of the initiative of February 2001 that aimed to liberalize the B-share market (the segregated equity class of domestic companies traded in foreign currencies and for foreign investors only), which had resulted in a near-calamity. The initiative was widely heralded at the time as offering a valuable investment opportunity to mainland investors, given the substantial price discounts between the B-shares and the renminbi-denominated A-shares only available to mainland investors.[8] The CSRC opened the market to domestic investors in June 2001 after a four-month rally that had doubled the B-share index, but this was followed by a deep adjustment that halved the market cap over the summer and resulted in serious financial losses for thousands of individual domestic investors. Although the regulator tried to shift the blame onto international investors, blaming them for cashing out when the Chinese investors joined the rally, it could not escape all criticism because the liberalizing move was seen as wrongfully conceived and executed.[9]

This was a painful lesson for the CSRC: investor protection had to be integral to the liberalization calculus, or there would be tremendous political liabilities and popular pressure in the event of policy failure. With such an unpleasant experience fresh in the memory, the regulator was wary of repeating the mistake with QDII. Moreover, the PBOC and SAFE were alerted to QDII's possible destabilizing capital outflow from the mainland financial system. Since the 1990s, capital had crossed the border through a variety of "gray" (and downright illegal) channels to foreign markets. Individuals with relatives or contacts in Hong Kong, and companies with offices in Hong Kong had been managing to invest in the city's equity market with few difficulties. Offshore brokerages and thousands of currency exchanges and underground financial entities also offered securities trading services to customers in southern China.[10]

Indeed, the financial community of southern China regarded illicit capital outflow as useful because it dampened excess domestic money supply and met the strong demand for the renminbi in Hong Kong caused by expectation of its appreciation.[11] The central bank and SAFE, however, were frustrated by their fledging capital monitoring system that rendered efforts to crack down on illegal investment ineffective. In their view, a legally sanctioned channel like QDII could only aggravate the extent of capital flight and complicate enforcement efforts.[12]

Besides these challenges from within the financial bureaucracy, QDII faced opposition from both onshore financial and local interests. Despite Hong Kong's extension of goodwill and consideration of the interests of onshore financiers, the financiers viewed QDII largely as a scheme that would primarily benefit offshore brokerages and argued that, if the scheme really was intended to help promote the international experience of the domestic securities industry running investment funds overseas, QDII's scope should go beyond Hong Kong and include truly global markets like New York and London.[13] Fang Xinghai, who represented the Shanghai Stock Exchange (SSE), questioned QDII's appeal to mainland investors after the significant losses accrued during the mainland investment bubble of the mid to late 1990s.[14]

These divergent policy priorities and assessments of QDII, together with the policy risk concerns widely held among bureaucratic actors, meant that Hong Kong was unable to garner the political patronage indispensable to forming a strong pro-opening coalition. Worse still, both the local and financiers' dissent also strengthened the opposing view, which effectively sank Hong Kong's initiative.

Bridging the markets with institutional investment channels

The setback, however, did not completely oust QDII from the agenda of the offshore community. Without much success, it capitalized on discussions between the mainland and Hong Kong authorities surrounding the Closer Economic Partnership Arrangement (CEPA), which concluded in June 2003, with the hope of incorporating QDII and the offshore renminbi business into the agreement to promote cross-border financial cooperation. But deliberations surrounding QDII stalled as the CSRC and PBOC were preoccupied by perceived policy risks, especially the systemic risk implications of capital outflow running out of control. The policy of introducing inbound investment through QFII took precedence, and allowed foreign institutional investors to purchase securities on the A-share markets after November 2002. In addition to strong bureaucratic support, the mainland brokerages, together with the Shanghai and Shenzhen local governments, were of the view that foreign investment could stimulate the bearish stock markets, boost turnover and prices, and elevate the international status of the domestic market (Li and Yuan 2003: 25–6).

It was not until 2004 that Hong Kong's initiative saw some hope of revival. Changing calculations surrounding QDII within the financial bureaucracy and among onshore financiers, together with Hong Kong's earlier concessionary attempt to incorporate the mainland financial industry interests into the initiative, contributed to a gradual unfastening of outbound investment restrictions imposed on domestic financial institutions. Starting in August 2004, insurance companies could purchase foreign securities through their own foreign currency holdings. The National Social Security Fund also ventured overseas in early 2006 and committed US$500–800 million (CIRC and PBOC 2004). While these easing moves were downplayed by Beijing as merely measures to diversify the investment portfolios of big financial institutions, they signaled a policy turn that had been driven by a rising sense of urgency within the central authorities caused by macroeconomic challenges.

Between 2002 and 2003, China's foreign exchange reserves jumped 85%— fueled by trade surpluses and expectations of the renminbi's appreciation. This warming of the domestic economy galvanized the PBOC to consider the possibility of introducing new channels of capital outflow like QDII. The securities regulator and brokers also came to recognize the possible business gains to be made from investing abroad. As bureaucratic actors once reserved about QDII took new stances, and onshore financiers began to extend their support to Hong Kong's liberalizing initiative, QDII took off. In what appeared to be preparation for outbound institutional investment, the CBRC signaled the readiness of domestic banks to provide custody services for QDII funds in mid-2004.[15]

Moreover, the Hong Kong-led pro-opening coalition met no local dissent. Shanghai did not voice its concern about the possible impact on the local financial industry interests in large part because the local stock market was buoyant and it was about to launch the IPOs of state-owned mega-firms. In the absence of a notable local rival or dissent over implementation specifics, QDII was rolled out with extensible scope that allowed the local authorities and financiers to acquire more flexibility and discretion over time.

Restrictions on outbound equity investment were formally relaxed in April 2006 when the PBOC permitted domestic financial firms to raise funds from individuals and institutions for overseas investment. For interests emanating from the different financial industries, regulation was not to be centrally managed by the central bank. Regulators would instead announce rules and oversee the investments of institutions under their oversight. Although financial institutions would have to obtain investment quotas from SAFE, there was no cap as was the case with QFII. This built into QDII considerable flexibility and made possible expansion whenever the authorities saw fit. While the scale and types of investment products the fund could engage in were limited in the early phase, restrictions were gradually lifted and financial institutions enjoyed increasing discretion in fund development and investment decisions (PBOC 2006). To balance the competing interests of the financial industry, while domestic banks took most of the quota, they were subject to specific rules that made room for securities firms to develop their own fund products. In QDII's first year, 15 banks and funds were given a quota of US$14.2 billion for overseas investment in debt instruments and money-market products. Stocks and derivatives remained barred until May 2007.[16]

The market monopoly of commercial banks was broken in June 2007 as securities and fund companies could develop QDII products that were not bound by the regulatory caps imposed on the banks. In doing so, the CSRC sought to promote the market appeal of brokerage-developed funds. Insurance companies also originated QDII funds after late July (CSRC 2007; CIRC, PBOC, and SAFE 2007). However, to better control the financial risks taken by QDII-operators and individual investors, there were restrictions on the asset allocation (for instance, no single stock could exceed 5% of the entire portfolio value) for each QDII product. Individuals also faced a 300,000 yuan entry requirement when investing in QDII funds. These regulatory barriers greatly reduced QDII's appeal; individual investors continued to resort to underground channels when accessing overseas investment opportunities.

From its inception, the QDII scheme was considered an important liberalizing channel sanctioning the indirect exposure of domestic investors to overseas markets like Hong Kong. Despite concerns at the time that QDII might attract capital inflow to China (as the scheme appeared to signal further capital decontrol by Beijing), and challenging the program's intent to limit the growth of foreign exchange holdings, the government remained committed to the initiative. Indeed, QDII became the primary *legal* pillar of outbound equity investment available to mainland investors despite most QDII products having yields much lower than domestic securities investments. It was only after November 2014 that access to Hong Kong equity markets was greatly eased with the launch of the Shanghai–Hong Kong Stock Connect scheme.

Such delays hardly served investors' interests, or did much to cushion "inexperienced" mainland investors from volatility in overseas markets. Indeed, QDII primarily catered to bureaucratic interests and their perceived policy challenges, rather than providing better investment options to individual investors. It also guaranteed the state's control of outbound investment and ensured the continuation of benefits available to domestic financiers of the pro-opening coalition.

The Through Train that was to depart

Introduction of QDII did represent a remarkable success for the offshore community in galvanizing the evolution of China's outbound equity investment regime through the shaping of Beijing's liberalizing agenda, and the solicitation of support from bureaucratic patrons and mainland financial industry interests. With QDII in place, Hong Kong wasted little time and advanced another liberalizing venture, calling for the direct access of individual mainland investors to offshore equity markets—an initiative that would eventually be known as the Through Train scheme.

In contrast to its quest for QDII, the offshore community found strong support for the Through Train from the central bureaucracy, onshore financial and local interests in relatively little time. The NDRC, the macroeconomic management body, viewed the proposal as a practicable response to imminent economic challenges; Tianjin and the banking industry were attracted by the scheme's promising market growth opportunities. These onshore parties worked closely with the offshore community in policy deliberation and implementation, and constituted a strong pro-opening coalition. However, within a few months dissenting parties within the financial industry and bureaucracy intervened, weakening the leverage of the coalition despite concessionary offers. This resulted in dramatic reversal and policy stasis.

Agenda-setting and leverage politics

A few months after QDII was inaugurated, Hong Kong lobbied the central authorities to consider granting a "free walk for foreign exchange" that would lift the restrictions on the use of foreign currency holdings by mainland residents in overseas investment, and remove the need to go through mainland financial institutions when accessing foreign capital markets through the free remittance of foreign currencies to offshore bank accounts (Central Policy Unit 2007: 36 and 65). From Hong Kong's perspective, the QDII scheme was grossly insufficient to help Beijing cool down the economy and relieve the appreciation pressures on the renminbi.

Joseph Yam, the founding HKMA Chief Executive, said at the time that even though domestic financial stability remained an important concern, there was "ample scope for imaginative financial liberalization on the mainland, without being imprudent." Yam (2006 October) elaborated:

> How about giving freedom to investors with their own foreign-currency holdings and the ability to protect themselves, to invest overseas and enjoy more attractive returns? This would provide the incentive to pursue, and be consistent with, the declared policy of 'storing foreign exchange with the people. Let us have a "free walk" for investors with foreign exchange along with the "free walk" for tourists.

Perhaps to the surprise of Hong Kong, this bold initiative found strong support among China's financial policymakers who were increasingly wary of the risks of economic overheating. After Wen Jiabao took the premiership in 2003, there was a surge of criticism from within government about his seeming inability to manage the ballooning liquidity of the domestic economy. In the three years after Wen took power, foreign reserves tripled and money supply (M1) grew 48%. Despite this maintained double-digit growth, expectation of renminbi appreciation following the exchange regime reform in July 2005 aggravated capital inflows and fueled overinvestment.[17] Concerns about an overheated economy running out of control intensified from 2006, as inflation in monthly consumer price index (CPI) terms spiked from 0.9% in January 2006 to a decade-high 6.5% in August 2007. The senior leadership repeatedly called for a gradual and slow cooling down of the economy to prevent any hard landing.

Wen's political protégé, Ma Kai, the then NDRC Chair, had to take on these economic challenges. The cost of policy inaction or delay in face of the challenges the administration faced seemed politically and economically unpalatable. Instead of going through established plans like the Eleventh Five-Year Plan (2006–2010)—which offered little help to the NDRC due to its domestic focus, imperative of gradually expanding investment channels, and its support of Hong Kong's international financial center status—Ma's NDRC was attracted by the offshore initiative that promised to offer a direct and swift response to the imminent problem (People's Bank of China et al. 2008).

Led by the NDRC, the Through Train proposal was deliberated in an inter-agency meeting in March 2007, which followed a lower-level discussion between SAFE and the Bank of China (BOC) in 2006 surrounding the facilitation of outbound investment beyond QDII.[18] Championed by the "super-ministry" and SAFE, the proposal was embedded in the "Package of Pilot Proposals for Financial Development and Reform" submitted to the State Council in early August 2007.[19] It outlined a rough time-frame for the lifting of China's capital controls, and contained implementation details like investment scope and pilot cities. According to the proposal, by late August 2007, the BOC's Tianjin Branch would be the first available channel for mainland residents to buy foreign currencies or stocks listed on the Hong Kong market. To solicit the support of local financial hubs and industries, BOC branches of other cities like Shanghai, Beijing and Guangzhou would take part in October; mainland investors would be able to buy foreign currencies or stock using the renminbi or foreign currencies through all state-owned banks from early 2008.[20]

If approved, the expansion of the scheme would have represented a big leap from a scheme where Tianjin was the sole exit to a scheme in which multiple localities participated in the opening initiatives. Reportedly, the NDRC's package also included ambitious liberalizing moves, such as relaxing the maximum foreign exchange holdings of individuals to US$200,000, and the freeing of the renminbi's convertibility and circulation outside China by summer 2008.[21] As the economy heated up, it was hoped these drastic liberalizing moves would lower the political risks that the NDRC confronted, and pull China away from the brink of a hard landing that would bring significant systemic risks to the domestic economy.

It is worth noting that Tianjin was slated to be the pilot host of the Through Train in its early phase before other leading onshore financial hubs like Shanghai and Shenzhen were brought into the scheme. This was largely due to the agenda-setting efforts of Tianjin's leaders and financiers after 2006, when the city's Binhai New Area was designated the "National Hub of Financial Innovation"—a proving ground in north China for financial sector reforms like the piloting of offshore financial services and derivative contracts.[22] This, however, would not have been possible without the strong connections between local officials and central decision-making elites. Tianjin's Party Secretary, Zhang Gaoli, who gained vast experience in Shenzhen and Guangdong in the late 1990s, and Mayor Dai Xianglong, who served as PBOC Governor before assuming the local position, lobbied central bureaucrats to endorse the Binhai New Area as the pioneer of financial reform.

Their efforts paid off when the local agenda became an integral part of the country's financial development in the eleventh five-year period that was to promote balanced regional development by fostering financial services in northern China.[23] Its success would also constitute a remarkable political achievement crucial to the career advancement of Tianjin officials. In the presence of strong onshore support from Tianjin, the offshore Through Train initiative was fast-tracked within the financial bureaucracy. This not only surprised the offshore community, the equity market also reacted fervently.

The premature announcement

Backed by the NDRC and PBOC, SAFE made public the "Pilot Scheme for Introducing Mainland Individual Direct Investment to Overseas Securities Markets" on August 20, 2007 while still awaiting the Premier's and other State Councilors' final approval. The scheme allowed investors to open a special foreign currency account in the Tianjin Branch of BOC, and entrusted the BOC International Securities in Hong Kong as the settlement bank for securities and foreign exchange (SAFE 2007).

SAFE explained that the access of individuals to overseas markets would facilitate manageable outbound investment, adjust the international balance of payments, promote the financial market development of China and Hong Kong, and help repress illegal overseas investment.[24] Offshore financial officials shared these views, seeing the Through Train scheme as an important response to ballooning domestic liquidity contributed to by the excessive foreign reserve accumulation that had increasingly complicated Beijing's macroeconomic management. It also benefited mainland investors by providing diverse investment opportunities using foreign currency holdings—especially in view of the considerable price discounts to be secured on shares of mainland companies traded in Hong Kong (the H-shares) when compared to over-valued A-shares.[25] The offshore community was convinced that the Through Train was ready to depart very soon (Yam 2007a, 2007b).

The Through Train was to have as little as one-third of the QDII minimum requirement (of about 100,000 yuan), and it was to be exempted from the established restriction limiting mainland individuals to exchange a maximum of US$50,000 (or equivalent amounts in other currencies) per year. In effect, this would have made the renminbi partially convertible to the Hong Kong dollar with respect to outbound equity investments, as the NDRC-PBOC proposals in early August envisioned, permitting investors to obtain as much foreign currency as they wished to make investments in a Hong Kong market that was slated to benefit enormously from increased market turnover and expansion of its financial industry. Indeed, the offshore community regarded the prompt endorsement of the Through Train proposal as an indication of Beijing's support for consolidating Hong Kong's status as an international financial center.[26]

This all suggested that the Through Train was, in essence, a political venture championed by a pro-opening coalition that consisted of the offshore community, supportive onshore financiers, and central bureaucratic actors. It climbed to the top of the central policy agenda and was promptly endorsed not purely because it would advance of the mainland investors' interests but also because it served the ends of the coalition and its constituents. Hong Kong and Tianjin, as well as the BOC and its securities subsidiary, lobbied hard with the prospect of reaping substantial material benefits. The NDRC and SAFE echoed their calls because it was thought that the Through Train would boost their problem-solving competence by addressing pressing economic challenges and mitigating the perceived potential political risks the two agencies confronted in the face of runaway economic overheating.

This generated an opening momentum that would result in drastic capital decontrol. The opening tendency, however, was not sustained. The concessions offered by the pro-opening coalition, to expand the scheme to other mainland financial hubs and industries and to accommodate dissent over technical arrangements, failed. Systemic risk concerns loomed over the economy and forced the top decision-making elites to halt the scheme and reverse the liberalizing tendency.

The concessionary politics of the opening advocates

In the days after the SAFE announcement, the Through Train rally not only excited investors inside and outside China, it also prompted some onshore banks and financial hubs to lobby for the same arrangement. Since the NDRC-led proposal in early August suggested the expansion of the Through Train to other financial hubs and interests only after it was introduced, almost every major state-owned bank and securities firm pressed for immediate expansion of the scheme so as not to miss potentially enormous financial gains. For instance, the Bank of Communication (BoCom) and its offshore investment branch in Hong Kong appealed to CBRC for the Through Train license operated by its Beijing branch.[27]

The constituents of the Through Train coalition attempted to adjust the original plan to enlist the support of other interested parties. For example, in addition to the designated branch of BOC in Tianjin, other state-owned banks and cities which were not part of SAFE's original plan would be invited to find their niche once the Through Train began operation. Shanghai and Shenzhen would partner with the Industrial and Commercial Bank and BoCom, respectively.[28] Through this concessionary offer, the coalition hoped to ward off charges of Tianjin "localism" or preferential treatment by the BOC.[29] To strengthen bureaucratic support and assuage wariness about political and systemic risks within the financial bureaucracy, SAFE and BOC proposed additional safeguards for the Through Train, including a threefold increase to HKD300,000 of the investment threshold, a cap of HKD1.5 million for individual accounts, and a mandatory risk tolerance assessment for all investors that would screen inexperienced investors and limit the extent of capital outflows. Also, only residents of Tianjin, Shanghai and Shenzhen with investment experience would be allowed to join the Through Train in its early phase via BOC's Tianjin branch.[30] By limiting scope and spatial scale in this way, the Through Train coalition hoped to ease worries about any unchecked capital outflows that might ensue.

As a result of such give-and-take from the Through Train coalition and opening advocates, reports emerged that the initiative would commence within two months.[31] Behind the scenes, however, vocal dissent and opposition from within the financial bureaucracy and industry posed significant challenges to the pro-opening coalition. Its concessionary moves were unable to secure any further political support at the central and industrial levels, and its liberalizing agenda was also dismissed by the top decision-making elites as politically unviable and detrimental to China's financial stability. This shattered any hope of launching the Through Train.

Opposition from within: the financial sector and bureaucracy strike back

From the moment SAFE announced the Through Train, the onshore financial community and their regulators had registered serious concerns even when appearing neutral to (or sometimes interested in) the scheme.[32] This resistance resulted in policy stalemate. Almost at the same time, intervention from the state's top decision-making elites, wary of the systemic risk ramifications to the financial system, led to a dramatic policy reversal that retreated from earlier commitments to and the preparation of the Through Train.

Concerted resistance of financiers and bureaucrats

Backed by financial regulators who were alarmed by the possible impact of the Through Train on industry interests, leading banks and securities firms petitioned the State Council for a halt to the scheme. The CBRC and banking executives were specifically warned of possible large-scale capital outflows from the banking system that might strain the banks' liquidity positions after going through major recapitalization in the mid-2000s. As the Through Train would remove the need for access to offshore markets to go through a financial intermediary, the banks also saw the Through Train as undercutting their nascent asset management business by drastically reducing the market appeal of bank-sponsored QDII products.[33]

Even though the BOC, one of the four leading state-owned banks, was involved in the Through Train, its industrial peers (especially the other three commercial banks which also maintained offshore securities subsidiaries), were reluctant to support the scheme.[34] This split the banking industry and forced the CBRC to hold a reserved position. The securities and fund industries were equally displeased. Like the banks, revenues of their QDII products would be depressed if the Through Train took off as investors found direct access to overseas markets. This might stunt the development of the new-born asset management fund industry in China.[35] On the technical front, both the SSE and Shenzhen Stock Exchange (SZSE) and CSRC questioned the wider readiness for the Through Train because harmonized securities settlements and clearing systems between the mainland and Hong Kong markets were still to be agreed.[36]

Considering the opposition within the industries, and concerns about its implications for the financial markets, both the CSRC and CBRC were disinclined to back the Through Train. The former withheld its approval crucial to the BOC kick-starting the securities business and significantly lowered the threshold of QDII funds managed by banks.[37] The two regulators also maintained that the Through Train scheme must be subjected to an overall quota approved by the authorities and not much different from that imposed on QDII to facilitate better risk management of the larger financial system. They also wanted detailed risk assessments and monitoring systems put in place before any funds crossed the border.[38]

As the policy deliberations unfolded, rifts between central bureaucratic patrons within the Through Train coalition further compromised the political and technical consensus, undermining the leverage of Tianjin, Hong Kong and the BOC, and called into question the opening agenda. The NDRC softened its support as unresolved technical and regulatory issues were raised within the financial bureaucracy.[39] The central bank also took an ambivalent stance, with Governor Zhou Xiaochuan and his deputy, Hu Xiaolian (who also led SAFE), showing sympathy for the Through Train, while other PBOC officials indicated otherwise. Another PBOC deputy governor, for example, publicly voiced their concern about the Through Train's impact on capital availability to the banking system.[40]

Indeed, although the PBOC had repeatedly raised interest rates and reserve requirements over the summer of 2007, capital outflows were aggravated after the Through Train plan was made public—a majority of this was believed to consist of unsanctioned transfers of funds through Shenzhen from late August as people looked to take advantage of the Hong Kong market surge ahead of the Through Train.[41] The PBOC was especially alarmed by the enormous amount of renminbi cash leaving Shenzhen. According to one estimate, the city took up 51% of the nationwide 195.8 billion yuan cash injection of the first three quarters of 2007, up 30% from the previous year. The same period also saw the dramatic exodus of foreign deposits from Shenzhen financial institutions to Hong Kong. The resultant fanfare among mainland investors, however, simply vindicated the concerns of the domestic banking industry, regulators, and the PBOC, raising serious question as to whether the banks could maintain sufficient funds for domestic needs.[42]

The Through Train agenda in doubt

Besides the strengthening dissent within the financial bureaucracy, the Through Train coalition faced a possibly fatal blow from top elites concerned by the scheme's impact on domestic financial stability. Their intervention reinforced the dissenting parties and derailed the opening agenda entirely as the original political economic imperative of the Through Train was called into question and the initiative appeared to entail systemic risk implications which no decision makers would find tolerable.

Weeks after the SAFE's Through Train announcement, in late August, the party senior leadership convened a Politburo study session (*jiti xeuxi*) to discuss issues pertinent to global financial markets and the deepening of China's financial reform. Hu Jintao stressed the importance of "national financial security" and suggested that the domestic financial system should be protected by a "stronger financial safety net" as it became more developed and liberalized.[43] Hu's remarks were widely read as indicative of the top elites' intent to pause the Through Train.

Shortly after the party meeting, CBRC Chair Liu Mingkang and Finance Minister Jin Renqing pointed to the escalation of risk in the domestic banking system caused by the Through Train. Both worried that easing access to overseas markets would unleash capital outflows and encourage illicit money laundering beyond Beijing's control, a situation that would pose a serious threat to China's financial stability.[44] The CSRC was particularly disturbed by the hype in the H-share market characterized by a surge of close to 40% and stoked by speculative capital in the weeks after SAFE's announcement. This brought back memories of its policy failure in the B-share market liberalization in 2001 when mainland investors had experienced unusually high financial risks and suffered substantial losses following a deep market adjustment. As investors withdrew their funds from China, the securities regulator was concerned about possible correction in the domestic stock markets.[45]

Senior economic advisers to Beijing also opposed the Through Train and challenged the core policy rationales of the Through Train peddled by the opening advocates. An internal study of the State Council, completed in October 2007, warned of the Through Train's risks to the domestic financial system and recommended that top decision makers keep a tight control of the short-term capital flows until China had completed its domestic liberalization to avoid a repeat of the painful experience of the East Asian economies during the 1990s crisis. The report also underscored the importance of "better coordination between government agencies in pursuing financial liberalization," and bluntly warned: "[although] some reforms might contribute to financial development, they should take into account the evolving domestic and international market situation and be sequenced better with other policy measures" (Chen 2007). Similarly, a member of the PBOC's Monetary Policy Committee expressed caution about the global economic uncertainties after mid-2007 that had emanated from the subprime credit crunch, and that any measure easing capital mobility might weaken China's crisis-management ability.[46] Another Beijing financial policy advisor also challenged the authority of SAFE to "appoint" the BOC to spearhead the Through Train.[47]

It is not important whether SAFE truly had legal grounds or whether the Through Train followed sound policy logic. The pro-opening coalition came into being because of material interests and the political will to manage policy problems. The dissenters gained strength because of adverse implications to their interests and concerns about political and systemic risks held by the financial regulators and top decision-making elites. These dashed any hope of the opening advocates for the speedy departure of the Through Train. Policy stalemate ensued.

Sealing the fate of the Through Train: policy reversal and stasis

As the dissenting parties gained strength, the leverage enjoyed by the Through Train coalition and opening advocates lessened dramatically. After two months of apparent indecision, the top decision-making elites intervened and explicitly renounced the Through Train initiative. The opening agenda was derailed and there was a reversal of the earlier public announcement. QDII stayed as the only officially sanctioned channel of outbound equity investment.

The top elites were wary of the looming systemic risk the domestic financial system might experience. According to PBOC research, between August 20 and October 11, 2007, an estimated 500 billion yuan left China for the Hong Kong stock market. This excluded outflows of comparable scale through illegal conduits like underground banks and currency exchange shops. Another estimate of capital outflow presented a much more disturbing picture—a figure as large as one trillion yuan, 75% of which was from state-owned enterprises and financial institutions, had flowed out from China; if unchecked, there were fears that the volume might triple by mid-October.[48] The massive exodus of capital drained the financial system, placing upward pressure on interest rates and reserve requirements that affected the capital adequacy of mainland banks.[49] This not only alerted the CBRC and PBOC about the health of the banking system and financial stability, it also prompted intervention from the top elites.

In a State Council meeting on October 13th, Premier Wen formally put a halt to the scheme. Wen blamed SAFE for prematurely announcing the Through Train in August and failing to consider its implications for domestic financial reforms and stability. Even before the Through Train was launched, China had already paid a heavy price in capital drain.[50] According to some reports, Wen even blamed the NDRC, the other leading agency which backed the initiative, for pushing ahead with the Through Train in the absence of consensus and the presence of strong reservations among bureaucratic peers. Indeed, the finance ministry and financial regulators, as well as the onshore banking and securities industries, were brought into discussions of implementation specifics only after the public announcement in August. As a result, despite the concessionary attempts of the Through Train coalition to adjust the scope, pace and location, the initiative was seriously challenged. What appeared to be a sound liberalizing initiative to cope with macroeconomic challenges at home was politically doomed.

Yet the offshore market continued to be confused by different policy messages as Hong Kong and Tianjin remained hopeful of the Through Train's launch. Central officials, however, downplayed and shied away from discussing the initiative. CSRC officials simply restated the agency's position that the Through Train was immature; Zhou Xiaochuan commented that the program had a "wide-ranging ramification on financial policies and markets."[51] To settle the lingering confusion, Wen broke his silence on November 4th and clearly stated Beijing's position for the first time since SAFE's announcement in August: no individual investment in the markets of Hong Kong would be possible in the short term. The Through Train, he argued, compromised China's capital control regime and the authorities had yet to develop the regulatory framework governing capital mobility that would mitigate market volatility in the mainland and offshore markets and best protect investors' well-being.[52]

The day after Wen's statement, the Hong Kong market slumped, losing 5% of market cap, and reversing the dramatic uptrend enjoyed after the summer, when the Hang Seng Index had shot up from 21,891 to 31,638 in anticipation of the launch of the Through Train. As a policy substitute, the mainland authorities continued to cling to QDII as a conduit for overseas investment. SAFE doubled the QDII quotas for securities firms and fund companies whereas the CSRC encouraged them to develop as many QDII funds as possible.[53] As the fate of the Through Train was sealed, SAFE officials reversed their position and warned of the "unparalleled" risk of overseas investment.[54] To stem capital outflows, the PBOC, SAFE and CBRC limited the daily withdrawal amount for individuals in Shenzhen and enforced a crackdown on exchange shops suspected of abetting illicit cross-border transfers.[55]

In just a few months, the policy tendency of the Through Train and the larger outbound equity investment had witnessed a dramatic turnabout. The opening momentum of the Through Train had by turns accelerated and then been dashed by dissenting bureaucratic actors backed by onshore financial and local interests. The interventions of top leaders had rolled back public commitments and QDII was left as the only legal pillar of overseas equity investment.

While it was (and is) impossible to appraise the possible impact of the Through Train on domestic financial stability had it been introduced as expected (especially the capital availability to banks), concerns about policy risk, both political and systemic, persisted within the financial bureaucracy. As the subprime credit crunch evolved into a global crisis, any liberalizing initiatives promoted by local and financial industry interests were halted. It would take years for another initiative of outbound equity investment to gain traction, but nothing that followed seemed as ambitious as the Through Train.

Futile local advocacy to resuscitate the Through Train

There remained some local liberalizing initiatives that aimed to promote financial market development. They generally strived to revive the Through Train in the same or similar fashion, but none led to any substantial policy change. Analytically, these failed attempts show that although local authorities might have been vocal when advancing and framing opening agendas, they were constrained by the lack of any interested and supportive bureaucratic patrons. As with the Through Train fanfare, Beijing's preoccupation with risk, especially the possible impact of systemic risks on the larger financial system, deterred any government agencies from supporting liberalizing moves even though they might be less ambitious than the Through Train.

Prominent among the different local policy initiatives were the efforts of the Shenzhen and Guangdong provincial governments to collaborate with Hong Kong less than a year after Wen called off the Through Train. They hoped to convince the offshore community to persuade Beijing to host the scheme put forward by Shenzhen, which benefited from its proximity to Hong Kong and an extensive cross-border network that handled massive amounts of cross-border financial transactions.[56] More importantly, it was hoped that a Shenzhen-based Through Train might boost the local securities and asset management industries in Qianhai, the district of the city bordering Hong Kong, which had been approved by Beijing as the "special zone" of Shenzhen SEZ and slated to pioneer financial reforms—a role analogous to that given to Tianjin's Binhai district and which had driven that city to help initiate the Through Train in 2007.[57] The provincial government also hoped to leverage Hong Kong's international status and transform the Pearl River Delta into a financial cluster of global standing that would rival the Shanghai financiers (NDRC 2008: 110–11).

Highly cautious of Beijing's policy stance due to the earlier Through Train disappointment, Hong Kong's officials did not respond enthusiastically to their neighbor's initiative.[58] It was not until 2009 and 2010, when the CEPA updates were concluded, that the offshore community became receptive to Shenzhen's initiative. Joseph Yam tossed the idea of the cross-listing of securities (i.e., making Hong Kong equities tradable on the mainland and vice versa) in June 2009, and this was followed by a call from the Guangdong securities bureau to provide brokerage services for overseas securities.[59] Shortly after Shenzhen's advocacy, Tianjin joined the local calls despite the embarrassing policy reversal of 2007. Backed by former mayor Dai Xianglong, Tianjin lobbied the center repeatedly to resume the scheme after 2009. To its frustration, however, SAFE policy guidance concerning the Through Train was declared to have expired in January 2010. This formally spelled its end after two years of expectations of revival.[60]

However, other financial hubs continued to pursue similar policy ideas to test their appeal to central financial policymakers. Less than a week after SAFE voided the 2007 initiative, Shanghai floated the idea of an expanded overseas securities investment scheme beyond Hong Kong. After a prolonged public denial of such proposal, the local financial services office confirmed it was preparing the Through Train, and was expecting its launch in the first half of 2010 alongside the international board beginning to trade the shares of overseas firms.[61] It was hoped this would elevate the city's status to that of a leading financial hub where domestic investors found exits to global investment opportunities, and where foreign companies would issue shares in China.

In early 2011,Wenzhou, a coastal city famous for its entrepreneurship, also sought Beijing's backing for a similar investment scheme that would allow local residents to set up, acquire shares, or invest in non-financial companies with a maximum yearly quota of up to US$3 million (and an overall project cap of US$200 million).[62] Like other locally sponsored initiatives, Wenzhou's policy venture was halted by SAFE, citing "procedural issues" shortly after it was made public.[63] Despite Wenzhou's success in securing Beijing's support for the piloting of a dozen financial reforms in March 2012, including channels for making "private direct investment" overseas, the city made little headway except for occasional local liberalizing rhetoric that drew some interest from investors.[64]

Although direct equity investment had once been seen as an important policy instrument for addressing domestic macroeconomic challenges, the success of these diverse, locally-originated, liberalizing initiatives ultimately depended on the ability to work with financial industry interests, to seek central bureaucratic patrons, and to engage in concessionary politics in response to dissenting parties. In the face of a financial bureaucracy sensitive to systemic risk concerns following the subprime crisis, none of the local authorities found any political backing for Through Train-related ventures.

The PBOC and SAFE turned to other policy agendas on their turf in the post-crisis years, notably promoting the renminbi internationalization discussed in Chapter 5. The CSRC also became averse to risking policy failure when mainland investors experienced substantial losses in an equity market crash, and believed that the Through Train no longer suited the needs of individual investors. As a CSRC official explained, since "the A-share [domestic market] has been bearish for year, it would appear to offer a much better return than overseas markets."[65] Moreover, the securities regulator came to recognize that feasible liberalizing initiatives must try to accommodate the interests of multiple parties, avoiding the charge leveled at SAFE of playing favorites with selected localities and financiers.

The CSRC therefore turned away from the possibility of bringing about a direct connection between mainland investors and offshore markets. Instead, it would eventually sponsor another initiative originally proposed by the offshore community back in 2001: the overseas ETF scheme that promised gains to multiple local and financial industry interests, and promised to boost the securities regulator's power and standing by expanding the overseas outreach of domestic securities firms and promoting domestic financial innovation—both slated as the regulator's policy priority in the Twelfth Five-Year Plan (2011–15) documents (Xia and Chen 2011).

Overseas ETFs as an emerging alternative

As the Through Train was no longer on the central agenda, a different initiative, originating from the offshore community and backed by the Shanghai and Shenzhen governments and the local exchanges, was gaining momentum. Although it did not immediately win support from the domestic securities industry or the CSRC, it would serve as a policy alternative to the Through Train, and was conceived as part of the offshore renminbi market breakthroughs of the late 2000s.

Together with QDII, trading overseas ETFs with Hong Kong equity underlying was part of the offshore community's policy recommendations to the central government in the early 2000s. Issued offshore, these ETFs could be made available to mainland investors akin to ordinary stocks traded on the mainland exchanges. Hong Kong officials described the program as an extension of CEPA's "free walk" of tourists, where offshore financial products would reach onshore investors.[66] As with QDII, the CSRC was unenthusiastic about the proposal at the time because it viewed the mainland market as simply unready for such innovation.

In fact, the first domestic equity-linked ETF emerged in China in 2005 but market growth was stagnant in the 2000s due to the lack of sufficient expertise among brokers and the seeming preference of individual investors for trading shares that appeared to provide the greatest opportunity for making short-term profits. At the local level, competition between SSE and SZSE also impeded the ETF market growth, with each imposing regulations prohibiting ETFs that "mixed" securities listed on the two bourses. It was not until late March 2012 that the two exchanges agreed to harmonize their rules and make cross-market ETFs possible.[67]

The stunted mainland ETF market contrasted with blossoming offshore developments. Strongly favored by Hong Kong's financial officials and community (notably the city's exchange), Hong Kong became a major marketplace of overseas ETFs in the region and lobbied Beijing to introduce overseas ETFs in 2007, even before the Through Train reversal.[68] Instead of peddling it as a means of easing cross-border investment, Hong Kong framed the initiative in strictly financial terms and as a means of promoting price convergence between the A- and H-shares, the different stock classes issued by mainland Chinese companies.[69] The CSRC, however, saw little urgency to address the market problem.

The offshore initiative, however, attracted Shenzhen, which saw the scheme as an alternative to the Through Train and as a catalyst to financial collaboration with Hong Kong.[70] Soon, ETFs were named as a priority for financial cooperation, and mainland securities firms were allowed to open offshore subsidiaries under the CEPA framework in 2009. This was followed by an agreement on product development between Hong Kong, Shenzhen and Guangdong that also elicited Shanghai's interest to lead the development of China's first overseas ETF that would track the performance of the Hong Kong market together with overseas stock indexes like the Dow Jones Industrial Average and the FTSE100 (PRC and HKSAR 2009, 2010). These products would represent a breakthrough in the internationalizing of the SSE with exclusive mainland China-linked products, complementing the pursuit of an international board that would bring in overseas firms to float shares in China.[71]

As the overseas ETF was brought onto the intergovernmental agenda, local governments and their financiers acted in concert to seek CSRC's support for what they dubbed the "mini-Through Train" that would offer indirect exposure to offshore stocks for mainland investors. The three exchanges also started considering technical issues associated with overseas ETF issuances to assuage the regulator's concerns about market risks and regulatory challenges.[72] This gave birth to a pro-opening coalition with complementary local interests. The CSRC, however, remained hesitant.

In fact, while the agency had once considered phasing in ETFs as a policy pilot, the unreadiness of the mainland capital market, notably its risk management measures underlying cross-border fund flows in buying and selling the ETFs, deterred any such pursuit.[73] For instance, trading overseas ETFs would involve transactions in two different and incompatible systems. The mainland market operated a T + 1 trade settlement arrangement (settlement after one day, in other words) whereas Hong Kong maintained a T + 2 system. Short of a harmonized mechanism, investors buying Hong Kong-linked ETFs would potentially experience volatility in the ETF prices and underlying securities between the trading and settlement dates.

More alarmingly to the agency, the mainland market did not have a well-developed market maker system critical to efficient pricing of ETFs, which had led to several market disorders involving mainland ETFs since 2009.[74] Although the SSE and SZSE considered having overseas ETFs following Hong Kong's settlement arrangement, still the CSRC was exceedingly wary of these technical matters that might result in policy failure. Within the financial industry, the CSRC also encountered resistance from domestic securities firms—most of which lacked competence in ETF product development for overseas markets—that held opposite views about the onshore bourses. They were concerned about losing market share to foreign firms generating Hong Kong-linked ETFs, and worried that the new product would depress domestic investors' interest in QDII funds, further hurting the firms' revenues.[75]

Despite the merits of the ETFs as an alternative to the Through Train, technical discord and dissenting views from brokerages deterred the CSRC from supporting the coordinated and strong local liberalizing initiative. The lack of a central bureaucratic patron deprived the local authorities and bourses of the political backing necessary to generate policy momentum that might lead to opening.

The coming of the "mini-Through Train"

Local interest in overseas ETFs stayed strong in the face of a reserved CSRC and an opposed securities industry. Policy breakthrough came after the onshore securities industry gained a foothold in Hong Kong's market, and the opening advocates framed and linked the liberalizing initiative with the offshore renminbi market development, successfully bringing in the PBOC's support. To assuage industry dissent, they also agreed to limit the initiative's scale and have mainland brokerages leading product development and marketing in both offshore and onshore markets. This subjected the scheme to more restrictions than the offshore community had initially envisioned.

While the CSRC was noncommittal, Shanghai and Shenzhen further strengthened their ties with the Hong Kong Exchange (HKEx) after 2010, all registering a strong interest in the program. Shanghai aspired to cement its international status as the prospect of the international board became uncertain (and was eventually adjourned in 2011), and Shenzhen sought to incorporate ETFs into the financial experimentation in the Qianhai area. At the same time, the CEPA made a larger offshore presence possible for mainland brokerages, and the brokerages quickly set up offshore subsidiaries that enabled them to compete with foreign firms in the ETF market.[76]

After 2011, in concert with local parties and bourses, the exchanges lobbied the CSRC to commence the mini-Through Train. Shortly afterwards, the regulator tasked a handful of mainland securities firms in which the government retained majority shareholding to build the fund portfolios underlying the ETFs, raise funds from mainland investors and, in turn, park them in the Hong Kong market.[77] The onshore brokerages were also to monopolize the marketing and distribution networks—a competitive edge unmatched and envied by foreign counterparts. This, in effect, excluded offshore players and limited the material gains to the domestic securities industry. Politically, it was hoped that a successful launch and development of overseas ETF products in China would help boost the CSRC's standing, as it represented a small but important milestone on the road to internationalizing the domestic stock market with new equity products entirely issued by, or linked with, mainland companies.

Despite the essentially preferential treatment of the domestic securities industry in both financial and political terms, to sustain the support of the CSRC and onshore financial authorities and financiers as coalition partners, the offshore community swallowed the arrangement even though it realized local and foreign brokerages would find only little gain under the scheme. This is not to suggest that Hong Kong registered no interest in promoting the mini-Through Train. As offshore renminbi business after 2010/2011 entered a new phase, with trade settlements and fixed income products in place, the Hong Kong financial community and PBOC were both looking for ways to bridge the onshore and offshore renminbi markets, to provide diverse investment opportunities to the expanding offshore renminbi pool.

The offshore community therefore tapped the central bank's support, taking the opportunity to link its push for overseas ETFs with the deliberations surrounding offshore renminbi market development. To allow offshore renminbi holders to circulate their holdings to the mainland, the renminbi QFII (RQFII) was introduced to give better yields than fixed income products offshore. Overseas ETFs, by contrast, offered a failsafe and indirect means of promoting offshore renminbi investment use.[78] The PBOC's backing, however, was contingent on the premise that overseas ETF products would generate little political or systemic risk. Since securities firms would take charge of product development and the buying of stocks in Hong Kong, and mainland investors would purchase ETFs like ordinary stocks in the domestic market, it was hoped the magnitude of capital outflow would be manageable to the PBOC and SAFE. To moderate the scale of overseas ETFs, the two agencies designated the capital quota for the scheme out of existing QDII ones for fund houses. In effect, there would barely be any increase of total fund outflow, even with the new products in place.

The cautious stance of the central bank and other pro-opening bureaucratic actors in scrutinizing overseas investment was translated into a relatively small-scale first batch of ETFs (around 20 billion yuan), especially when compared to similar offshore products like the X-Ishares A50 or Tracker Fund—both valued above HKD50 billion (or 43 billion yuan). With the scope limited and the extent of the investment capped and closely calibrated by the authorities, the fears of other bureaucratic actors and decision-making elites that direct overseas access for ordinary investors would pose significant challenges to the regulation and monitoring of cross-border capital flows and lead to excessive speculation and volatility in the Hong Kong market, as experienced in 2007, were soothed.

In mid-August 2011, the ETF scheme was inaugurated by the then Vice Premier Li Keqiang during his visit to Hong Kong, alongside other liberalizing initiatives such as RQFII, discussed in Chapter 5. The first cohort of Hong Kong-linked ETFs was rolled out in late 2011.[79] However, for a year after the announcement, only two domestic securities firms developed the products to the value of about US$6 billion. Onshore market participants were lukewarm and, as the global market faced considerable uncertainties after 2011, investors had mostly lost interest and confidence in overseas market-linked products.[80] Leading asset management fund houses also questioned the value of limiting overseas ETFs to Hong Kong equities in view of the many QDII funds, and turned to originating ETFs that tracked other international markets. As of March 2017, among the 150 ETFs traded on mainland bourses, only four were Hong Kong-linked and five others tracked the US and German markets. This reflected both weak demand among mainland investors and the low regard the scheme was held in by the mainland fund industry.

This is hardly surprising since the much belated program represents the most politically feasible liberalizing initiative that served the interests of mini-Through Train advocates, including onshore and offshore financial hubs and exchanges, as well as the CSRC and PBOC, rather than that of ordinary investors in the mainland. Nonetheless, Hong Kong's success in making concessions with the CSRC, framing the agenda as an integral element of renminbi internationalization, and securing the PBOC's support helped engender another opening initiative in late 2014—the Stock Connects between Hong Kong and the two onshore stock exchanges.

Yet another quest for the Through Train: QDII2's waiting game

With the introduction of the overseas ETFs, and after a few fruitless policy endeavors, offshore and onshore local authorities no longer saw a viable prospect of creating a direct outbound equity investment channel. However, after January 2013, the PBOC and CSRC became advocates from within the financial bureaucracy for creating QDII2—a scheme that would permit individual mainland investors to invest in offshore capital markets. To the central bank, QDII2 would encourage renminbi internationalization, relieve onshore liquidity build-up, and ultimately catalyze more capital market opening.[81] The CSRC was motivated to relax inbound equity investment through initiatives such as QFII2 and RQFII2 and permit offshore individuals to invest in China's capital markets using their foreign currency and renminbi holdings.[82]

QDII2 was to start from Hong Kong and be expanded to other foreign jurisdictions where mainland Chinese individuals could invest their funds with considerable latitude in other offshore markets, not only in stocks but also in other asset classes such as derivatives and real estate, galvanizing the internationalization of domestic capital. This supportive liberalizing posture from the center excited every onshore financial hub that had for years been eager to take part in a Through Train-like scheme and establish a niche in China's globalizing financial footprint. Local lobbying to the PBOC and CSRC intensified and the market anticipated the launch of QDII2 as early as mid-2013. The regulatory hurdles and surge of competing local interests, including a head-on competition between Shenzhen/Guangzhou and Shanghai to be the first mover, however, once again postponed the scheme.

Whereas Shanghai aimed to incorporate QDII2 into part of the Shanghai Free Trade Zone's (FTZ) liberalizing initiative, Shenzhen and Guangzhou's plan to introduce QDII2 as a closed-loop pilot with a minimum investment amount of half a million yuan was backed by the PBOC.[83] Offshore, the HKEx and newly created Financial Service Development Council (FSDC), comprised of the financial industry and government officials, supported Shenzhen's initiative and even proposed running a Qianhai Qualified Individual Investor (QDII3) scheme that would galvanize more lifting of control in Shenzhen's Qianhai reform zone (FSDC 2013). The parallel quests for QDII2 did not result in any policy breakthroughs, as Shanghai and Shenzhen/Guangzhou set themselves at loggerheads, and the central financial policymakers were unable to reach consensus with other onshore contenders over the scope and pace of implementation.[84]

To balance competing local interests and galvanize China's capital easing, the PBOC was reportedly considering starting QDII2 in the Shanghai FTZ, followed by similar pilots in Shanghai, Tianjin, Chongqing, Wuhan, Shenzhen and Wenzhou, which would abandon restrictions on outbound investments in offshore securities and fixed income products, real estate, and industrial investment projects.[85] The central bank also reassured the market by signaling that QDII2 would come forth after the launch of the Shanghai–Hong Kong Stock Connect that would provide access to fewer than 20% of all Stock Exchange of Hong Kong (SEHK) main board stocks in its early phase.[86] QDII2, however, was sidetracked by the deteriorating domestic economy that witnessed financial market volatility after the onshore stock market crash of the summer of 2015, and unprecedented capital outflows following the central bank-initiated exchange regime reform that challenged the outlook of renminbi internationalization.[87]

As systemic risk concerns assumed the utmost importance, the PBOC's agenda of fostering renminbi's investment use by easing outbound equity investment was overridden. Although the State Council suggested in late 2015 that QDII2 would be launched at some future appropriate time, the PBOC and CSRC had little choice other than to shelve the scheme. This not only disappointed the offshore community that had been working extensively with the PBOC over regulatory and technical matters relating to QDII2, it also frustrated onshore local and financial industry interests.[88] In order not to stoke even more capital exodus than was already posing a grave challenge to domestic financial stability, the PBOC formally terminated the QDII2 deliberations in March 2016, together with several other liberalizing initiatives.

As a Shanghai official remarked: "Apparently, the focus is now on reining in capital outflows.... No concrete step would be taken in the coming months towards the launch of QDII2."[89] To stem capital outflows through established outbound investment channels, SAFE also capped the QDII quota at US$90 billion and did not issue any new licenses after 2015. Similarly, new investment in RQDII, a scheme that channeled renminbi funds from onshore financial institutions to offshore investment, was stopped in late 2015 after its first year to block the routes allowing capital to be moved offshore and stop firms from engaging in high risk investments (Karolczuk 2017).[90]

Mutual market access through the Stock Connects

While the offshore community was waiting for the PBOC's green light to start QDII2, the onshore and offshore authorities and financiers became opening advocates for another equity market liberalizing initiative. Building on earlier discussion of the cross-listing of stocks in 2009, HKEx and Hong Kong financial officials again became the backbone of a pro-opening policy coalition, championing what would become known as a Stock Connect.

Although differences of cross-border regulatory arrangements and technical issues such as exchange rate risks had impeded the direct listing of shares among the SEHK, SSE, and SZSE, as Hong Kong-linked ETFs were introduced, the offshore authorities were searching for a plausible way of individual outbound equity investment that would involve little easing of China's capital control regime. As the offshore renminbi market flourished after the late 2000s, the HKEx (2013) aimed to become the "global exchange of choice" for both Chinese and international investors. In addition to developing the renminbi-denominated financial products Chapter 5 discusses, the HKEx promoted "mutual market access" that would make possible two-way investment traffic that connected the onshore and offshore bourses operated in a closed-end system. It was hoped that this would not only ease China's outbound investment and promote renminbi internationalization, but also boost the HKEx's global competitiveness as the "one-stop shop for Chinese investors" together with widening Hong Kong's position as the gateway that allowed domestic investors to access multiple asset classes offshore.[91]

The initiative elicited strong interest from its onshore counterparts who were eager to expand their international connectivity. The SSE was especially keen to work with the HKEx after its failed quest for an international board in 2011. As a first step to cross-border exchange cooperation, the HKEx, SSE and SZSE founded China Exchange Services in October 2012, a joint venture that would develop cross-market stock indexes and index-linked derivatives.[92] Throughout 2013, a series of meetings were convened among exchanges and their regulators to develop a cross-border trading and clearing system. The SFC and CSRC conducted a review of the regulatory implications associated with mutual market access before promoting the agenda to other financial policymakers. Shenzhen and Hong Kong securities officials also explored how to develop a Stock Connect via the Qianhai special zone.[93]

In contrast to QDII2 and the Through Train linking up brokers from between the originating and target economies, the exchange-based initiative would have onshore (and offshore) brokers taking investors' orders and executing trades with the offshore (and onshore) bourses instead of offshore securities firms. In outbound investment, brokerages which were members of the mainland bourses would execute trading for domestic investors and carry out settlements and clearing via the offshore subsidiaries of the mainland exchanges in the HKEx. This circumvented the linkage with offshore securities firms and ensured that outbound funds would be handled exclusively by parties supervised by the mainland authorities.

Although this limited the entry of foreign securities firms into the onshore capital market by having the SEHK assume the intermediary role, it facilitated a reciprocal arrangement by which offshore brokers would take charge of all inbound investments through the SEHK's mainland subsidiaries. This benefited both the offshore subsidiaries of the Chinese securities industry as well as their Hong Kong and global peers whose material interests would not be compromised by the exclusive participation of onshore brokerages as it had been in the development of overseas ETFs. As such, the mutual market access proposal originated by the offshore financiers quickly won the support of onshore counterparts who, in turn, lobbied the CSRC for endorsement.

To ensure a sufficiently high level of investor protection for reassuring the CSRC, mainland individual investors were to have a minimum securities and cash value of over half a million yuan—a threshold slightly higher than the 2007 Through Train proposal. They would use their existing securities accounts and trade using their own renminbi holdings that would not be bound by the annual foreign exchange purchase limit of US$50,000. Although onshore institutional investors (and offshore investors) faced no eligibility requirements, trading and clearing would be subject to the regulations and operational rules of the home markets, therefore maintaining the regulatory authority of the CSRC and SFC. In effect, this expanded the QDII's scale while allowing for outbound equity investment by individual investors within a restricted channel, which would barely weaken China's capital control, as was feared would happen in cases of open-end and multi-asset class initiatives.

In fact, the SAFE and PBOC found the Stock Connect scheme particularly appealing since it would simply be a close circuit that bridged mainland and offshore exchanges (and their trading and settlement entities). To minimize policy risks emanating from cross-border capital flows, southbound onshore investors would settle their trades in renminbi via the China Securities Depository and

Clearing Corporation (ChinaClear), the onshore clearing institution, or its participants. The funds generated would be remitted back to onshore securities accounts. In northbound investment, offshore investors were to use offshore renminbi funds and proceeds would return offshore. Such an arrangement barred the use of outbound investment funds to acquire other asset classes, drastically lowering the risk of capital flight (for the southbound channel). It also mitigated the risks of hot money inflows (for the northbound route) which the QDII2 or Through Train-like schemes might entail (CSRC and SFC 2014).

Since all Stock Connect transactions would use the renminbi, the PBOC was very supportive of the CSRC and offshore community. Notably, private investment uses of the renminbi could surge in the northbound conduit, greatly broadening the foreign investor base of mainland Chinese equities that no existing initiatives (like QFII and RQFII) could match. To maintain stable market conditions and hedge against the policy risks, the early phase of Stock Connect was subject to a daily quota of 13 billion yuan (northbound) and 10.5 billion yuan (southbound), as well as an overall scale limit of 300 billion yuan (northbound) and 250 billion yuan (southbound). No new order would be accepted after the daily quota was met, smoothing out market volatility.

To guarantee a successful debut in the interests of the central patrons of the Stock Connect scheme, Shanghai was slated to pioneer the first Stock Connect with Hong Kong despite Shenzhen's desire to be the first mover. This was particularly welcomed by the Shanghai government and financiers as they were keen to break new ground after the Shanghai FTZ was inaugurated and to conclude a global investment conduit that linked up SSE and offshore peers.[94] The CSRC and PBOC hoped that onshore and offshore investors would find the eligible shares of the SSE and SEHK, mostly stable, blue-chip companies with a large market cap, attractive and good value investments.[95]

In April 2014, Premier Li Keqiang finally endorsed the mutual market access scheme and announced that the Shanghai–Hong Kong Stock Connect would start within six months after the completion of trading tests and the finalizing of the roster of eligible stocks. Trading commenced in November 2014, with 269 selected stocks listed on SEHK main board (representative of 83% of SEHK market cap) available for southbound trades. This included all constituent stocks of the Hang Seng large- and mid-cap indexes as well as H-shares not listed on the two indexes. Over 560 stocks, including all blue-chips and companies dual-listed as A- and H-shares (or 90% of SSE market cap), were investible through the northbound Shanghai Connect. A conversion limit of 20,000 yuan for Hong Kong residents was also abolished to encourage northbound investment.[96] After the launch, the southbound utilization rate averaged 80%, which reflected the strong demand of domestic investors trying to diversify their portfolio.

Shortly afterwards, the Shenzhen and Guangdong provincial authorities embedded the Shenzhen–Hong Kong Stock Connect into their agenda for the development of Shenzhen's Qianhai and the larger Guangdong FTZ, and pressed the central financial policymakers to approve the Shenzhen–Hong Kong

Stock Connect as early as 2015.[97] Although the CSRC, SAFE and PBOC were supportive, the second Stock Connect was considerably delayed because of the fluctuating market conditions that followed China's stock crash crisis and capital flight of summer 2015.[98] To thoroughly stem the risks associated with capital outflows, the HKEx and SZSE put on hold much of the preparatory work until early 2016, when the Premier and CSRC senior officials signaled a liberalizing outlook.

After multiple tests and upgrades of the cross-market trading and settlement system among the regulators and bourses, the State Council approved the Shenzhen–Hong Kong Stock Connect in August 2016. An inter-agency working group led by the CSRC soon decided to scrap the aggregate quota of the Shenzhen– and Shanghai–Hong Kong Stock Connects that had restricted the scale of mutual market access (SZSE 2016). This significantly eased investors' access to the onshore and offshore markets, and attested to the PBOC's commitment to heighten renminbi investment even after the domestic market turbulence. But to stabilize short-term capital flows, daily quotas for the northbound and southbound trades were maintained.[99]

The second Stock Connect commenced trading in December 2016. Through the SZSE, mainland investors could trade 416 SEHK-listed stocks, including all the companies under the Shanghai–Hong Kong Stock Connect, as well as small-cap companies of more than HKD5 billion. Global investors could access stocks of 881 Shenzhen-listed companies, many in new economy and high growth sectors not available in the SSE. Shares floated on the ChiNext, however, could only be traded by qualified institutional investors. The two Stock Connects created the world's second largest market, with a combined market cap close to US$7.5 trillion.

The launching of the two Stock Connects emboldened the offshore community to articulate more ambitious liberalizing initiatives that went beyond the secondary market, and to promote them to the central financial policymakers. For example, the HKEx and FSDC explored mutual access arrangements that would cover the primary market (i.e., IPOs), ETFs, bonds, and exchange-traded derivatives. The SSE and SZSE also conceived of the Hong Kong Stock Connects as a template that would help develop similar conduits with global stock markets such as London, internationalizing the global profile of China's bourses (ASIFMA 2016).

However, the closed-loop nature of the Stock Connects means that a true easing of outbound equity investment still lies some way in the distance. The single asset class channel structure connecting the three exchanges with markets under the oversight of China and Hong Kong seems designed always to allow re-regulation by the authorities if future market conditions generate serious concern of policy risk that give rise to strong dissent from the financial bureaucracy.

Conclusion

This chapter has analyzed the policy shifts underlying China's outbound equity investment regime from its earliest discussions in the early 2000s. Early policy stasis gave way to opening initiatives following one after another in the middle of the decade. The institution-based QDII program was followed by the Through Train that would promote a direct connection between mainland investors and overseas markets. The Through Train, however, was canceled months after being made public, leaving QDII as the only established conduit. It was not until 2011 that the financial opening gained momentum, as overseas ETFs were made available to the mainland markets with Hong Kong equity underlying. Stock Connects bridging the three stock markets across the border were introduced in late 2014. It remains unlikely that policy endeavors which would enable direct individual access to offshore markets will come to fruition.

Rather than ascribing these policy changes entirely to shifts of economic conditions, this chapter argues that pro-opening policy coalitions consisting of offshore authorities, financiers and patrons within the financial bureaucracy were instrumental to driving various policy changes. They shaped the policy agenda and framed the initiatives to their favor, sought political leverage and extended concessions of different kinds to dissenting parties. This, in turn, resulted in different policy tendencies and opening outcomes.

Whereas the coalitions' compositions were not permanent and were contingent on actors' preferences in response to the distributional and policy risk implications of each opening initiative, Hong Kong's authorities and financiers remained the primary constituents of pro-opening coalitions that advanced several opening initiatives for China's outbound equity investment regime. Since the 2000s, they have capitalized on Hong Kong's niche as an international financial hub by putting forward many policy initiatives to the mainland authorities, and have hoped to consolidate a role as China's leading financial center.

These concerns were behind the discussions of QDII in the early 2000s that failed to gain backing from onshore financiers and central bureaucratic actors due to divergent policy priorities, political ends, risk implications, and challenges from Shanghai. This foiled the attempt of the pro-opening coalition to shape the opening agenda and QDII remained a non-starter until the mid-2000s, when Hong Kong re-defined QDII not just as a means of outbound investment but also as a policy remedy that addressed domestic economic overheating. This immediately found support within the financial bureaucracy that recognized QDII's policy relevance. Shanghai raised no objection and domestic financiers found their niche in the business. A lack of dissenting voices catalyzed QDII's launch in 2006 with extensible scope, in which financiers were granted increasing flexibility to sponsor QDII funds.

An escalating risk of economic overheating motivated the NDRC, PBOC and SAFE to look for more direct means of channeling domestic liquidity overseas. Once again, they were interested in an offshore initiative—the Through Train scheme. Hong Kong and its central bureaucratic patrons, together with Tianjin and the BOC, who were eager to expand their material interests, constituted a strong pro-opening coalition that had the hubris to bypass their counterparts and prematurely announce the Through Train scheme in August 2007.

To maximize support from local interests and financiers, the opening advocates envisioned an expansion of the scheme's scope and reach after its early phase, and tinkered with the regulatory content to allay financial regulators' concerns of policy risk and competing financiers' interests. This failed because the Through Train coalition met fierce opposition from major state-owned banks and securities industries excluded from the scheme. Enormous capital outflows after the premature policy announcement, together with warnings of imminent financial crisis, intensified the division within the bureaucracy and weakened consensus among the constituents of the pro-opening coalition. This also alerted the top party state decision makers to the imminent systemic risks the domestic economy confronted, making the Through Train politically and financially unviable and leading to an abrupt turnaround of the earlier policy commitment, and a policy stasis that perpetuated QDII.

Although this confused market participants and tarnished Beijing's credibility, the reversal arguably cushioned China from the capital flight that afflicted some emerging economies in the crisis years. As the brunt of the crisis receded, the Through Train scheme was raised again by local financial hubs. Motivated by their own developmental agendas, nearly all of China's domestic financial hubs jockeyed for the support of central bureaucratic actors, but none succeeded in gaining any backing. The offshore initiatives listing Hong Kong-linked ETFs, by contrast, witnessed slow advances. Both Shanghai and Shenzhen saw the introduction of overseas ETFs as important to increasing the product diversity of their exchanges. The PBOC was also willing to extend its support since it would constitute a breakthrough in the offshore renminbi market development with little departure from established capital controls. The securities regulator, however, insisted that domestic brokers and fund houses be eligible for the scheme to foster a niche developing new financial products. Only after the opening advocates agreed to moderate the scope of the initiative was it introduced.

A recent quest for QDII2, championed by the PBOC and CSRC and multiple localities, faced a similar setback to the Through Train, due to the escalating policy risks of easing outbound investment. At the time, the Chinese economy faced strong headwinds and considerable uncertainty. Nonetheless, Stock Connects founded on the mutual market access roadmap led by the HKEx and offshore financial community quickly gained broad support from onshore counterparts and the CSRC, who viewed the scheme as a failsafe arrangement that could ease capital outflows and encourage global capital flows into the domestic stock markets. The SAFE and PBOC shared this view, and saw a valuable strategic opportunity to promote the investment uses of a fledging internationalized renminbi through orderly and expandable capital flows across mainland and Hong Kong exchanges. This culminated in the Shanghai– and Shenzhen–Hong Kong Stock Connects of late 2014 that are poised to maximize market efficiency with minimum systemic risk (Li 2014).

This analysis suggests that the evolution of China's outbound portfolio investment regime is a quintessentially political process involving a myriad of domestic actors. This was best evidenced in the launches of QDII, overseas

ETFs, and the Stock Connects, where central bureaucratic actors, financiers, and local interests were all catered to. By contrast, the Through Train (and proposals like QDII2/3) that might better meet investors' needs met with cancellation or reversal because of the unmet needs of the financial industry, local interests and bureaucratic actors.

To ensure a successful opening, advocates had to frame initiatives in ways that best helped solicit central patronage in policy formation, extended concessions over implementation specifics to allay dissent, and expanded the basis of support in deliberations. Yet, precisely because such a process of give-and-take and a willingness to divide spoils were necessary to the success of opening endeavors, the liberalization of outbound equity investment in China has remained partial and fostered parochial well-being at the expense of capital market efficiency and the interests of investors. The drastic lifting of outflow controls might be possible but only with a substantially reduced sense of inherent policy risk to bureaucratic actors, and concomitant gains available to the financial hubs and industry interests.

Notes

1 "Gang fu jinrong daji, xu zhengming neng huli" (Financial planning document from Hong Kong should prove beneficial to both parties), *Hong Kong Economic Times*, July 3, 2001.These investment banks were exclusively foreign, including Credit Suisse, Goldman Sachs, HSBC, JP Morgan Chase, Merrill Lynch, and Morgan Stanley.
2 "Song jianyi she zhongguo yingfu, cheng Guowuyuan, cheng ta texu touzi jigou zhu neidi ren mai ganggu" (Anthony Leung suggested setting up a type of Tracker-Fund for the Chinese market and designated institutions that might enable mainland investors trying to buy Hong Kong equities; the proposal was submitted to the State Council), *Hong Kong Economic Times*, July 3, 2001.
3 "QDII liao yi Gang zuo shidian" (Hong Kong expected to pilot the QDII), *Apple Daily*, October 31, 2001.
4 "QDII liao yi Gang zuo shidian."
5 Lin, Meifen and Hong Xiaojing, "Zhong Zhengjian yan yun neidi ke mai ganggu" (CSRC to study whether to allow mainland residents to buy Hong Kong equities), *Hong Kong Economic Times*, October 30, 2001.
6 "'Bei shui nian diao' shang wei chengshu, renxing cheng muqian tui QDII zhidu hai bu jubei tiaojian" (PBOC said conditions not ripe for QDII, capital diversion from north to south remains immature), *Wenweipo*, November 7, 2001.
7 QFII was introduced in Taiwan in 1991 when the equity market was already fully liberalized. It was abolished and replaced by a simplified registration-based system in 2003. "Taiwan QFII zhidu jingyan du dailu de qishi" (Lessons of Taiwan QFII program to the mainland), *Shanghai Securities News*, June 25, 2003. QFII in South Korea commenced in the 1980s, gradually phasing in investment from foreign firms. See Kwon (2004).
8 "Jinfang B-gu kaifang jiaoxun, Gang gu zhitong che huan kai" (Beware of the lesson of B-share market opening and slow down the Through Train), *Caijing*, September 3, 2007.
9 Hang, Zhiguo, "Congmang tuichui biduo lishao, CDR yu QDII ying huang xing" (Problems outweighed merits in prompt introduction, CDR and QDII should be deferred), *Securities Daily*, March 28, 2002.

10 Interviews with Shenzhen securities officials, Shenzhen, January 2012. See also "Fang quanshang jigou touzizhe: jiemi yinxing QDII" (Visit to institutional investors of securities industry reveals "hidden" QDII), *New Finance Economics*, June 13, 2002.
11 "Shenzhen zhiye tichao ren huazhengweiling taobi jinrong jiangguan" (Shenzhen residents breaking large cash withdrawals into small sums to evade financial regulation), *First Financial Daily*, November 19, 2007.
12 "Fang quanshang jigou touzizhe: jiemi yinxing QDII"
13 "QDII buying zhi xian Gang gu" (QDII shall not be restricted to Hong Kong equities), *Mingpao*, November 7, 2001.
14 "Fang Xinghai: 90 niandai lai Gang chaogu wei qiye dailai buliang daikuan" (Fang Xinghai: non-performing loans accrued by mainland enterprises in their speculation of Hong Kong stocks in the 1990s), *Wenweipo*, October 31, 2001.
15 "Zhongguo Yingjianhui zhuxi Liu Mingkang cheng QDII guanli banfa jijang chutai" (CBRC Chair Liu Mingkang claimed that QDII procedure is forthcoming), *Shanghai Securities News*, June 1, 2004.
16 "Miaozhun jingwai gupiao shichang, QDII chanpin huode touzizhe gaodu guanzhu" (Overseas stock markets targeted, QDII products highly regarded by mainland investors), *Xinhua News*, June 15, 2007.
17 The 2005 exchange rate reform abandoned the peg with the US dollar in favor of a currency basket of unannounced weights. After this, the renminbi maintained an appreciating tendency against the US dollar, moving from a value of 8.11 yuan per dollar to 7.8 per dollar in just one year. For details, see Bell and Feng (2013).
18 Interview with PBOC Research Bureau researcher, Beijing, February 2012.
19 "Xie Yonghai jie zhitong che shating zhi mi" (Xie Yonghai explained the abrupt turnaround of the Through Train), *Apple Daily*, July 26, 2010.
20 "Neizi jisu liuzou, Wen zong youlu Gang gu zhitong che jiting" (Domestic capital fled, Through Train halted as Premier Wen worried), *Singtao Daily*, November 4, 2007.
21 "Neizi jisu liuzou."
22 A review of the city's quest for financial development can be found in: "Tianjin Binhai: Jinrong tequ you dai po ti" (Tianjin Binhai: financial special region awaiting a beginning), *Caijing Magazine Finance Series*, no. 11, November 10, 2008.
23 "Gang gu zhitong che Tianjin shixing you yin" (Sound basis of Tianjin hosting the Through Train), *Hong Kong Economic Journal*, November 16, 2007.
24 "Hu-Wen gao pingheng, ting Binhai mian hu du da" (Hu and Wen seek balancing, supportive of Binhai to prevent Shanghai's dominance), *Hong Kong Economic Times*, August 22, 2007.
25 Consider, for example, that the price-to-earnings ratio of the Shenzhen and Shanghai markets were 60 and 68 respectively, at the time, more than triple that of the Hang Seng Index of Hong Kong.
26 SAFE (2007).
27 "Zhitong che menkan ni tigao zhi 30 wan" (Minimum commitment amount of Through Train increases to 300,000 yuan), *Hong Kong Economic Times*, September 4, 2007.
28 "Ganggu zhitongche chuqi jiang da 500yi meiyuan, jiang caiqu san xing sanshi moshi" (Through Train scheme would reach US$50 billion in early phase, and adopt a "three-bank-three-cities" model), *Jinrong Jie*, October 29, 2007, http://big5.jrj.com.cn/gate/big5/stock.jrj.com.cn/2007–10–29/000002846396.shtml.
29 "Zuixin fangan pingheng ge fang liyi" (Latest plan balances different interests), *Hong Kong Economic Times*, September 6, 2007.
30 "Zuixin fangan pingheng ge fang liyi."
31 "Gang gu zhitong che zonge shangxian kaifang zhengce da hui yuanxing" (Through Train would be subjected to an overall cap, financial opening returned to original shape), *Hong Kong Economic Journal*, September 22, 2007

32 Wen, Wenjun, "Zhongyingjian kaiqiang zheng yan zhitong che fengxian" (CBRC speaks of grappling with the risk of the Through Train at the moment), *Hong Kong Economic Times*, September 1, 2007.

33 Ye, Tan, "Gang gu zhitong che de Zhongguo tese" (Chinese characteristics of the Through Train scheme), *Yazhou Zhoukan* 27, no. 31, September 23, 2007.

34 "Zhong zi yinhang bao dipan zhengduo zhan" (Chinese banks compete for business), *Hong Kong Economic Times*, August 22, 2007.

35 Guo, Qiongcai, "Gang gu zhitong che chongjibo," (Impacts of the Through Train), *Caijing*, September 3, 2007, www.caing.com/2007–09–03/100189318.html.

36 Deng, Guoqiang and Peng, Lin, "She waihui guanli fengxian dangju jinshen" (Authorities turn prudent as foreign exchange risk involved), *Hong Kong Economic Times*, October 18, 2007.

37 Deng and Peng, "She waihui guanli fengxian dangju jinshen."

38 "Liu Mingkang: Gang gu zhi tou jiang she xiane" (Liu Mingkang: direct investment to Hong Kong would be capped), *First Financial Daily*, September 24, 2007.

39 "Fagaiwen guanyuan: gou Gang gu shang yu xijie xu jiejue" (NDRC officials: details to be worked out for purchasing Hong Kong equities), *Wenweipo*, August 29, 2007.

40 "Zhitong che shenpi yan" (Stringent screening on Through Train), *Hong Kong Economic Times*, August 31, 2007.

41 PBOC raised interest rates from 3.06% to 3.33% in July and to 3.6% and 3.87% by the end of August and September, respectively. Reserve requirements were upped 0.5% from 11.5% to 12% in mid-August and another 0.5% in early September.

42 Zhang, Bagnsong, "Gang gu zhitong che de beihou boyi" (Bargaining behind the Through Train), *New Century Weekly*, issue 24, 2007, pp. 101–2.

43 Yu, Mu, "Hu zong chang jinrong anquan, zu zhitong che" (Hu Jintao stresses financial security, blocking the Through Train), *Hong Kong Economic Times*, August 30, 2007.

44 "Jinrong anquan jia lidu, zhitong che zenban" (Increasing emphasis on financial security, whither the Through Train?), *Hong Kong Economic Times*, September 4, 2007.

45 The market hype and overpricing of Hong Kong's market was best evidenced in the price-to-earnings ratio of the Hang Seng index that climbed beyond 20 in late October, greatly deviating from its average at 15–17 in the previous two years. HKEx (2007a), p. 10.

46 Yu, Yongding, "Wo zhichi jiaoting Gang gu zhitong che" (I support suspending the Through Train scheme), *Financial Times Chinese*, November 20, 2007, www.ftchinese.com/story/001015622.

47 "Zuixin fangan pingheng ge fang liyi."

48 Interview with PBOC Research Bureau researcher, Beijing, February 2012.

49 "Wen Jiabao tan Gang gu 'zhetong che'" (Wen Jiabao speaks about the Through Train), *The Trend Magazine*, September, 2007, pp. 7–8.

50 "Neizi jisu liuzou Wen zong youlu Gang gu 'zhitong che' jiting" (Domestic capital fled, "Through Train" halted as Premier Wen worried), *Singtao Daily*, November 4, 2007.

51 "Tsang Chun-wah: zhitong che huo niandi kaidong; Zhongzhenjian san da xing taidu shenshen" (John Tsang: Through Train expected to come at the end of the year; CSRC and three major banks now reserved), *Mingpao*, October 18, 2007; "Yanghang: Gang gu zhitong che reng xu shiri" (Central Bank: Through Train takes more time), *Wenweipo*, November 2, 2007.

52 "Gang gu zhitong che kaitong wuqi" (No departure time for Through Train), *Mingpao*, November 4, 2007.

53 Between September and November 2007, the QDII quota doubled to US$40 billion. Individual funds raised by securities companies in the period averaged US$5 billion, tenfold the earlier ones. "Zhitong che sui chikai wu gai beishuinandiao" (North water

diverting south continued after Through Train is delayed), *Hong Kong Economic Times*, November 5, 2007.

54 Wen, Tao, "'Zhongguo Wahui' zazhi kanzai wenzhang cheng Gang gu zhitong che shidian ying fangfan liu da fengxian" (*China Forex Magazine* carries an article on the Through Train, warning of six major sources of risk), *Securities Times*, November 17, 2007.

55 "Lanjie 'feifa zhitong che' peiyi hefa shudao" (Interception of "illegal Through Train" complemented by legal diversion), *Wenweipo*, November 17, 2007.

56 Xiao, Chengcong, "Yue-Gang jinrong hezuo qu fangan yi shangbao zhongyang" (Guangdong-Hong Kong financial cooperation plan submitted to the central government), *21st century Business Herald*, October 22, 2008.

57 "Shen chang hezuo dajian Ganggu zhitong che" (Shenzhen called for collaboration to build Through Train), *Mingpao*, July 11, 2009.

58 Interview with Shenzhen securities official, Shenzhen, January 2012.

59 Leung, Pak Yee, "Ren zong: Gang Ye hezuo kexun sanhu wutong" (Joseph Yam: Guangdong-Hong Kong cooperation could be based on "three exchanges and five links"), *Hong Kong Economic Times*, June 25, 2010.

60 "Gang gu zhitong che zhong yaozhe" ('Through Train' scheme terminated in the end), *Hong Kong Economic Journal*, January 15, 2010.

61 "Hu queren yan ban geren haiwai touzi shidian" (Shanghai acknowledged pilot program for individual investment overseas under study), *Wenweipo*, January 23, 2010.

62 Jamil Anderlini, "Chinese city allows personal investing abroad," *Financial Times*, January 10, 2011.

63 Li, Xinwen, "Wenzhou geren haiwai zhitou bei jiaoting" (Direct investment scheme of Wenzhou halted), *21st century Business Herald*, February 14, 2011.

64 Cheng, Zhouxi, "Wenxzhou geren jingwai zhijie touzi shidian fangan shangbao Guowuyuan" (Proposal of direct investment scheme of Wenzhou submitted to the State Council), *First Financial Daily*, March 22, 2012.

65 Interview with CSRC official, Beijing, February 2012.

66 "Gousi 6 nian shixian Gang gu ETF" (Six years of deliberation in preparing for the Hong Kong ETF), *Hong Kong Economic Journal*, October 24, 2011.
Wang, Xiaolu and Mo Li, "Kuajing ETF puojian" (Cross-border ETF breaks the cocoon), *Caijing Magazine*, January 16, 2012.

67 Interview with mainland securities professionals, Shanghai, January 2012, and Beijing, February 2012. Consider, for example, that ETF products constituted only about 1% of the market turnover on the Shanghai and Shenzhen exchanges in 2012, compared to an average of 20% in well-developed markets like Hong Kong.

68 Throughout the 2000s, offshore financial institutions developed synthetic ETFs mimicking the market and share performances of A-shares unavailable outside China, and had a wide appeal to global investors. In 2012, the Hong Kong market was ranked the best for issuing ETFs in Asia, with the highest number of ETFs tracking securities and asset classes of different kinds and markets in the region.

69 He, Ji, "Shenzhen tuichu Xianggang ETF jiema" (Understanding Shenzhen's push for Hong Kong ETF), *21st century Business Herald*, July 18, 2008. Price convergence is made possible by overseas ETFs as mainland investors could short overvalued A-shares and long ETFs with H-shares listed in Hong Kong. Both traded within China and eventually the price differentials between the two share classes narrowed.

70 Wen, Weijun, "ETF ji CDR tang tui, Shen Gang ke chuang shuangying" (If ETF and CDR are introduced, both Hong Kong and Shenzhen benefit), *Hong Kong Economic Times*, July 16, 2008.

71 "Hu Gang jinrong hezuo, ETF ying xianxing" (Shanghai–Hong Kong financial cooperation, ETF should take precedence), *Wenweipo*, January 20, 2010.

72 Robert Cookson, "Shanghai to Launch Foreign Tracker Fund," *Financial Times*, January 22, 2010.

73 "Gang gu ETF Hu guapai yu zuzhi" (Hong Kong ETFs listed as Shanghai obstacle), *Mingpao*, March 24, 2010.
74 Liu, Debin, "Gang gu ETF jinjun neidi kong shouzu" (Hong Kong ETFs entry to the mainland likely be delayed), *Hong Kong Economic Times*, February 26, 2010.
75 Interview with mainland securities professional, Shanghai, January 2012; and with CSRC official, Beijing, February 2012.
76 Sun, Yuan, "Jinzhui guoji ban Gang gu zhitong che zaodong" (Following international board, the Through Train gains momentum), *Securities Times*, June 16, 2011.
77 "ETF hu gua hai kan jianguan qutai" (Cross-listing of ETFs depends on regulator's position), *Hong Kong Commercial Daily*, July 12, 2010.
78 Shi, Na, "RQFII + Ganggu ETF shuang lun qudong renminbi guojihua jincheng tisu" (Renminbi QFII and Hong Kong ETFs as the two wheels accelerating the pace of renminbi internationalization), *Shanghai Securities News*, August 18, 2011.
79 Wang and Mo, "Kuajing ETF puojian."
80 "Ganggu ETF shidian jijin niyong QDII yue" (Hong Kong ETF pilot scheme fund likely to use the QDII quota), *Jinrong Jie*, August 29, 2011.
81 Yang, Lu and Zhang Bing, "QDII2 laile" (QDII2 is coming), *Caixin Weekly*, January 28, 2013.
82 "QFII, QDII shengji huo niannei qidong, Hu Shen Jin youwang shuaixian shidian QDII2" (QFII and QDII to upgrade in a year, Shanghai, Shenzhen and Tianjin to pilot QDII2), *Shanghai Securities News*, January 16, 2013.
83 Zhu, Wenbin, "Yanghang tongyi Guang Shen shidian QDII2" (PBOC agreed Guangzhou and Shenzhen to pilot QDII2), *Shanghai Securities News*, June 25, 2013; Xu, Jinzhong, "Shanghai Zimaoqu zhengqu niannei qidong QDII2" (Shanghai FTZ aiming for QDII2's launch this year) *Securities Times*, March 18, 2015.
84 Interview with Shenzhen and Guangdong financial officials, May 2014.
85 Gabriel Wildau, "China to allow individuals to buy overseas financial assets" *Financial Times*, May 29, 2015.
86 "QDII2 qidong zaiji shou pi liu cheng" (QDII2 is about to inaugurate in six cities), *Hong Kong Economic Times*, May 27, 2015
87 "Lu Lei: QDII2 xu shenshen yanjiu caineng tuichu" (Lu Lei: QDII2 needs careful research before launch), *Caixin*, October 23, 2015, http://economy.caixin.com/2015-10-23/100866178.html.
88 "Chen Delin yinshu Ma Kai QDII2 Zimaoqu shitui" (Norman Chan cited Ma Kai that QDII2 to launch in the FTZ), *Hong Kong Economic Times*, December 4, 2015.
89 Daniel Ren, "Yuan scare: Why China is putting on hold a major cross-border investment scheme," *South China Morning Post*, February 1, 2016.
90 Unlike QDII, RQDII maintained a simplified registration system with no overall investment quota regulated by SAFE. Onshore financial institutions could invent as many RQDII fund products as investors demanded, and file the related documentations to the authorities. For details, see PBOC (2014).
91 Josh Noble, "HKEx seeks to be 'gateway for China'," *Financial Times*, January 16, 2013.
92 "Gang jiao suo dashidai" (HKEx's critical juncture), *China Entrepreneur*, April 7, 2013.
93 "Jiaoyi suo 'Shen Gang Tong' qian jing liao ren" (Exchange-based Shenzhen–Hong Kong Stock Connect has a promising future), *Ta Kung Pao*, July 12, 2013.
94 "Hu Gang jiaoyisuo fouren dacheng hulian hutong xieyi" (SSE and HKEx deny reaching mutual market access arrangement), *Securities Times*, April 3, 2014.
95 "Jigou changxiang Shen Gang Tong" (Institutions conceiving Shenzhen–Hong Kong Stock Connect), *China Securities Journal*, August 28, 2014.
96 Enoch Yiu, "HKMA scraps 20,000 yuan daily conversion cap in landmark reform," *South China Morning Post*, November 12, 2014.

97 Shi, Na, "Yue Gang qi fasheng: Shen Gang Tong haoshi linjin?" (Guangdong and Hong Kong turn vocal: is Shenzhen–Hong Kong Stock Connect coming?), *Shanghai Securities News*, April 19, 2016.
98 Lin, Jinbing and Jiang Fei, "Gongtong shichang xin chongjing" (Prospect of a common market), *Caixin Weekly*, April 13, 2015.
99 Interview with Shenzhen and Guangdong financial officials, July 2016.

4 Let the global brands in
Failed pushes to internationalize China's stock market

Introduction

While Chapter 3 examined the evolution of China's outbound equity investment regime, this chapter studies a complementary dimension: the internationalization of the domestic stock market through securities issuance by foreign firms. Instead of looking into the interplay between foreign firms, domestic firms and regulatory authorities during China's financial services opening (Schlichting 2008; Hsueh 2011), the chapter focuses on initiatives that promoted the presence of foreign firms in the domestic capital market and its degree of internationalization.

The analysis centers on the efforts—led by Shanghai since the mid-2000s—to bring home red-chip companies and create an international board (*guoji ban*) that might foster the city's international profile, promote China's capital market competitiveness, and bring quality investment opportunities to mainland investors. By creating a new listing platform, foreign firms might also be given further opportunities to expand their footprint in China beyond FDI and the inbound investment channels.

The Shanghai government and stock exchange were the principal architects of these liberalizing initiatives and constituted the backbone of the pro-opening coalition. Together, they pushed ahead and framed agendas to solicit the support of bureaucratic actors and top decision-making elites. The Shanghai-based interests embedded their agenda alongside Beijing's promotion of capital market internationalization, to secure central support and accelerate the opening momentum. However, at the point where the liberalizing pursuit appeared ready to go, the entire endeavor was sidetracked and called into question. The opening tendency was terminated and rolled back. There is, to date, no platform for foreign firms to list on China's domestic stock market.

The rise and fall of the international board is incomprehensible with sole reference to market factors or the leverage of foreign firms. Indeed, despite a sound financial rationale, the opening tendency shifted as the dynamics between the pro-opening coalition (composed of local and financial industry interests) and dissenting parties unraveled and were complicated by the intervention of the central elites at critical junctures. The liberalizing commitment to introduce foreign shares in China was not irrevocable.

In the mid-2000s, the Shanghai authorities and financiers called for red-chip companies to pursue secondary listings on domestic exchanges. Despite a lack of strong market interest, the onshore parties pressed hard and found support from the CSRC, the securities regulator, which was eager to elevate the status of Shanghai as a leading securities market. However, disagreements between the onshore and offshore communities over the way the red-chip homecoming might be introduced resulted in a standoff between the Shanghai and CSRC-led pro-opening coalition and dissenting offshore parties. Policy stalemate ensued. This, however, did not frustrate the Shanghai authorities and financiers. Almost immediately, they put forward an international board initiative that was deliberately framed to be in line with the CSRC's stock market internationalization agenda to solicit the regulator's backing.

Soon after the 2008 global financial crisis the proposal won the blessing of China's top elites and the PBOC, who were also seeking to promote the international profile of China's capital market and currency. These developments strengthened the pro-opening coalition and brought the international board to global attention. Nonetheless, the proposed international board lacked important regulatory frameworks and listing requirements. Within the pro-opening coalition, Shanghai and the CSRC took different stances but were soon able to resolve their disagreements in response to a surge in market expectation both at home and abroad, and they expected the debut of the international board in mid-2011. Progress, however, was complicated by parallel local calls and strong dissent over implementation specifics.

Whereas Shenzhen failed to rival Shanghai's initiative due to a lack of political support at the local level, Hong Kong's renminbi debt and equity markets had made advances, thanks to the PBOC's backing in the late 2000s that undercut the basis of creating an international board onshore. Within the financial bureaucracy, the "false consensus" maintained by the Shanghai and CSRC-led coalition collapsed as deliberations over listing methods, accounting standards and the pricing currency of shares generated stronger dissent from other bureaucratic heavyweights. The unyielding position of the opening advocates wasted important opportunities to solicit the support of potential bureaucratic actors like the banking regulator, PBOC and the finance ministry—all of them preferring to delay the board's launch until their regulatory concerns were resolved.

Although the insistence of Shanghai and the CSRC appealed to investors and buoyed market confidence, it substantially weakened political support for the international board within the financial bureaucracy. Debate over the pricing currency of shares saw the pro-opening coalition at odds with the PBOC and SAFE, and brought the regulatory challenges concerning the renminbi's convertibility and adverse implications for China's capital control and investor protection to the fore. This exhausted the central bank's support and eroded the CSRC's commitment to Shanghai's agenda.

Table 4.1 Major developments in the internationalizing quest of the domestic stock market

Late 1990s to mid-2000s	Red-chip and "mega-size" state-owned companies are listed on the SEHK, causing a bull market.
	The Shanghai authorities and onshore financiers propose in the mid-2000s to bring home the red-chip firms through listing on the SSE
2005–2007	Backed by the CSRC, Shanghai-based interests press for red-chip homecoming but fail to solicit offshore support.
	SAFE also opposes the initiative, causing stalemate.
	Shanghai presses for the establishment of an international board as the centerpiece of its efforts to internationalize its capital market and wins CSRC support (early 2007).
2008–2011	The idea of an international board gains momentum because of the political backing of top decision-making elites and the PBOC.
	Shanghai is slated to become China's international financial center (April 2009).
	A Shanghai and CSRC-led coalition works on regulatory and technical matters (from mid-2009), but is unable to reach consensus or obtain wider support from within the financial bureaucracy.
2010–2011	Shenzhen's quest for a second international board and Hong Kong's plans to advance the offshore renminbi equity market are overshadowed by Shanghai's pursuit.
	Disagreement over methods of listing, accounting standards, and the currencies the shares of foreign firms will be priced in on the international board intensify a split in financial bureaucracy support.
Mid-2011	A looming domestic credit crisis and a switch in policy priority toward domestic capital market development significantly weakens the support of the top elites and financial bureaucracy.
	The idea of an international board increasingly called into question and falls off the central agenda (late 2011).
2013 onwards	Efforts by Shanghai to resurrect the international board as a renminbi internationalization initiative fail to gain traction.
	Launch of the Shanghai-Hong Kong Stock Connect makes the creation of a separate listing platform for foreign firms in the SEE moot. No foreign firms float shares on the domestic exchange.

Even worse, the entire pursuit was sidetracked and reversed by the competing political priorities of bureaucratic actors already skeptical about the international board, that arose in response to the domestic crisis of late 2011. The Stock Connects, which bridged the mainland and Hong Kong bourses after late 2014, became the de facto international board open to mainland investors without substantially loosening the onshore market regulations. This spelled the end of Shanghai's quest.

The myriad share classes of Chinese companies

Before continuing, it is worth introducing the different classes of shares issued by Chinese companies, in particular the red-chips and H-shares so pertinent to Shanghai's liberalizing pursuit. The Shanghai and Shenzhen exchanges float shares of companies incorporated in China only, and house both A- and B-share markets (traded respectively in the renminbi and foreign currencies). In addition to the main board, the SZSE also hosts the Small and Medium Enterprises Board (SMEB) and ChiNext, which meet the financing needs of small and medium enterprises and high-tech firms.

Even with these multiple listing platforms available, since the early 1990s thousands of Chinese firms had been seeking overseas listings. This was not purely to tap foreign capital and sell their shares at higher prices, they also sought to evade regulatory strictures and send assets overseas. Despite sporadic scandals, overseas listings in general promoted better corporate governance standards and better regulatory competition in the domestic market (Tobin and Sun 2009; Zhang and King 2010).

Pertinent to China's endeavor to internationalize its domestic stock markets were two offshore equity species of Chinese firms that often confused investors—the red-chip and H-share. They had different origins and legal status and were subject to different regulatory requirements. The red-chip referred to stocks of Chinese companies incorporated and listed outside China but which had most of their revenues generated from businesses on the mainland. H-shares, by contrast, were issued by mainland-incorporated companies listed on SEHK but maintaining most of their business onshore. Early red-chips were comprised of Hong Kong-based Chinese enterprises and the "window companies" of local governments seeking to raise funds for their budgets and infrastructure projects. Some large SOEs also joined the crowded market in the mid-1990s by way of industrial restructuring and repackaging, including China Mobile and the China National Offshore Oil Corporation (CNOOC) (Walter and Howie 2006: 101–16).

The two equity products emerged not merely due to the choice of the listed firms, but also as the result of different political economic considerations. With Beijing's acquiescence, in the late 1980s, when China's securities market was virtually non-existent and absent of any regulation, some Chinese companies created offshore entities that were incorporated in Hong Kong or other popular destinations like the British Virgin Islands. Through strategies like acquiring onshore assets and business, these entities then went public and became red-chips (Li, Su, and Zhu 2011). The birth of the H-share, by contrast, was formally sanctioned by then Vice Premier Zhu Rongji in 1992 after he was convinced by the Hong Kong financial community that having mainland firms raising funds on the Hong Kong stock market would improve the corporate governance of mainland companies and do little to challenge the interests of the then nascent Shanghai and Shenzhen markets.[1]

The two species were subjected to different regulatory requirements prior to and after listing. H-share companies stayed under the purview of the Chinese

Table 4.2 Market cap of red-chips and H-shares in the SEHK main board

Year-end	H shares		Red-chips		H-share + Red-chips	
	Market Cap (billion HKD)	*% of Market*	*Market Cap (billion HKD)*	*% of Market*	*Market Cap (billion HKD)*	*% of Market*
1993	18.23	0.61	124.13	4.17	142.36	4.78
1994	19.98	0.96	84.28	4.04	104.26	5.00
1995	16.46	0.70	110.70	4.71	127.17	5.42
1996	31.53	0.91	263.33	7.58	294.86	8.48
1997	48.62	1.52	472.97	14.77	521.59	16.29
1998	33.53	1.26	334.97	12.58	368.50	13.84
1999	41.89	0.89	956.94	20.24	998.83	21.13
2000	85.14	1.78	1,203.55	25.10	1,288.69	26.87
2001	99.81	2.57	908.85	23.39	1,008.67	25.96
2002	129.25	3.63	806.41	22.66	935.66	26.29
2003	403.12	7.36	1,197.77	21.87	1,600.89	29.23
2004	455.15	6.87	1,409.36	21.26	1,864.51	28.13
2005	1,280.50	15.78	1,709.96	21.08	2,990.46	36.86
2006	3,363.79	25.39	2,951.58	22.28	6,315.37	47.67
2007	5,056.82	24.62	5,514.06	26.85	10,570.88	51.47
2008	2,720.19	26.53	2,874.91	28.04	5,595.10	54.57
2009	4,686.42	26.37	3,862.14	21.73	8,548.56	48.11
2010	5,210.32	24.88	4,380.69	20.92	9,591.01	45.80
2011	4,096.66	23.47	3,999.09	22.91	8,095.75	46.39
2012	4,890.93	22.36	4,835.26	22.11	9,726.18	44.47
2013	4,906.58	20.52	4,815.32	20.14	9,721.90	40.66
2014	5,723.99	22.99	5,214.97	20.95	10,938.96	43.94
2015	5,157.11	21.11	5,137.71	21.03	10,294.82	42.15
2016	5,316.16	21.74	4,898.95	20.04	10,215.11	41.78

Source: HKEx, "Market Capitalisation of China-related Stocks (Main Board and GEM)," www.hkex. com.hk/eng/stat/smstat/chidimen/cd_mc.htm.

authorities. Important corporate actions had to be approved by the CSRC and other agencies like the PBOC, SAFE, and the powerful state-owned Assets Supervision and Administration Commission. Red-chip firms, by contrast, were not bound by the mainland regulatory requirements and had more flexibility when taking corporate action.

This resulted in Beijing's extensive restrictions on aspiring firms listed as red-chips and H-shares that were intended to stem the loss of corporate assets in the late 1990s. Multiple vetting and approvals by regulatory bodies, sometimes involving conflicting interpretations of regulations, became a prerequisite.[2] Yet this did little to discourage Chinese firms from listing offshore. By the end of 2016, there were 153 and 241 red-chip and H-share firms, respectively, making up close to 42% of the city's main board market cap (see Table 4.2 for composition and trend from the 1990s).[3]

Prelude to a bigger quest: homecoming call to the red-chips

Discussion of securities issuances by foreign firms was originated by the Shanghai authorities and financiers in the mid-2000s as a reaction to the market hype of red-chip listings in Hong Kong. They successfully drew support from the CSRC as a central patron, but failed to come to terms with the offshore community over listing methods, or to allay the policy risk concerns held by SAFE in the wake of the Through Train initiative. This derailed Shanghai's quest to bring red-chips home.

The waves of Chinese companies that landed in Hong Kong before the handover unleashed an investment boom that rode on the enormous growth opportunities of China. The craze over red-chips peaked in the mid-1990s in Hong Kong and was followed by a similar rally of H-shares for Chinese SOEs. Companies with China-related assets and businesses had drawn extraordinary attention from international investors and had raised far more capital than was possible on the mainland markets. The Asian financial crisis and internet bubble briefly cooled the China craze, but the bull run returned in the early 2000s as mega-sized SOEs, the "national teams" in the financial, energy and resource sectors, listed in Hong Kong in order to "broaden their international exposure." Often their IPOs placed a chunk of shares for international investors while keeping a smaller portion for subsequent offerings on the mainland.[4] Except for the gray channels that exploited regulatory loopholes, only overseas investors could freely trade shares on the Hong Kong market, which left mainland investors excluded from direct exposure until the advent of the QDII scheme for institutional investors in 2006.

Against such a backdrop, mainland investors and, more vocally, the Shanghai government and SSE, repeatedly called for the return to China of quality enterprises listed in Hong Kong, and saw fund-raising in the offshore market as a mere stepping stone to the eventual return to domestic exchanges. Their calls were echoed by the CSRC, which was keen to transform the Shanghai bourse into a world-class blue-chip market with flagship Chinese companies, and to make the city the primary destination for the listings of SOEs.[5] As Shanghai's initiatives were aligned with the regulator's agenda, the homecoming of the red-chips to the domestic A-share market became a matter of "political imperative," rather than the mere financial decision of individual firms.

In view of the much higher valuation in the mainland market than offshore platforms, together with unsatisfying share performance in Hong Kong, several red-chip companies considered the homecoming option.[6] China Mobile, for example, repeatedly discussed floating shares in China as its share values offshore lost 50% of their value between 2000 and 2001; CNOOC was also keen to join the ranks of its industrial counterparts, Sinopec and China National Petroleum Corporation, in selling shares on the A-share market.[7] Yet for many others, the homecoming option had little appeal because it was feared it would simply burden the firms with the regulatory straitjackets of the CSRC and other government agencies, as the H-share companies were seen to experience.

However, the drive to bring home the red-chips elicited much attention from other financial hubs and interests. Several policy alternatives were proposed and deliberated at the time, including IPOs, the issuance of China Depository Receipts (CDR), and the creation of a segregated trading platform for foreign companies. While these were not exclusive choices, the first two capital market practices were favored by a different set of parties for material and political reasons. This pitted the offshore and onshore interests against each other throughout the 2000s, making impossible any technical consensus essential to foreign securities issuances.

CDR issuance was strongly championed by the offshore authorities and financial community in view of clear market convenience and political advantage. Not only was it an integral part of the financial development proposal Hong Kong forwarded to Beijing in 2001, it was also favored by Hong Kong-based foreign financiers that had the product development expertise. Simply put, depository receipts are securities representing the underlying stock of foreign companies traded on other markets and can be structured and priced to represent different numbers of original shares. Since their price generally trends with that of their home market, Chinese investors would be able to buy securities of foreign companies without facing the concomitant exchange rate risks of moving funds across different jurisdictions.[8] For depository receipt-issuing companies, this would promote international exposure and capital access to overseas investors without going through the lengthy and costly IPO process, especially the extensive due diligence and compliance with foreign regulatory standards.[9] As no new shares were to be raised, existing shareholding structures would be maintained. In practice, issuing depository receipts was (and is) carried out by domestic depository banks acting as brokers to purchase the outstanding shares in a market local to the foreign company. The underlying shares were then deposited in foreign custodian banks (Gande 1997; J. P. Morgan 2005).

Despite these evident financial conveniences, the Shanghai-based financiers resisted CDR issuance and adhered to the IPO option. In their view, CDR issuance would simply serve the interests of the Hong Kong authorities and financial institutions because of the edge commanded by offshore firms in product development that no mainland counterparts could match. Mainland companies would also be disadvantaged since offshore Chinese firms could reach domestic investors by way of a much easier process than domestic enterprises issuing A-shares (Li and Yuan 2003: 234–7).[10]

To broker political and technical consensus among competing local and industrial parties, the CSRC convened a meeting with representatives of the SSE, SZSE, SFC, SEHK (and its holding company, the HKEx), in March 2007, hoping to find an agreeable way that red-chip companies could list in China. A tentative list of eligible red-chip companies was prepared and it was scheduled that the first red-chip would return to the domestic market by summer of 2007.[11] Shortly afterwards, the CSRC circulated a draft regulation outlining the requirements and listing thresholds of red-chips among domestic securities firms. Eligible firms were to have been listed in the SEHK for at least a year, have capitalization above HKD20 billion, and an accumulated profit of above HKD2 billion for the past three years. Half of the firms' operating profit (or asset) should come from (or be located in) China.[12] In what appeared to signal CSRC's support for the onshore interests, IPO was preferred ostensibly because it would subject red-chips to comparable regulation to domestic firms and contribute to the market cap of the local market, boosting the standing of Shanghai.

The regulator's stance clearly dismissed the stronger financial rationales for CDRs that had been advocated by the Hong Kong financial community. However, the wait for the first red-chip homecoming became endless. The emergent subprime mortgage crisis froze the initiative in the same way it had halted the Through Train. Although the CSRC was supportive of Shanghai's initiative, the regulator softened its support as it was wary of the political risks it would accrue from A-share market adjustment if the red-chip homecoming stressed capital supply.[13] Shanghai's plan was further challenged by the "counter-offensive" of SAFE and Hong Kong.

After experiencing a dramatic policy setback in launching the Through Train, the foreign exchange administrator swung to the other extreme and was highly cautious of capital decontrol.[14] Hong Kong was also vocally opposed to the CSRC's proposal of adopting CDRs, fearing the secondary listings of the mega red-chips would threaten the city's market position.[15] Indeed, the regulator had simply frustrated the offshore community, which sought to ward off competition for listing resources with the mainland bourses by way of a series of collaborations with onshore counterparts and regulators after 2007 that promised better cross-market policy coordination.[16] The tug-of-war between local financial hubs, onshore and offshore financiers, and the CSRC resulted in policy stasis. No red-chip company ever returned to the A-share market.

As the issue ran into stalemate in 2007, Shanghai unleashed a different advocacy effort that successfully re-framed the red-chip homecoming agenda as a means of promoting China's capital market internationalization, and embedded it within a larger local pursuit—an international board hosting global multinationals that would strengthen Shanghai's status as a rising international financial center. This eventually found strong interest and support from the city's staunch ally, the CSRC.

Local origination of the international board

As in the evolution of China's outbound equity investment regime, initiatives dealing with foreign securities issuance originated from and were steered by local authorities and financiers. Shanghai therefore assumed a pivotal role in the pursuit of an international board by way of its endeavors to promote the agenda with and without the government, framing the initiative in its favor, and leveraging its connections with onshore financial interests and central patrons.

Shanghai's pursuit of the international board began almost as soon as its red-chip homecoming call faced lingering dissent. In face of the policy stalemate, local financial officials explored the less fashionable option of creating a separate platform for red-chips on the Shanghai A-share market, and outlined their plan in an unassuming report in March 2007 (SSE Innovation Laboratory 2007). Noting the increasing competition from regional exchanges (especially Hong Kong and Singapore), and the lack of market depth and liquidity in China's main board, the report, amongst other recommendations, envisioned an international board that might realize the city's ambition of internationalizing the local capital market—a goal enshrined in Shanghai's Eleventh Five-Year Plan for Financial Development (Shanghai People's Government 2006: 13).

It was hoped the board would bring several advantages to the local and central authorities, the listed firms and mainland investors. Foremost, it was hoped it would enhance the competitiveness and influence of the domestic securities markets. Though China's stock market was the second largest worldwide by the end of 2010, it was dwarfed by that of New York and there were no foreign enterprises listed on the SSE or SZSE. This contrasted with regional exchanges like SEHK and Singapore Exchange that already housed 17 and 317 non-local firms in 2010, respectively.

To Shanghai officials and financiers, this revealed how seriously China's financial system was lagging behind its Asian counterparts in terms of openness and its extent of internationalization. Although foreign financial institutions gained partial entry to the domestic financial sector, and the QFII scheme and B-share market opening permitted foreign investment in China's capital markets, the absence of non-Chinese firms floating shares on domestic bourses rendered China's internationalizing pursuit incomplete even though its exchanges were among the world's largest by market cap (see Table 4.3 on market cap and composition of listed firms in the world's top exchanges).[17]

Second, the report expected that an international board with quality shares of foreign firms would attract domestic capital and therefore help generate higher returns than liquidity lying idle in banks, and reduce volatility in the real-estate and stock markets. Third, just as the overseas listings of Chinese firms was supposed to achieve, foreign firms landing in China might introduce the international best practices of corporate governance and, in the longer term, promote value investment in China. Lastly, as some loosening of capital control measures would be necessary for foreign firm listings in China, this might promote the international use of the renminbi beyond the onshore market as investors acquired shares with fewer constraints. Such expectations, however, turned out to be unfounded: a loosening of capital control was barely acceptable to financial policymakers even though denominating shares in renminbi might enable China's currency internationalization. Indeed, the pricing currency was central to the policy deliberations of later years, and became a major source of disagreement between the Shanghai and CSRC-led pro-opening coalition and dissenting parties.

To obtain central political support, the SSE began endeavors that aimed beyond the mainland market. It set up overseas trading terminals for China's market after the mid-2000s that facilitated market access from abroad (SSE Innovation Laboratory 2007: 53).[18] To ease the regulatory barrier of floating shares in China, local financial officials lobbied the CSRC to consider substantially lowering the regulatory and compliance standards applicable to as many as 407 red-chip enterprises, most of them listed in Hong Kong. Among them, only 38 could meet the listing requirements of China's main boards. It was

Table 4.3 Market cap and number of listed companies of selected stock exchanges

	Market Cap (billion US$)	Total Listed Companies	Domestic	Foreign	% Domestic	% Foreign
NYSE Group	19,573.1	2,307	1,822	485	78.98	21.02
Nasdaq	7,779.1	2,897	2,509	388	86.61	13.39
Japan Exchange Group	4,955.3	3,541	3,535	6	99.83	0.17
Shanghai Stock Exchange	4,098.8	1,182	1,182	0	100	0
LSE Group	3,496.2	2,590	2,111	479	81.5	18.5
Euronext	3,459.9	1,051	936	115	89.06	10.94
Shenzhen Stock Exchange	3,212.7	1,870	1,870	0	100	0
Hong Kong Exchanges*	3,193.2	1,973	1,872	101	94.88	5.12
Deutsche Börse	1,716.0	592	531	61	89.70	10.30
Bombay Stock Exchange	1,566.7	5,821	5,820	1	99.98	0.02
National Stock Exchange of India	1,539.6	1,840	1,839	1	99.95	0.05
Australian Securities Exchange	1,268.5	2,095	1,969	126	93.99	6.01
Korea Exchange	1,254.5	2,059	2,039	20	99.03	0.97
Taiwan Stock Exchange	844.0	911	833	78	91.44	8.56
Singapore Exchange	640.4	757	479	278	63.28	36.72

Source: World Federation of Stock Exchanges Annual Statistics 2016, www.world-exchanges.org/home/index.php/statistics/annual-statistics.

Note
* Chinese firms are classified as domestic firms in computing the company figures here.

hoped the less stringent requirements championed by Shanghai might have translated into a much larger pool of eligible firms (about 120–30) floating shares on the platform.[19]

However, Shanghai's suggestion was not well-received by the CSRC at first, which saw no rationale for lowering the bar and was inclined to have foreign companies land in China ahead of the red-chips.[20] From the regulator's perspective, firms from leading financial centers often maintained comparable, if not more stringent, disclosure and corporate governance standards to China, and might therefore experience fewer difficulties in meeting the CSRC's expectations. This set high standards for listing on the international board and firms—red-chips or otherwise—could expect to be subjected to high regulatory benchmarks.[21]

The divergent positions of local and central parties, however, did not noticeably slow down policy deliberation. The CSRC acknowledged the merits of Shanghai's international board initiative, finding it important to the fostering of its policy agenda surrounding securities market development and the SSE. The shared policy objectives of Shanghai interests and the securities regulator, therefore, made room for accommodation and bargaining within the emergent pro-opening coalition of the international board.

In May 2007, the CSRC responded to Shanghai's proposal with a consultation paper for domestic securities firms on the subject of the possible listing requirements and trading rules of red-chip and foreign firms (Trusted Sources 2010: 28–9). The paper, instead of resolving technical issues before moving forward, relegated regulatory disagreements to a secondary importance and left them for resolution at a later stage. Although specific firm-level feedback was not publicly known, the domestic securities industry strongly welcomed the listing of red-chip and foreign companies with their apparent competence to execute the IPO process in the A-share market. In view of favorable financial industry interests, in 2008 the CSRC embraced Shanghai's initiative and, for the first time, incorporated the international board into its annual agenda. Shanghai's officials seemed emboldened by the center's support. A senior exchange official claimed that there were no longer any technical barriers to foreign firms listing, and saw the launch of the international board as a "matter of resolve and time" for the regulator.[22]

However, as it turned out, such an assessment was grossly over-optimistic and failed to anticipate the political implications inherent in the seemingly undisputed regulatory issues of domestic constituents. The global crisis temporarily interrupted Shanghai's venture despite the strong backing of the CSRC and securities industry. As had happened with the Through Train, the systemic risks which China's financial system faced deterred the central authorities from pursuing any liberalizing initiative. The CSRC would also confront grave political liabilities arising from domestic market adjustments if the IPOs of newly listed firms depressed the capital levels of domestic financial institutions. This, however, did not completely stall the quest of the Shanghai and CSRC-led coalition for an international board.

Center elites weighing in: toward a stronger opening coalition

In fact, Shanghai's pursuit of an international board received stronger blessing from the center. The new framing of the opening initiative by local interests as a means of internationalizing China's stock exchanges was supported by top decision makers, like the then Vice Premier Wang Qishan, who recognized the move as an important strategy that might boost the global profile of China's financial markets and consolidate Shanghai's niche as the country's international financial center. This strengthened the leverage of the pro-opening coalition comprised of Shanghai, the mainland securities firms, and the CSRC.

With patronage from Beijing's top elites, Shanghai's agenda was extensively marketed abroad. Wang Qishan, for example, encouraged foreign companies to list on China's exchange in the fourth China–US Strategic Economic Dialogue of June 2008, and the UK–China Economic and Financial Dialogue in May 2009 (Ministry of Foreign Affairs (China) 2009).[23] This drew intense market attention as the two leading economies held most of the top global firms and were the preferred destinations, other than Hong Kong, for overseas listings by Chinese firms. Companies like NYSE–Euronext and HSBC soon expressed their interest in listing in China. The strong market reaction further boosted the leverage of the international board coalition.

This galvanized additional political impetus from the center when the State Council of China (2009) released its "Opinion on Promoting the Accelerated

Development of the Modern Service Industries and Advanced Manufacturing to Establish Shanghai as an International Financial Center and International Shipping Center." The document referenced Deng Xiaoping's vision of transforming Shanghai into one of the "twin global centers" of finance and shipping by 2020 and anticipated the city's capital market would provide a wide range of new financial services and products available to both domestic and foreign investors. In addition to the international board relished by Shanghai, financial futures and derivatives, as well as credit default swaps, would be gradually introduced.[24]

As the central elites weighed in, no longer was the international board merely a parochial quest of Shanghai and the CSRC for a global profile. The initiative had also become symbolic of China's increasingly globalized capital market of the future. Such excitement was shared by the PBOC as its renminbi internationalization agenda was compatible with the pursuit of an international board. The central bank's International Financial Market Report, for example, discussed how an international board would serve to promote the global standing of China's securities market and the international profile of the renminbi (Shanghai Head Office, PBOC 2009: 134). Despite such public endorsements, however, there remained several technical issues that needed to be resolved before the international board's debut. These included, for example, the method of listing and the pricing currency. Accordingly, the PBOC did not provide any details of the timing and implementation specifics.

Yet within the pro-opening coalition, this brought its constituents—the Shanghai government, SSE and CSRC—much closer together in policy deliberation. The CSRC founded a special working group (*gongzuo zu*) in mid-2009 to oversee the development of listing regulations and rules, and participated in a similar taskforce with the Shanghai bourse. It was hoped the two in-house platforms would also be the focal point for soliciting wider support to maintain the essential political and technical consensus within government.

Indeed, Shanghai officials were so convinced that the launch of the international board was beyond question that they queued one after another to share their optimism in public. Mayor Hang Zhang, and Fang Xinghai, Director of the Shanghai Financial Service Office, said that they expected that several overseas firms would start floating shares in Shanghai in 2010. The SSE even speculated that Beijing was orchestrating a "master game plan" of financial internationalization, as part of which the international board was set to commence operations following the launch of ChiNext—China's NASDAQ—in Shenzhen in 2009.[25]

Concessionary politics within the coalition

Despite the central elites' support and the synergistic efforts of the CSRC and Shanghai to address operational aspects of the international board, wider consensus beyond the pro-opening coalition was conspicuous by its absence. Within the coalition, Shanghai and the CSRC had yet to reconcile their disagreements over listing requirements and procedures despite their shared commitment to the international board.

Opening advocates finding accommodation among themselves was to be crucial to sustaining their drive. However, a number of political and technical difficulties beyond the regulatory realm of the CSRC resulted in a rift with its local partner. The CSRC capitalized on the annual agenda-setting National Working Conference on Securities and Futures Regulation in January 2010 to galvanize support from the securities industry and other bureaucratic stakeholders. The meeting did not bring any breakthrough, however, but simply revealed more problems within the financial bureaucracy that would eventually foil the ambition for an international board.[26] This, though, did not entirely derail the international board from the policy agenda due to the continuing support from the top decision makers. An "opinion note" of the State Council of China (2010), for instance, stated that the issuance of shares and other securities instruments by foreign firms was one of the principal ways to better utilize foreign capital, alongside FDI, joint venture projects and QFII, and the note encouraged relevant government agencies to pursue the initiative.

In view of the apparently committed center, the SSE (2010) presented a more concrete timeframe, making the international board one of its near-term objectives to be achieved by 2013, together with initiatives to launch new financial products and expand its global outreach. As it kept restating throughout the policy formation, it hoped these initiatives would elevate China's capital market competitiveness and transform Shanghai into a top IPO destination in the region by 2016. The CSRC also kept the international board as one of its 2011 key policy priorities (CSRC 2011). To accelerate policy momentum, Shanghai interests presented a "fait accompli" to the CSRC even while there was a lack of agreement between the securities regulator and other bureaucratic stakeholders regarding implementation specifics.

The SSE officials publicly discussed the regulatory frameworks governing share issuance, listing, trading and settlement of foreign firms. Listing and trading regulations were completed while they were still waiting for the center's approval. The bourse also upgraded its trading system to cope with the expected significant expansion of trading turnover following the IPO of leading global firms. Local banking officials foresaw the listing of foreign banks with a significant presence in China, such as HSBC and the Bank of East Asia, as early as April 2011.[27]

These moves to cement the ties with the CSRC paid off in part. The regulator ratcheted up its political commitment and promoted the "working group" on the international board to be the "leading group" (*lingdao xiaozu*) under the Department of International Cooperation in January 2011. This group was comprised of the Shanghai government and exchange officials and counterparts from other bureaucratic actors. The group would address regulatory issues that required the inter-departmental coordination crucial to the launch of the international board.

The Shanghai and CSRC-led coalition also found new partners outside the government, notably foreign financial institutions that had some presence in

China or an eagerness to issue shares on the international board. During the 2011 annual meeting of the National People's Congress and Political Consultative Conference, representatives with a financial background such as Li Jiange, Chairman of China International Capital Corporation (CICC), and former CSRC Vice Chair Laura Cha, urged the center to launch the international board within a year or two. As the non-executive deputy chair of HSBC, Cha sought to make the bank the first foreign company landing on the new platform. Indeed, her view was typical among the overseas financial community, which sought a bigger foothold in China's markets. Financial services companies, especially joint venture investment banks and brokers, reached out to prospective companies.[28] Goldman Sachs–Gao Hua and CITIC securities, two leading domestic brokers, struck a deal with CNOOC as its underwriters, and CICC was appointed the financial adviser for Royal Dutch Shell and HSBC.[29] Goldman Sachs and UBS also assembled lists of prospective multinational clients, including leading brands like Coca Cola, General Electric and Unilever, to prepare their landings on the SSE (Zhu et al. 2011 May).[30]

In April 2011, a CSRC draft on the particulars of the international board revealed the compromise between the central and local parties over implementation specifics. It corroborated earlier local officials' remarks about listing requirements and approval from the securities regulator. The first cohort of foreign firms listing in China would consist of about ten companies, a larger scale than the Shanghai authorities had expected. Each firm was to have a market cap over 30 billion yuan and to have made net profits of three and one billion yuan in their last three and one years, respectively, before listing on the SSE. Issuing prices would be determined with reference to share prices in the overseas markets. The funds raised could be used within or outside China, but approval was to be obtained from the PBOC and SAFE for the latter case.[31]

These major clauses aside, the CSRC made important accommodations with Shanghai interests to sustain the liberalizing momentum. Shanghai's proposal to introduce two-tier regulatory requirements for red-chip and foreign companies, once turned down by the securities regulator, was revived and endorsed. Red-chip companies would meet a lower listing threshold with their issuance and listing applications being assessed by CSRC's Department of Public Offering Supervision, due to the firms' business affiliations with China. Foreign firms, by contrast, would be supervised by the Department of International Affairs, the same unit that scrutinized the overseas listings of domestic firms. They would also enter the international board ahead of the red-chips in the early stage.[32]

This regulatory compromise evidenced the regulator's policy and political commitment, and went in Shanghai's favor. Listing of foreign enterprises would help the city's brand as an upcoming global financial center, serve the CSRC's agenda of internationalizing China's capital market, and improve corporate governance of domestic firms through the role modeling of foreign companies.[33] In a Shanghai–CSRC sponsored forum in May 2011, the top securities regulator stated that the international board was "getting close" to China. His deputies also foresaw the board's "natural delivery."[34]

These official endorsements unmistakably hinted at the imminent arrival of the international board and further stoked market expectations. But they disguised lingering and escalating disagreements within the Shanghai and CSRC-led coalition. Supportive policy rhetoric failed to increase the political leverage of the pro-opening coalition and secure wider support from within the financial bureaucracy. Rival initiatives also emerged from Shenzhen and Hong Kong, breaking Shanghai's agenda-setting monopoly and undercutting its presentation of itself as the default destination for foreign firms listing in China. Even worse, the Shanghai and CSRC-led coalition resisted accommodating bureaucratic actors who were growing wary of the political and technical complications underlying the international board. This deprived Shanghai of local allies, and effectively led to a breakdown of consensus within the financial bureaucracy, generating a much stronger dissenting force that would eventually roll back Shanghai's ambition.

Parallel opening calls from local interests

As Shanghai was forging its tie with the CSRC in 2010, Shenzhen and Hong Kong pursued different initiatives that rivaled Shanghai's quest for an international board. Shenzhen wanted to inaugurate a second international board for foreign SMEs and high-tech firms in a similar way to that set out in Shanghai's initiative, whereas Hong Kong avoided head-on competition with the Shanghai and CSRC-led coalition and capitalized on its advance in offshore renminbi business backed by the PBOC to present itself as an alternative destination, issuing renminbi-denominated securities. This put Shanghai on the defensive, forcing it to intensify its courtship of central elites.

With a small market cap, Shenzhen was initially no match for Shanghai in stock market development. The SZSE, however, grew dramatically in the late 2000s due to the fast-growing SMEB and ChiNext, tripling its market cap. In 2010 alone, the exchange raised a total of 298.1 billion yuan (or US$45.4 billion) for 321 companies, representing 62.8% of the total equity funds raised and 92% of all newly listed companies in mainland China. This made Shenzhen the leading IPO destination in China and the world's second largest after Hong Kong (SZSE 2010; PricewaterhouseCoopers 2011: 3). By contrast, the SSE only executed 28 IPOs totaling about 180.2 billion yuan in 2010, and was running short of mega-size IPOs of blue-chip companies because most SOEs had already gone public in the 2000s.

The ascending status of Shenzhen emboldened local financiers and officials to expand beyond the existing market niche and to look for a secondary international board serving foreign SMEs that might fail to meet the strict listing requirements of Shanghai. Senior executives of local firms, financiers and exchange officials lobbied the Shenzhen government in early 2011, hoping that the initiative would gain traction as the city had acquired strong credentials in serving non-blue chip companies on the SMEB and ChiNext.[35] The SZSE also proposed a secondary listing of overseas Chinese high-tech firms like Baidu and

Tencent (two of China's IT giants) in the ChiNext that would significantly boost the city's global finance profile.[36]

Jockeying from Shenzhen's financiers, however, was coolly-received. Though the city had strengthened its ties to Hong Kong under CEPA and was capitalizing on the Qianhai area to foster cross-border financial development, it still failed to elicit wider political support from local and provincial authorities. The Shenzhen officials appeared to realize that, short of the establishment of a "primary" international board in Shanghai, Shenzhen would have little leverage to pursue its agenda. After all, Shanghai had been ceaselessly defending its role as China's global financial hub throughout the deliberations surrounding the red-chip homecoming and the international board by linking the local pursuit to the central financial policy agenda and had apparently obtained strong bureaucratic support. With no backing from the central or provincial governments, Shenzhen could do little to rival Shanghai's opening initiative, or to seek international boards in the two onshore financial hubs at the same time.

Perhaps more worrisome than Shenzhen's endeavors was Hong Kong's transformation into an offshore renminbi center. It undercut Shanghai's agenda-setting monopoly and leverage over central bureaucratic actors. Instead of aiming to establish another international board like Shenzhen and seeking the patronage of the CSRC, Hong Kong's advance was intertwined with the PBOC-sponsored renminbi internationalization of the mid-2000s. After offshore renminbi bond issuance and trade settlement were phased in, the offshore community was planning for renminbi-denominated stock issuance by foreign companies in the SEHK. Although some offshore financial officials and the HKEx were reportedly unsettled by Shanghai's pursuit, they raised no explicit dissent to the international board. Publicly, the Hong Kong authorities even commented that the platform would be complementary to the SEHK.[37]

This conciliatory posture avoided a clash with Shanghai over opening agendas, and afforded some leeway to Hong Kong to enlist political support from its onshore counterpart regarding offshore renminbi market development. Indeed, the quid pro quo exchanges preempted dissent from Shanghai-based interests, and helped buy time for Hong Kong to gradually position itself as a failsafe alternative destination for foreign firm listings as its renminbi financial product development made advances.

Although the city's renminbi market was not yet fully fledged, Hong Kong promised to be a better candidate than Shanghai due to its world-class regulatory infrastructure, talent pool of professional financial services, and an economy without capital controls. Even for renminbi transactions, the offshore market imposed far fewer restrictions than the mainland, and benefited from the rapidly expanding renminbi funds that grew ninefold between 2009 and April 2011, enabling the HKEx to execute IPO projects for foreign multinationals.[38] In the same period, 45 companies issued offshore renminbi bonds (or "dim sum bonds" as they are vividly known) and raised 55 billion yuan. The HKEx also welcomed the first offshore renminbi IPO in April 2011 with a scale of US$1.7 billion.[39]

Although this was relatively small compared to most blue-chips, it represented a breakthrough from Hong Kong in broadening the variety of renminbi financial products in response to the dramatically expanding pool of renminbi deposits with little use except as interest-bearing instruments. To encourage more renminbi IPOs offshore, the HKEx and Hong Kong officials simplified secondary listing regulations, targeting companies listed in bourses of acceptable overseas jurisdictions, and developed the "dual tranche, dual counter" model for companies issuing shares in either renminbi or Hong Kong dollars.[40] This not only attested to Hong Kong's status as the leading offshore renminbi center, it also demonstrated to China's financial bureaucracy that the city was a plausible alternative to Shanghai for foreign companies issuing renminbi stocks, and would not compromise China's securities regulations and capital controls. As the following sections show, these regulatory concerns would bleed away the PBOC's commitment to Shanghai, further aggravating the resistance of dissenting parties within the financial bureaucracy to the international board.

Breakdown of the "false" technical consensus from within

As the market was anticipating an imminent announcement from CSRC about the international board's regulatory particulars, the Shanghai and CSRC-led coalition encountered a significant challenge from within the financial bureaucracy alongside the parallel local initiatives. Three important issues—method of listing, accounting standards, and the pricing currency of shares—stood out and disrupted the efforts of Shanghai and the CSRC after 2010. Bureaucratic actors were also at odds because of policy priorities and they questioned the relevance of the platform as adverse distributional implications and policy risks of both kinds became more salient to their policy deliberations. This stronger resistance to the international board resulted in a policy turnabout just a few years after the abrupt suspension of the Through Train.

It is as well to analyze the political considerations that loomed over the method of listing, accounting standards, and the pricing currency. For each issue, constituents of the pro-opening coalition failed to address dissent from financial bureaucracy stakeholders over implementation specifics. This limited the extent of the political support Shanghai and the CSRC could obtain, and shattered the apparent technical consensus driving forward the international board. Together, these issues show how disagreements over operational aspects of the liberalizing initiative sparked political contests within and without the pro-opening coalition and illustrate the great importance of concessionary politics in policy deliberation.

Method of listing: depository receipt or IPO?

IPOs of red-chips and overseas companies had been seen as the default, if not the only, method of listing throughout Shanghai's quest for the international board. Nonetheless, the issuance of depository receipts in the A-share market (i.e., CDRs) remained a plausible alternative despite Hong Kong's failure to challenge the CSRC's position in 2007. As the international board entered the national agenda, the regulator and Shanghai dismissed the alternative and insisted on floating shares through IPOs.[41] Their intransigence meant they missed important opportunities to expand their leverage and the wider support it might obtain.

To the CSRC, CDRs were simply proxies for foreign shares, not much different from the ETFs tracking the performance of foreign markets. It was thought that, even if CDRs were issued with fund-raising purposes like certain species in the US market, they would not contribute to the market cap of China's stock market and so would do little to boost global standing.[42] Strongly motivated to internationalize its financial sector, Shanghai shared the regulator's position and insisted IPOs were the best, if not the only, way of listing.[43] To undermine the advocates of CDRs, the CSRC highlighted a number of operational challenges, including the lack of precise regulations governing how original shares of foreign companies could be converted to CDRs, as well as investors' confusion over the way CDRs might be priced and valued and their difference from ordinary shares.

To avoid CDR-issuing companies simply selling their outstanding shares (a secondary offering), where the proceeds would be of benefit primarily to existing shareholders, the regulator required foreign companies to issue new shares (an incremental offering) as the underlying of CDRs. This, however, was largely unacceptable to foreign firms since it would dilute existing shareholding and thereby reduce the appeal of listing in China. The CSRC was also wary of placing higher demands on China's settlement and clearing mechanisms because CDRs would necessitate the domestic banks serving as depository units issuing negotiable certificates to foreign custodian banks (Trusted Sources 2010: 18).

Whereas some of these concerns were valid, they were not insurmountable technical obstacles beyond the policy capacity of the CSRC and domestic securities industry. For example, better investor education and risk profiling could lower the investment risks, and regulations guiding share conversion and trading could be developed jointly with domestic brokers in the same way the red-chip and international board requirements were crafted. As mainland securities professionals commented, the CSRC was holding double standards as it had encouraged American Depository Receipt (ADR) issuances of China's SOEs like China Insurance simultaneously with their IPOs in Hong Kong. The offerings in the US market were officially celebrated as a milestone of Chinese firms joining the global marketplace.[44]

It had been the CSRC's political concerns, especially its interests in the securities industry and within the financial bureaucracy, that explained its reluctance to consider CDRs. Since issuance would involve domestic commercial banks buying stocks in markets where foreign companies were listed and then becoming depository institutions, securities firms, most with far less capital than banks, would be unlikely to play much of a role in CDR issuance and custody. This would disadvantage the domestic securities industry and politically usurp the

CSRC's stake in the matter relative to its regulatory counterpart, the CBRC.[45] Moreover, the fact that CDRs were primarily advocated by the offshore financial community also reinforced Shanghai and CSRC's disapproval, as offshore firms would benefit from their edge in managing the product's development. IPOs, in contrast, would promise huge material benefits to onshore brokerages and the SSE, and expand the CSRC's regulatory leverage over the new listing platform.

The insistence on IPOs, however, challenged the international board endeavor as Shanghai barely obtained any support beyond the CSRC and PBOC, and prevented the possibility of reaching a compromise with other bureaucratic actors who regarded CDRs as a simpler option for foreign companies to float shares in China. SAFE, and to some extent the PBOC, for example, saw fewer technical hassles with CDR issuance since it would not involve compliance with China's incorporation requirements for firms issuing shares in China, and would not necessitate loosening capital control regimes.[46] Indeed, once the PBOC and SAFE approved the size and quota of CDR issuances, foreign firms might quickly establish their presence on China's stock market. In the longer term, when CDRs could be converted into ordinary shares traded on overseas markets (the two-way fungible CDR), the investment uses of the renminbi worldwide might see a big leap in the central bank's favor (Ba 2011: 2–3).

Since IPOs brought no ancillary benefits to other bureaucratic actors, they saw little or no interest in strongly supporting Shanghai and the CSRC, who might at least have forged ties with CBRC, SAFE and PBOC if they had been less devoted to their preferred way of listing. This weakened the political consensus for the international board and relegated it to a mere liberalizing initiative boosting China's stock market internationalization. Although this political concern had engendered support from the PBOC and other central elites in the mid-2000s, the unaddressed (or downplayed) technical issues eventually left the pro-opening coalition much more exposed to political challenges.

Valuing foreign firms: Chinese or international accounting standards?

Another important but unresolved technical issue in foreign securities issuance concerned the accounting standards that were used to appraise the values of foreign companies. While the Shanghai and CSRC-led coalition preferred the adoption of the International Financial Reporting Standards (IFRS), the authority to settle the issue was beyond their remit. The CSRC and the SSE, however, attempted to present a "false" consensus on the matter and seemed unwilling to consider the view of other bureaucratic stakeholders. This provoked opposition within the financial bureaucracy.

Instead of adopting domestic practices, the Chinese Accounting Standards (CAS), the pro-opening coalition endorsed the IFRS in the 2011 draft regulations. Yet accounting standards governing the listing of foreign firms continued to be a contentious and unresolved issue, despite the mutual recognition agreements of CAS and IFRS being concluded in the 2000s between the Ministry of Finance (MOF)—the agency that oversaw the China Accounting Standards Committee—and its foreign counterparts. The MOF was particularly sensitive to the adoption of overseas accounting standards and had been striving to promote the international recognition and use of CAS beyond China since the 2000s.[47]

Although this frustrated foreign institutions issuing renminbi-denominated bonds in China (i.e., the panda bond)—as when the Asian Development Bank (ADB) and International Finance Corporation (IFC) were required in 2005 to follow the CAS and have their bonds rated by domestic credit-rating agencies—this did little to extract a compromise from the MOF. Only after protracted negotiation were the panda bonds made available to investors and the finance ministry forced to grant exemptions to the two foreign institutions. The MOF's recalcitrance, however, irked the issuers and depressed the panda bond market due to China's tax reporting requirements and associated compliance costs.[48]

Even then, the finance ministry sought to revive the market and promote CAS overseas, and expected foreign firms listing in China to follow domestic standards. Since the mid-2000s the MOF had signed agreements with major economies to reconcile divergent accounting standards, but essential reciprocal arrangements were still lacking. The MOF eased the reporting requirement of Chinese firms listed in Hong Kong by having the offshore regulator recognize CAS in late 2007. An equivalence agreement about CAS and European Union (EU) IFRS in 2008 also enabled Chinese firms listed on EU markets to comply with CAS only (Trusted Sources 2010: 28–9). These efforts in effect lowered the regulations of publicly traded Chinese firms overseas without reciprocal treatment to foreign companies floating shares in China.[49]

The MOF position invariably complicated that of the Shanghai and CSRC-led coalition. The Shanghai bourse and financial officials were concerned that CAS would burden foreign firms with additional compliance costs and taint the global appeal of the international board in the same way the panda bond initiative had suffered. A financial industry estimate suggested that complying with the CAS accounting and reporting framework would cost as much as five to six million US$ and could jump to over ten million for larger multinationals in the IPO process. This excluded follow-on audit fees to meet reporting requirements.[50] To defend their preference for IFRS, the opening advocates drew on the lessons of the Tokyo Stock Exchange Foreign Section founded in December 1973. Serving a similar purpose as the international board, the section expected compliance with the Japanese accounting requirements from foreign companies listed in Japan. Although this did not initially affect the platform's appeal, it shrank significantly after the domestic economy peaked in the 1980s. Only around a dozen companies stayed, down from 120 in its heyday.[51]

The MOF was initially receptive to IFRS in view of the strengthening pro-opening coalition and the central elites' support. It even considered working with the CSRC and SSE to devise appropriate accounting practices for the international board if they would hold back their push for a while until the technical issues were resolved. But, as the CSRC and Shanghai made occasional public declarations that the issue was settled, the MOF saw little chance of narrowing its divergence with the pro-opening coalition without registering opposition to the larger liberalizing pursuit. In what would pierce the false technical consensus, the head of the MOF's Enterprise Department explicitly rejected adoption of IFRS in October 2011.[52] This escalated tension with the pro-opening coalition which now saw little hope of coming to terms with the MOF over the accounting standards of the international board.

The preference for IPO and IFRS did serve the best interests of the Shanghai and CSRC-led coalition, but this squandered opportunities to enlist the backing of SAFE and the PBOC over methods of listing, and to compromise with the MOF on accounting standards. As these bureaucratic heavyweights were alienated and provoked in policy deliberation, any apparent consensus over technical specifics essential to the platform's operation were noticeably lacking—even though the political commitment of the top decision makers appeared to remain.

Contestation over the pricing currencies of shares

Technical issues like the method of listing and accounting standards were not merely arcane subjects of finance with few political implications. They became "politicized" as the quest of the pro-opening coalition to launch the international board on its own terms generated dissent and opposition. It is also worth examining another equally, if not more, important operational parameter—the pricing currency of shares. Two possibilities stood out: the US dollar and the renminbi. As with the deliberation over accounting standards, Shanghai and the CSRC's inclination toward the renminbi were at odds with the PBOC's preference for pricing shares in US dollars that would advance its own policy agenda. Following the breakdown of apparent technical agreements, the political consensus on the international board was dealt a heavy blow by this further division within the financial bureaucracy, which in turn further weakened the leverage of the pro-opening coalition.

A "non-issue" becomes contested

Choosing a pricing currency for stocks is a non-issue for most countries as stocks are denominated and traded in the local currency. Even in Tokyo's Foreign Section, the shares of US companies are quoted and traded in yen. In China, since the advent of the B-share market in 1991, pricing shares in non-local currencies (US and Hong Kong dollars) had become a peculiar practice. In early discussions surrounding the red-chip homecoming, floating shares or issuing CDRs in renminbi was uncontroversial—just as it had been for the IPOs of domestic firms on the A-share market. The international board brought the financial subject to the center of policy deliberation with implications that reached beyond company valuation (which shaped the earnings multiples and offering prices) and influenced appeals to investors.

The pro-opening coalition of the international board, however, had been convinced that the issue was settled in mid-2010 after senior SAFE officials remarked that the agency did not foresee any implications for foreign exchange management arising from the international board, and was considering granting full convertibility of up-front costs for listing as well as partially lifting capital controls for firms' capital transfers before and after their IPOs.[53] This, however, did not actually address the choice of pricing currency. Some viewed SAFE as being in favor of the US dollar; others read into the remarks the opposite and anticipated shares to be denominated in renminbi.

Pricing in US dollars was primarily backed by onshore investors and broker-ages who sought to revitalize a B-share market plagued by low turnover and liquidity following the fanfare of the early 2000s when the market had opened to domestic investors. Onshore securities firms hoped that a US dollar-denominated international board would stimulate the appeal of the B-share market, and lobbied the CSRC to merge it with the international board. To solicit the CSRC's support, the domestic securities industry also argued that pricing shares in US dollars would address the regulator's concern about adjust-ment in the A-share market "crowded out" by listings of foreign firms. Domestic investors with foreign currency holdings would also find more prom-ising returns in the international board than in deposit interest and B-shares.[54]

Despite these potential merits, the Shanghai and CSRC-led coalition did not find pricing shares in US dollars an appealing arrangement. Instead, the CSRC saw no urgency in reviving the B-share market and repudiated the proposal to merge the B-share market with the international board. The draft regulation in April 2011 clarified the CSRC's stance of pricing shares in renminbi, and valuing them with reference to their average price over a period of time in over-seas exchanges prior to their China IPO, adjusted to compensate for exchange rates.[55] This rocked the A-share market as investors were unsettled by the pro-spect of more favorably valued quality shares on the international board. The Shanghai index dropped by 3% on a single day of May 2011.[56]

Push for renminbi shares but weakening political leverage

The push of the pro-opening coalition to price shares in renminbi was not sur-prising, however, given the several immediate benefits this entailed and the pro-spect of strengthening the PBOC's support for the international board. In the interests of Shanghai and the CSRC, pricing shares in renminbi guaranteed a high market turnover due to the nearly cost-free access of investors to the market. The US dollar option, by contrast, necessitated the holding of foreign currencies that would mean individual purchases were subject to an annual limit of US$50,000, and thus would be of little appeal.

Indeed, the pro-opening coalition likened an international board with renminbi-priced shares to QDII, since it was hoped that if companies could remit funds overseas in foreign currencies, this would remove excess liquidity, help ease pressures on the PBOC to tackle the overheating economy, and slow down the reserve buildup. [57] This new framing of the liberalizing pursuit found sympathy among senior PBOC and SAFE officials who considered creating a "hot money pool" to contain short-term capital inflows and excess domestic liquidity so as to keep inflation and market volatility in check. First proposed by the PBOC Governor Zhou Xiaochuan in November 2010, his deputies found in Shanghai's international board an example of the "hot money pool" and urged the CSRC and Shanghai to start the board as soon as possible. This would cool down the economy that had witnessed phenomenal growth in money supply and asset prices after the global crisis, contributed to by loose monetary policy and capital inflows. [58]

Nevertheless, this did not bring unqualified support from the PBOC to the Shanghai and CSRC-led coalition. Although the international board might represent a timely policy response to macroeconomic challenges, it was soon complicated by the regulatory void and the perceived political risk with adverse ramifications that the CSRC and the supportive PBOC and SAFE had not recognized earlier. Despite having policy goals compatible with Shanghai's pursuit, the central bank was quick to see the lack of regulations on how funds raised in the platform might be allocated and transferred across markets, even though SAFE appeared to come close with the CSRC to agree on procedures about post-listing capital remittance. [59] This was understandable, as it had been assumed that foreign companies listing in China should have considerable China-based business operations and most of the proceeds should stay onshore rather than be taken out of the country. [60]

Meanwhile, the development of Hong Kong's offshore market also detracted from the PBOC's backing of Shanghai's pursuit. Having foreign firms issuing renminbi-denominated shares offshore was deemed a more practicable option without the concomitant easing of China's capital control regime, and at the same time might help encourage private international uses of the renminbi. To the PBOC and SAFE, this represented significant political gains easily attained in a failsafe context, and the two agencies preferred to delay the launch of the international board pursuit until all related regulatory and technical challenges had been resolved. [61] The Shanghai and CSRC-led coalition, however, pressed on and expected to receive their continuing support and prompt approval on regulatory matters. This intensified the divide between the pro-opening and dissenting parties, and the PBOC and SAFE became more reserved than ever.

In fact, since the renminbi was not fully convertible, the platform would likely be accessible by domestic investors and selected foreign parties for some time to come. [62] However, persistently high valuations in China's stock market might lead to the over-valuation of shares in Shanghai compared to shares of the same company listed on overseas markets. To the PBOC and SAFE, this would make the international board a virtually cost-free ATM for foreign firms if they were allowed to remit the funds with ease. Shares traded at a price premium in the SSE would also be convenient and low-cost arbitrage instruments if capital controls were to loosen in the future. [63] Although this might facilitate share price convergence across different capital markets, the two agencies might experience severe political liabilities because of ensuing market instabilities. Equally, the CSRC might be blamed for its failure to protect investors if heavy losses were incurred by domestic traders. This presented the CSRC with costly political risks, putting the agency in a dilemma over whether to continue its support for the international board, or to postpone its launch.

Accordingly, although the pro-opening coalition had obtained the PBOC's support in earlier phases of policy deliberation, this did not quite translate into agreements over technical specifics or tolerance of policy risks. The unready state of regulations and the associated policy risks alarmed the PBOC and SAFE, which had initially backed the international board, and resulted in their hesitation. Implications for stock market stability and the likely exposure to risk of domestic investors (for which the CSRC would be held accountable) challenged the regulator's patronage of Shanghai's international board. All this dampened political commitment within the financial bureaucracy, and called into question the leverage of the pro-opening coalition.

Shifting central political priorities; waning opening agenda

Weakening bureaucratic support aside, the Shanghai and CSRC-led coalition met with a significant setback when competing policy agendas emerged in 2011 that sidetracked the critical backing it had obtained from top decision makers in the State Council. As political commitment to the international board waned and resistance piled up, the venture was terminated and fell off the central agenda.

As Shanghai was counting down to the board's debut, its agenda was rivaled and overtaken by competing policy priorities originating from within the financial bureaucracy and galvanized by the worsening domestic economic conditions after late 2010 that deprived millions of private SMEs of the capital essential to their survival. Despite the expanding money supply, capital allocation remained grossly skewed to state-owned financial institutions and enterprises. Cash-strapped firms unable to obtain funds from equity markets or banks turned to underground channels, spurring a significant growth of the shadow banking market stoked by funds from financial institutions, SOEs, and local governments. This resulted in several large-scale defaults across China after early 2011 and posed escalating systemic risks that foreshadowed a looming crisis in the wider financial system.[64]

In response, China turned away from financial opening and prioritized its domestic challenges. To address the SME financing challenges and rein in the growth of shadow banking activities, the National Development and Reform Commission (NDRC), the super-ministry of macroeconomic management, reshuffled the annual financial development agenda of 2011 and stressed that a new Over-the-Counter Bulletin Board (OTCBB, or *xin san ban*) should take precedence.[65] The NDRC reasoned that provisioning new financing channels to domestic firms should assume a higher priority than pursuing financial opening that might usher China's capital market into contingencies it was unready for.

As such, the OTCBB was "accelerated" and the international board was left waiting for "further debate and study" (State Council of China 2011).

As the scale of shadow banking loomed large and domestic banks accumulated more debt, the NDRC soon found strong support from the MOF and PBOC. Its plan to expand the OTCBB's scale was also promptly endorsed by top decision makers and approved by the State Council in June 2011, shortly after the CSRC had publicly declared the international board was imminent.[66] This inward policy turn effectively relegated the international board to a secondary policy concern and restricted any further pursuit of the Shanghai and CSRC-led coalition.

Worse still, the imperative of internationalizing the domestic stock exchange through the listing of foreign firms was seriously called into question. Some PBOC officials recommended liberalizing the domestic bond market for foreign companies issuing bonds in the Shanghai-based interbank market before creating an international board. This would introduce product diversity for the domestic investors and invigorate the inactive panda bond market. The agenda was quickly favored by the NDRC and finance ministry, who had strong political stakes in bond issuance and larger fixed income product market development.[67]

The success of the NDRC's intervention was seemingly indicative of its preponderance over the lower-level ministries and agencies, given its overarching role in economic policymaking. But its leverage was far from unconditional as the Through Train setback in 2007 had demonstrated. The "coup" of derailing the international board gained traction to a large extent due to the increasingly divergent policy priorities and assessments of the international board within the financial bureaucracy, all reinforced by the failure of the pro-opening coalition to accommodate the concerns of dissidents over implementation particulars. As a result, no longer could Shanghai or the CSRC sustain backing in policy deliberation and they lost favor almost entirely at the central level.

This unquestionably embarrassed Shanghai and the CSRC, and there was little hope that the international board would be revived. Indeed, it disappeared from the securities regulator's annual plan altogether after a new CSRC chief took power in October 2011.[68] In view of a far less supportive central patron, the Shanghai authorities and exchange dropped their pursuit and conceded that a separate platform for red-chip and foreign firms was probably unnecessary. The mayor acknowledged that the city was not ready due to complicated technical and regulatory issues.[69]

Fang Xinghai, head of the Shanghai finance office, even confessed that the international board would be halted for a long period, and commented: "if you ask me why it's so difficult, all I can say is that it's always been difficult to implement any liberalization in the finance sector."[70] He likened Shanghai's pursuit to China's non-tradable share reform of the late 1990s in which Beijing had taken almost seven years to devise an agreeable resolution among regulators and shareholders after failing twice due to strong opposition from shareholders and a dramatic loss of stock values.[71] The endeavor to launch the international board similarly confronted a deep division within the financial bureaucracy arising from the lack of political and technical consensus and the changing central agenda of financial reforms. As local ambitions were foiled, the opening tendency was halted for a long time.

Internationalization via the offshore connector

Despite lingering petitions from domestic and foreign financial industry interests throughout 2011, the international board was not revived. Yet investors remained confused by the competing policy signals coming from Beijing. The Twelfth Five-Year Plan (2011–2015), for example, still referred to the platform as an issue of further inquiry (PBOC et al. 2012). In 2013, however, the agenda was entirely overshadowed by the more pressing priority of developing a multi-layered capital market that might better serve domestic enterprises (Central Committee of the Communist Party of China 2013).

The Shanghai authorities, however, continued their liberalizing quest. Employing a similar strategy to Hong Kong when it had catalyzed the debut of the offshore renminbi IPO, Shanghai conceived and marketed the international board pursuit to the PBOC as a possible channel for foreign investors to use their offshore renminbi funds in the onshore market in a similar fashion to the way RQFII operated, and hoped to solicit the central bank's support. As the Shanghai FTZ was inaugurated in September 2013 and easing renminbi convertibility was slated as an important reform area, Shanghai FTZ officials capitalized on the agenda and launched a proposal in 2014 to found an over-the-counter international board for private domestic firms selling equity stakes to foreign investors and vice versa.[72] The stagnant pace of introducing financial opening initiatives in the FTZ since inception, due largely to domestic economic uncertainties and escalating risks of capital flight after late 2014, extinguished any hope Shanghai nurtured to reintroduce the international board onto the agenda, whether on its original scale or with a limited scope.[73]

More importantly, the launch of the Shanghai–Hong Kong Stock Connect in late 2014 made irrelevant the creation of a separate listing platform for foreign firms on the SSE. The southbound trading link for mainland institutional and individual investors represented a substitute for an international board, making available to mainland investors not only shares of foreign firms listed on the SEHK but also most red-chip companies floating shares on Hong Kong's market. An even larger menu of offshore companies became available to onshore investors when the Shenzhen Connect commenced in late 2016. This rendered any pursuit of red-chip homecoming obsolete.

Politically, the Stock Connects brought the CSRC market acclaim for successfully collaborating with the offshore regulator and exchange, and circumvented the complicated regulatory matters associated with the international board that had elicited dissent from the PBOC and SAFE. As discussed in Chapter 3, both agencies regarded the Stock Connects as an important measure that might enhance investment uses of the offshore renminbi. Reservations among Shanghai-based financiers, notably the SSE and securities firms, were allayed by the material benefits of executing southbound investment to Hong Kong, and they saw the prospect of linking up with other bourses like London in the future as one that would heighten the SSE and Shanghai's global connections.

With its niche as China's de facto international board established, the HKEx has been courting more foreign firms to float shares on the Hong Kong market, and exploring a "Primary Equity Connect" that would allow mainland investors to participate in offshore IPOs and vice versa. In the words of Charles Li (2016), the HKEx Chief Executive:

> The Shanghai and Shenzhen exchanges both have their sights set on building international boards to welcome foreign listings and investors, however we expect this to take considerable time, if it happens at all. The urgent need for the Mainland is to diversify its investor base ... and to allow Mainland investors to have greater access to high-quality international investment assets.... Both of these key objectives can be met by opening up the primary markets on both sides of the boundary to investors from the other side.

To lure high-tech Chinese IT giants to list on the SEHK, the exchange has even considered creating a new listing board for "new economy companies" that would adopt a dual-share structure—shares of different voting rights common among start-ups—despite its deviance from the established "one share, one vote" principle upheld by the SFC, the offshore securities regulator (HKEx 2017).[74] If successful, this could position Hong Kong as a "truly global IPO center" where multinationals might tap China's massive domestic savings without much associated loosening of the mainland's outbound capital controls—a market edge that would be unmatched by any onshore financial center or regional peer like Singapore.

Conclusion

This chapter traced the fruitless quest of Shanghai and the CSRC to internationalize China's stock market through the listing of foreign companies. The policy deliberation process was perhaps just as dramatic as the ill-fated Through Train scheme examined in Chapter 3.

Early efforts to promote the homecoming of red-chip companies to the mainland exchanges were initiated by the Shanghai-based financial community and found support from the CSRC. But their split with offshore interests and the reservations of the securities regulator in the face of the subprime crisis dashed market expectations. While red-chip homecoming became a non-starter, this was soon embedded in Shanghai's pursuit of an international board that would invite red-chips and foreign multinationals to list on the SSE in order to internationalize China's capital market and boost the city's standing as a global financial center. Despite the lack of essential agreements on regulatory and technical issues, the CSRC strongly backed the initiative, constituting a strong pro-opening coalition. The central decision-making elites, eager to transform Shanghai into China's international financial center, also weighed in, seeing the board as a symbol of such status, and they marketed it at home and overseas.

The strong market expectations that ensued were frustrated by an abrupt termination and unwinding of the agenda in late 2011. Endeavors to re-introduce the agenda by linking the board to renminbi internationalization and the financial reforms of the Shanghai FTZ after 2013 made no headway as the financial bureaucracy saw a rise in systemic risks to the domestic economy. The *raison d'être* of the international board was entirely lost with the advent of the Shanghai– and Shenzhen–Hong Kong Stock Connects that provided a conduit for domestic investors to trade stocks of red-chip and foreign companies listed offshore.

The policy trajectory, while puzzling, is not incomprehensible. As the coalition politics perspective suggests, the Shanghai and CSRC-pioneered opening initiative would have had the best chance of becoming reality if the coalition and its constituents could have successfully managed dissent or expanded political support through concessionary maneuvers. The breakdown of false consensus within the financial bureaucracy over technical matters illustrates how these important opportunities were missed due to the preference of Shanghai and the CSRC to implement their desired arrangements for the international board. This might indeed have served most of their interests and retained their policy "monopoly," but given the level of complexity not uncommon in the experience of financial opening, successful policy deliberation inevitably necessitates some give-and-take and an attempt to reach compromise with dissenting parties.

Shanghai and the CSRC's reluctance led to a narrow base of bureaucratic support as the concerns and interests of the CBRC, PBOC, SAFE, and the MOF were barely considered. The finance ministry was even provoked by the coalition's preference for the adoption of IFRS and lack of consultation. Contestation over the pricing currency similarly weakened backing from the PBOC and SAFE and challenged the CSRC's patronage of the international board. It is true that concessionary offers do not necessarily garner the support, or even the acquiescence, of other local, industrial and bureaucratic actors, but their absence certainly engenders stronger dissent and opposition.

Hong Kong's stance throughout Shanghai's pursuit is also instructive about the different ways concessionary politics can play out. Hong Kong raised no opposition, despite its concerns about diverting companies to the Shanghai-based platform, in order not to affect the offshore renminbi market development. Deliberately framed as an outgrowth of the renminbi fixed income products, its budding niche in renminbi securities issuance was not viewed by Shanghai as a challenge. This provided the necessary leeway for Hong Kong to develop new liberalizing initiatives, including the Stock Connect schemes, that ultimately rendered the international board (and red-chip homecoming) unnecessary.

As with the evolution of outbound equity investment regimes, Shanghai's pursuit of stock market internationalization reveals the importance of local and financial interests in agenda-setting politics. Local and financial industry interests originated the liberalizing initiatives and linked issues with relevance to central bureaucratic parties to solicit their attention and patronage. Stalled by policy stalemate with the offshore community over red-chip homecoming, the Shanghai authorities and bourse advanced the international board and presented the issue as a strategy for promoting China's capital market internationalization. This successfully appealed to the CSRC and eventually led to the top elites sharing the same agenda.

The simple congruence of policy priorities between the Shanghai and CSRC-led coalition, the initially supportive PBOC, and the top decision-making elites to foster capital market internationalization was eventually weakened by the lack of technical agreement and the seeming inability of the pro-opening coalition to offer concessions and reach compromise with dissenting parties. This illustrates the imperative of achieving consensus over technical regulatory matters, and its equal importance to the political commitment in pursuing a financial opening. In fact, as the technical consensus of the international board thinned, Shanghai's pursuit met a significant setback when the NDRC championed a competing agenda in late 2011 in response to pressing domestic policy challenges and the escalating systemic risks in the domestic financial system.

This resulted in a reshuffling of the central agenda, and the international board was relegated to a much lower priority. As the central patron of the pro-opening coalition walked away from the local and industrial constituents, and in the face of strong dissent and a waning agenda, the international board shared the fate of the Through Train. Shanghai's aspiration to introduce foreign and red-chip companies onshore was finally dashed by the inception of the Stock Connect with Hong Kong.

Notes

1 "Liu Hongru and Gao Xiqing: weile H-gu de chuangli" (Liu Hongru and Gaoxiqing: for the genesis of the H-share), *Caijing Magazine*, issue 31, October 5, 2000. pp. 62–74.
2 "Liu Hongru and Gao Xiqing: weile H-gu de chuangli."
3 Together with a sizable number (608 by 2016 year-end) of non-H-share mainland private enterprises (NHMPEs), all China-related companies would come to make up 63.3% of SEHK. The latest data can be found at: www.hkex.com.hk/eng/stat/statrpt/mkthl/mkthl201706.htm.
4 The Chinese government (and its entities) retained majority ownership of the H-share companies even after the IPOs that made part of the shares tradable. For details of Beijing's buildup of the "national team" in the 2000s, see Walter and Howie (2011), chapter 7.
5 "Zheng Jian Hui Zhuxi zhuli Yao Gang: jiji yanjiu hongchou gongsi huigui A-gu" (Assistant to CSRC Chairman Yao Gang: Exploring ways to bring red-chips to A-share market), *China Securities Journal*, December 25, 2006.
6 Consider, for example, the average price-earnings ratios of the stock indexes of the Shanghai and Hong Kong markets. From January 2000 to December 2004, Shanghai Composite recorded 41.59 whereas the Hang Seng Index had a ratio of 16.19.

7 Oliver Chung, "Beijing ponders red-chip dual-listing," *Asia Times*, March 15, 2007.
8 "Xianggang jinrong gaoguan xiang neidi pinpao xiuqiu dali tuidong QDII, CDR ji shuangchong shangshi" (High-ranking Hong Kong financial officials floated ideas of QDII, CDR and dual-listing to the mainland authorities), *Securities Times*, March 24, 2006.
9 There are, however, exceptions to this case. Some issuances of ADR in the US market, for example, must comply with almost the same public offering regulations as the Securities and Exchange Commission (SEC) if companies release new stocks (and therefore raise funds).
10 Interview with mainland securities professional, Shanghai, May 2011.
11 Liu, Honggang, "Hongchou A-gu IPO" (Red-chip companies A-share IPO), *21st century Business Herald*, March 27, 2007.
12 Qiao, Xiaohui and Song Yanhua, "Choumou guoji ban" (Preparing for the international board), *Caijing Magazine*, October 11, 2009.
13 Interview with CSRC officials, February 2012.
14 Interview with mainland securities professional, Shanghai, May 2011.
15 Daniel Ren and Enoch Yiu, "Shanghai fast-tracks return of red chips," *South China Morning Post*, November 13, 2007.
16 "You daji jinrong diwei, Gangfu chengdong youshuo zhongyang hongchou huigui A-gu yanzhi mingnian" (Concerned with undermining Hong Kong's financial center status, the government has convinced the central government to defer red-chip homecoming to next year), *Singtao Daily*, August 15, 2007. The HKEx even considered taking over the SSE and/or the SZSE in a similar fashion to the merger of NYSE and Euronext. However, the "non-profit making" status of the two mainland exchanges, under the oversight of the CSRC, made a merger with the publicly listed HKEx impossible.
17 The QFII program was announced in November 2002 by the PBOC and CSRC to introduce overseas institutional investors into the domestic securities market in an orderly manner. Since the first two QFII licenses extended to UBS and Nomura Securities in May 2003, a total of 278 foreign institutions have obtained the status with a total approved investment quota of US$87.31 billion (as of December 2016).
18 The overseas terminals would enable foreign investors trading shares listed in the SSE. The proposal, however, did not ease investment restrictions of mainland or foreign investments until the inception of the Shanghai–Hong Kong Stock Connects in late 2014.
19 Tang, Zhenlong, "Guoji ban jianshe tisu," (International board accelerates), *Shanghai Securities News*, February 5, 2010.
20 "Fang Xinghai: Guoji ban guize niandi shi diang wan" (Fang Xinghai: regulations for international board to be completed by the end of the year), *Hong Kong Economic Journal*, February 9, 2010.
21 Interview with CSRC official, Beijing, February 2012; Fan, Junli, "Guoji ban linpen" (International board about to be born), *Century Weekly*, no. 21, May 30, 2011
22 Wang, Meili, "Shanghai zhengquan jiaoyi suo yanjiu zhongxin zhuren Hu Ruyin: tui guoji ban yi wu jishu zhangai" (SSE Research Director Hu Ruyin: no technical barriers for the launch of international board), *South Metropolis Daily*, January 21, 2008.
23 "China-US Strategic Economic Dialogue eye-catching," *People's Daily Online*, June 23, 2008, http://english.people.com.cn/90001/90780/91344/6435313.html.
24 These proposals of product innovation were first raised by Shanghai as early as 2007, as strategies that might help it become the "blue-chip market of China." See Tang, Wei, "Shangzhengsuo: kuaguo gongsi youwang da Hu shangshi" (SSE: multinationals could list in Shanghai), *China Economic Times*, November 19, 2007.
25 Qiao and Song, "Choumou guoji ban" (Preparing for the international board); "Hanzheng: Jinrong zhongxin jianshe you da tupo, guojiban kending yao chu lai" (Hanzheng: international board is a requisite for breakthrough in the making of an international financial center), *Dongfang Daily*, March 8, 2010.

26 "Guoji ban ningju gongshi" (Consensus building for international board), *Securities Times*, June 24, 2011.

27 Wang, Lu and Ma Jingyu, "Shangjiaosuo chubu wancheng guoji ban zhunbei gongzuo" (SSE completed preliminary works for the international board), *Shanghai Securities News*, December 20, 2010; "Shanghai Guoji Ban xushi" (Shanghai international board ready to go), *21st century Business Herald*, April 22, 2011.

28 "Gaoceng songkou Huifeng huo cheng "di yi gu" guoji ban neng rang shui zhuanqian" (Senior HSBC officials reveal it could be the first stock in the international board, so who could profit from it?), *China Economic Weekly*, June 7, 2011.

29 "Zhongxintaifu chuan wei chengxiaoshang huigui A-gu" (CITIC Pacific reportedly appointed underwriters in preparation for listing in A-share market), *Hong Kong Economic Journal*, September 17, 2009.

30 Yang, Dong, "Chao 60 jia gongsi youyi guapai guoji ban," (More than 60 companies interested in listing on international board), *Securities Times*, May 25, 2011.

31 "Shanghai Guoji Ban xushi".

32 Fan, "Guoji ban linpen."

33 Interview with CSRC official, Beijing, February 2012.

34 Zhu, Baochen, "Shang Fulin: Tuichu guoji ban yue lai yue jin le" (Shang Fulin: international board is getting closer), *Securities Daily*, May 21, 2011.

35 "Jiji zhenhggu zai Shenzhen chuangjian Guojiban" (Fight strongly to create an international board in Shenzhen), *Shenzhen Economic Daily*, January 18, 2011, p. A7.

36 Baidu floated shares on NASDAQ in 2005 whereas Tencent went public on HKEx in 2004. Li, Qing, "Qiewu rang guoji ban zou chuangye ban lao lu" (Don't let the international board repeat the mistakes of the ChiNext), *Caixin Media*, May 26, 2011.

37 Su, Jiang, "Geng Liang: Hongchou gu huigui bingbu yiding fei yao deng guojiban tuichu" (Geng Liang: Red-chip homecoming does not need to wait for the international board), *21st century Business Herald*, March 15, 2010

38 Samuel Shen and Kazunori Takada, "Analysis: Shanghai, HK bourses set for faceoff on yuan listings," *Reuters*, March 1, 2011

39 Robert Jackson, "Keen appetite for Hong Kong's dim sum bonds," *Financial Times*, April 26, 2011. Unlike most primary offering of companies, the first renminbi equity involved share issuance of a real estate investment trust, which generates revenue through investing, financing or mortgaging real estate. For details, see Philippe Espinasse, "A Primer on Hui Xian REIT," *Dow Jones Investment Banker*, March 23, 2011.

40 Chen, Jianjia, "Caiku Ju: yan jianhua dier shangshi" (Financial Services & Treasury Bureau: Studying to simplify secondary listing procedures), *Mingpao*, April 18, 2011. As of March 2017, there are 25 acceptable overseas jurisdictions recognized by the HKEx. The latest list is accessible at: www.hkex.com.hk/eng/rulesreg/listrules/list sptop/listoc/list_of_aoj.htm. Denise Law, "To list in renminbi or HKD: how about both?" *Financial Times Tilt*, June 23, 2011.

41 "Faishen wu chu dangang yanjiu niding hongchou huigui banfa" (Department of Public Offering and Supervision Five taking the lead to study methods of red-chip homecoming), *Shanghai Financial News*, April 5, 2007.

42 "CDR ranglu shangshi, hongchou gu 6 yue wangzhe guilai" (CDR giving way, red-chip homecoming in June), *21st century Business Herald*, March 5, 2007. Most depository receipts in the US market serve no financing ends, except those that also raise funds like stocks. See J. P. Morgan 2005.

43 Wang, Ziwu and Fang Junli, "Guoji Ban xin fangxiang" (New direction of the international board), *Century Weekly*, no. 27, July 11, 2011.

44 Interview with mainland securities professionals, Shanghai, March 2012.

45 Wang and Fang, "Guoji Ban xin fangxiang."

46 For example, China's company law requires half of the promoters of joint stock corporations to be residents of China.

47 Xu, Ming, "Tu Gangshao: guoji ban suoyou tiaojian yi zhunbei daowei" (Tu Gangshao: all conditions for international board have been met), *Caixin Media*, June 7, 2011, http://finance.caing.com/2011–06–07/100266690.html.

48 Qiao and Song, "Choumou guoji ban" (Preparing for the international board). On development of domestic credit-rating industry, see Kennedy (2008).

49 Interview with CSRC officials and mainland securities professionals, Beijing, February and March 2012.

50 Qiao and Song, "Choumou guoji ban."

51 Zhang, Hui, "Hu Shen dazhan guoji ban" (Shanghai–Shenzhen rivaling for the international board), *Outlook Weekly*, January 30, 2011.

52 Liu, Yuting, "Zhongguan buyi zhijie caiyong Guoji kuaiji zhunze" (China should not adopt directly the IFRS), *China Securities Journal*, October 17, 2011.

53 These include, for example, expenses to carry out due diligence by accounting firms, auditing firms, and other professional consultancies, to prepare sales agreements, and to offer documents to underwriters. Wu, Qi, "Waihui ju: guoji ban meiyou waihui guanli zhangai," (SAFE: international board poses no challenge to foreign exchange management), *Securities Times*, June 28, 2010.

54 Fan, Junli, "B-gu mingyun zhuanji" (Chances for B-shares to change their fate), *Century Weekly*, no. 24, June 20, 2011.

55 Fan, "B-gu mingyun zhuanji"; Fan, "Guoji ban linpen."

56 Li, Qing, "Qiewu rang guoji ban zou chuangye ban laolu" (Don't repeat the mistake of the ChiNext in international board), *Caixin Media*, May 26, 2011.

57 Dinny McMahon and Amy Li, "Shanghai's International Board: Some New Clarity," *The Wall Street Journal*, July 4, 2011.

58 The risks of hot money inflows spiked after late 2010 as inflation and price measures like CPI and housing indexes returned to similar levels they had been before the subprime crisis. See Liu, Yuan and Li Bin, "Yanghang cuisheng guoji ban" (The central bank urged for an international board), *First Financial Daily*, November 30, 2010. For Zhou's original discussion, see "Zhou Xiaochuan: ba rujing reqian fangjin chizi" (Zhou Xiaochuan: Put the hot money inflow into the pool), *Caixin Media*, November 5, 2010.

59 Fan, Junli, "Shichang dimi huo zhi guoji ban tuiyan" (Market downturn might delay the launch of international board), *Caixin Media*, June 10, 2011.

60 Interview with mainland securities professionals, Beijing and Shanghai, February and March 2012.

61 Fan, "Shichang dimi huo zhi guoji ban tuiyan."

62 This includes firms under the QFII and renminbi QFII (RQFII) scheme.

63 In practice, short of easing the renminbi's convertibility, this could happen even when domestic and foreign bourses conclude mutual settlement and custody arrangements, making possible the short-selling of A-shares and subsequently purchasing shares of the same company in overseas exchanges at a lower price. The foreign shares could then be converted to domestic species, deposited with securities brokers and returned to the lenders in China. See Liu, Yutian, "Guoji ban tuichu bu ke caozhi guo gi" (No haste in the launch of the international board), *Shanghai Financial News*, May 27, 2011.

64 It was estimated that the underground market handled US$630 billion of loans in 2011, equivalent to 10% of China's GDP. See Sun Yu, "Underground banks squeeze business," *Financial Times China Confidential*, July 21, 2011.

65 Unlike existing listing platforms, the new OTCBB had markedly lower listing requirements and thresholds for high-value-added SMEs and firms in the "new industries."

66 "Xin san ban qiang pao, guoji ban keneng tuihou" (OTCBB taking the lead, international board might be postponed), *Investor Journal*, August 28, 2011.

67 Tang, Zhenglong, "Xia Bin: Ying jinkuai kaifang renminbi zhaiquan shicang" (Xia Bin: renminbi bond market should be further open), *Shanghai Securities News*, July 21, 2010.

68 "Guo Shuqing xin siwei, QFII sho repeng, guoji ban bei lengluo" (New thinking of Guo Shuqing, QFII promoted and international board sidetracked), *Securities Times*, January 11, 2012

69 Daniel Ren, "Wait goes on for Shanghai's new board," *South China Morning Post*, January 18, 2012.

70 Daniel Ren, "Foreign Listings in Shanghai still a long way off," *South China Morning Post*, September 16, 2011

71 On non-tradable share reform and its impact on capital market development, see Walter and Howie (2006), chapters 8–9.

72 "Shanghai zimaoqu chouhua xinxing guoji ban" (Shanghai FTZ planning for a new kind of international board), *21st century Business Herald*, September 6, 2013.

73 Lin, Jingbing and Wang Xiaoqing, "Zimaoqu kuowei waqian" (Shanghai FTZ to explore more potentials), *Caixin Weekly*, January 12, 2015.

74 Enoch Yiu, "Pain of Alibaba loss prompts HKEX to examine new measures," *South China Morning Post*, September 1, 2016.

5 Let the red-back go global

The ascent of the offshore renminbi market in Hong Kong

Introduction

The previous two chapters have examined the evolution of outbound equity investment regimes and the attempt to internationalize China's securities market through the listing of foreign firms on domestic exchanges, both cases exhibiting alternating policy tendencies between opening, stasis, and reversal. Together, they show how important local authorities and financial industry interests were to the origination of financial opening initiatives through the shaping of policy agendas and the way they defined and framed the issues in their favor. To build policy support and minimize dissent, they leveraged connections with central bureaucratic actors and top elites, and offered concessions to dissenting parties over implementation specifics.

This chapter turns to a broader, and arguably more important, facet of China's financial opening—currency internationalization. The research of recent years has tended to focus on the external implications of the renminbi's ascent, such as its perceived challenge to the existing global monetary system and its connections with China's projection of monetary and financial power abroad. While the general economic rationales of renminbi internationalization have been widely appreciated within the economic and financial community (for example, slowing down China's massive US dollar foreign reserves, redenominating trade flows from US dollars into renminbi, and channeling offshore renminbi funds back onshore in a manageable non-disruptive way while retaining the onshore capital controls), the domestic political dynamics, especially the political sources of the internationalizing initiatives that founded the offshore renminbi center in Hong Kong, have received scant attention (Ramos and Sahi 2010; Overholt, Ma, and Law 2016; Prasad 2016; Subacchi 2016).

Most studies have examined the national motivation for renminbi internationalization and the associated central-level politics. A common thread of the arguments sees the project as China's method of fostering its monetary and financial powers abroad while reducing its dependence on the US/West-centric system (McNally 2012, 2015; Kirshner 2014; McNally and Gruin 2017). Others have argued that China has been motivated by nationalist sentiment to promote its international reputation and standing (Subramanian 2011a). Other researchers have conceived renminbi internationalization as a "lever" of domestic reform, driven primarily by the PBOC's desire to seek an "exit" from mercantilist policies and ward off domestic resistance to further capital market reforms at home (Kroeber 2012; Thornton 2012; Bowles and Wang 2013; Chin 2013).

The divides within the financial bureaucracy, however, have made the process a partial and incomplete one (Mallaby and Wethington 2012; Yang 2014; Otero-Iglesias and Vermeiren 2015) and resulted in the Chinese government riding "on the cheap—to make as few concessions as possible in terms of either political or financial reform" (Cohen 2012b). As the prospects for financial reform have become gloomier in recent years, the PBOC has taken risks to reassert its policy control (Pettis 2012), and has played the "Trojan horse" strategy of soliciting the support of the top elites through nationalist language (Bell and Feng 2013).

Although these studies have shed light on the domestic sources of policymaking, they have failed to adequately map out the contours of a playing field that has accounted for policy tendency and outcomes, and have been too ready to assume unchanging preferences among bureaucratic actors. It would be more appropriate to conceive of renminbi internationalization as a totality of separate but related liberalizing episodes, each involving different sets of constituents in the policymaking process. It is this that has gradually made the renminbi an invoicing medium and a reserve currency for trade and investment in various public uses and private transactions (Cohen 2012a, 2012b).

Studies of China's financiers have revealed the context-specificity of private groups' interests, and challenged the views of Broz (1999) and Henning (1994) regarding the roles of financiers as promoter of currency internationalization in other national contexts. But these studies have also failed to appreciate the diversity of positions amongst financiers about the different facets of the renminbi's international outreach (Helleiner and Malkin 2012). More importantly, there has been virtually no discussion about the roles of local authorities. Even though Hong Kong's position as the premier offshore renminbi hub is globally recognized, its role in initiating and strategizing the endeavor is rarely recognized (notable exceptions are, perhaps, McNally 2012; and Green and Gruin 2017). Shanghai and other onshore financial hubs have also escaped researchers' attention. Such research misses the subnational developments and cannot fully account for much of the policy trajectory and political dynamics underlying renminbi internationalization. For example, Subramanian (2011a: 112) describes the Chinese liberalizing strategy as "controlled, discretionary and micromanaged" and characterized by "interventionist opening" and "liberalization via enclaves." This downplays the agency of local authorities in the inherently *political* process underlying offshore renminbi market development.[1]

This chapter presents a different formulation. It centers on the takeoff of offshore renminbi business in Hong Kong, where most of the breakthroughs of the 2000s originated and were implemented, and unravels the political economic dynamics that cut across the local, financial industry, and bureaucratic levels. In disaggregating the development into separate but related facets, it finds a policy trajectory distinctive from the other two financial opening episodes, instead showing a punctuated pattern in which incremental moves in the early phase were overtaken by rapid growth in later years. The period between the late 1990s and 2007 that witnessed the slow introduction of individual renminbi businesses was overtaken by a leap into offshore renminbi bond issuance, a trade settlement scheme involving both Hong Kong and Shanghai, progress in financial product development, and increasing connections between the offshore and onshore currency markets. These aspects associated with renminbi internationalization entailed varying levels of local and industrial discretion and involved shifting contestations within the financial bureaucracy.

Hong Kong's maturation as an offshore renminbi center began with the endeavors of the city's authorities and financiers to originate a liberalizing agenda. They constituted a pro-opening coalition that would eventually be joined by sympathetic central bureaucratic actors in the mid-2000s. The efforts of the early days, however, met setbacks due to onshore dissent and a failure to solicit support from the financial bureaucracy until the breakthrough of 2003/2004, when individual renminbi businesses were introduced after a successful reframing and the offshore community's concessionary offers to scale down its ambition and restrict the liberalizing scope.

A burgeoning renminbi fixed income market and trade settlement emerged after going through contrasting political contestations. Regarding the fixed income market, the pro-opening coalition met challenges primarily from within the financial bureaucracy, but found gradual support from some onshore financiers. Offshore concessionary moves also paid off and galvanized the birth of the offshore renminbi bond market. The push for a renminbi trade settlement scheme was fast-tracked after the subprime crisis and backed almost unanimously within the financial bureaucracy, but it met with a challenge from onshore constituents, notably Shanghai. The pro-opening coalition agreed to expand the initiative that made Shanghai an alternative hub of trade settlement, but this did not do away with all dissent during implementation, especially that caused by risk concerns emanating from the possible abuse of the system. This resulted in tightening moves to preempt stronger resistance from within the financial bureaucracy.

After the late 2000s, the offshore renminbi business was complicated by subnational dynamics onshore. Shanghai was poised to rival Hong Kong while the two minor financial hubs, Shenzhen and Tianjin, sought collaboration with the offshore community and reinforced the offshore initiative with new opening advocates. The opening momentum was also slowed down by discord within the Hong Kong and PBOC-led coalition over technical matters essential to the financial product development of the equity and derivatives markets. Notwithstanding the doubt surrounding the larger opening agenda in 2011, which decelerated the liberalizing initiatives bridging the offshore and onshore renminbi markets, a dramatic easing spearheaded by the PBOC unfolded after 2012 at a time when the mainland economy was meeting headwinds. This not

Table 5.1 Major developments of the offshore renminbi center in Hong Kong

Late 1990s–2003	Sizable renminbi funds begin to pool in Hong Kong (1990s). Offshore authorities and financiers call for the establishment of channels to return renminbi to the onshore market (2001), but the idea is not well-received by the financial bureaucracy. Shanghai and onshore financial interests are also opposed to Hong Kong's initiative.
2003–2006	CEPA is concluded between Hong Kong and mainland China (June 2003). Offshore renminbi businesses are an integral part of the agreement but trading is confined to personal uses. The introduction of offshore individual renminbi business is sanctioned by the central bank (November 2003). Bank of China (Hong Kong) is designated the sole clearing bank. The scope of offshore renminbi services is gradually expanded. Offshore authorities push for renminbi bond issuance and trade settlement (2004).
2006–2007	Onshore financiers and firms favor offshore renminbi bond issuance, but are met with resistance from within the financial bureaucracy. The State Council sanctions renminbi bond issuance offshore (January 2007). The first offshore renminbi bond is issued (July 2007). The market grows exponentially.
2007–2009	A renminbi trade settlement scheme is proposed by the offshore community and makes headway, catalyzed by the effects of the subprime credit crunch on domestic exporters, support from the financial bureaucracy, and the interest of onshore financial institutions. The State Council approves the scheme (December 2008), and it begins operation (July 2009).
2008–2010	Tianjin and Shenzhen seek renminbi business collaboration with Hong Kong. Shanghai emerges as a strong rival. Disagreements between Hong Kong and mainland authorities over the scope and pace of financial innovation and technical concerns slow offshore market development.
2011–2012	First renminbi stock listed in Hong Kong (April 2011). RQFII, RFDI and overseas ETFs launched (late 2011) and intended to form a renminbi circulation mechanism between onshore and offshore markets. Reservations about renminbi internationalization grow. New initiatives are slowed.
Mid-2012 onwards	Increasing numbers of asymmetric connections develop between the onshore and offshore currency markets. The RQFII quota is significantly expanded and onshore interbank bond market access is greatly eased. Hong Kong's status as the leading offshore renminbi center is largely unchallenged despite the emergence of several rival offshore centers.

only channeled funds to the domestic market, but also strengthened Hong Kong's role as the premier renminbi center and sustained the opening momentum started in the early 2000s.

"One country, two systems, three currencies"[2]

Prior to tracking the policy trajectory of the offshore renminbi center in Hong Kong, it is instructive to introduce the different renminbi markets and their operations. The renminbi is the official currency of China and its level and convertibility has been tightly controlled by the PBOC under the guidance of the State Council of China and the Politburo. Prior to economic reforms, the external use of the renminbi was virtually non-existent, except for a miniscule circulation in bordering economies like Hong Kong, Macau, and some Southeast Asian states, where traders sometimes accepted the currency. Even though on current accounts, the renminbi has been convertible since 1996, cross-border capital flows remained strictly controlled except through institutional (i.e., QDII, QFII, and FDI) and informal conduits. The onshore renminbi market (the CNY market), where all domestic transactions and settlements take place, has been a distinct sphere and has been governed by domestic economic conditions and, more importantly, state intervention. In jurisdictions beyond the mainland, the renminbi's values have been influenced by a host of different factors. The Hong Kong offshore renminbi market (also known as the CNH market) emerged in 2003 and was the first offshore marketplace created with Beijing's support. Exchange and interest rates were determined primarily by market forces and implicitly moderated by mainland monetary policies. Renminbi banknotes and coins in the onshore and offshore markets were identical, but their value, mobility and settlement have been situated in two different political economies (see Figure 5.1 for a schematic illustration of the setup).

A non-deliverable forward (NDF) market has been in existence since the mid-1990s. First flourished in Singapore, the market allowed foreign financial institutions to offer renminbi-linked products on an unregulated and over-the-counter basis. Hong Kong took over as the region's top renminbi NDF market in the early 2000s, when major banks relocated their trading to the city, and has since played an important role managing the currency risk offshore. With a daily turnover of billions, the NDF market has a market-based pricing mechanism that allows participants to bet on the expected values of the renminbi offshore without settlement. Thus, the NDF forward curve is often viewed as a useful indicator of future onshore currency trends, changes in which signal shifts in market expectations of the renminbi's value (Peng, Shu, and Yip 2007).

Offshore currency businesses were not entirely new to Hong Kong. Far from being a "spontaneous" offshore center as Palan (2006: 33) conceived, Hong Kong's eurodollar business took off in the late 1970s with the colonial government's lifting of capital control measures. This allowed Hong Kong to rival Singapore's Asian Currency Unit and handle non-resident foreign currency holdings (Schenk 2011). Mainland financial institutions and businesses also

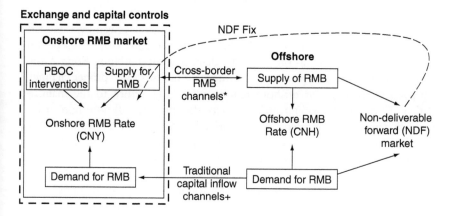

Figure 5.1 "One country, two systems, three currencies."

Source: Adapted with modification from Mackel et al. (2011)

Notes
* Including individual RMB business, RMB trade settlement, RMB QFII, RMB FDI, Stock Connects, interbankmarket opening, Bond Connect, and central bank swaps.
+ Including FDI, QFII.

entered the city in the mid-1990s, when Shenzhen branches of state-owned banks provided offshore financial services to offshore subsidiaries of SOEs. The experience, however, resulted in the piling up of non-performing loans and losses of banks; some companies also engaged in speculative activities unrelated to their main business. Therefore, the PBOC (the banking supervisor before the CBRC was founded in 2003) halted these offshore activities.[3]

The local origination of offshore renminbi business

Like the other two aspects of China's financial opening, offshore renminbi business had its origin at the local level. However, the Hong Kong government and offshore financers displayed little interest until the renminbi fund grew in scale in the late 1990s. The Tung Chee-hwa administration was joined by the offshore financers in setting the policy agenda, framing the initiative in their favor and soliciting the support of central government.

After the handover in 1997, Hong Kong's economy was increasingly permeable to the renminbi as individuals were allowed to carry up to 6,000 yuan in cash across the border after 1993 for personal use or to settle business transactions.[4] An estimated 50 to 70 billion yuan accumulated outside the city's formal financial system (this excluded the inflows facilitated by the underground channels located in Guangdong province).[5] The situation alerted the PBOC in 2002, which found a dramatic increase of cash injection into Shenzhen that equaled 40% nationwide, and a strong correlation between Guangdong's money supply and the growth of offshore renminbi cash (Zhang 2008). These funds eventually became the money base for an offshore renminbi business critical to the takeoff of renminbi internationalization in the late 2000s.

Hong Kong's offshore renminbi initiative was primarily driven by a quest for financial gains and local interests. This began with the 2001 visit of Joseph Yam to Beijing in his capacity as the head of a delegation of the Hong Kong Association of Banks, where he proposed that there should be some "proper channel," approved by Beijing, for offshore renminbi funds to return to the mainland market. In effect, this would make the city the first ever offshore hub of renminbi business and promised both exclusive business opportunities to offshore financial institutions and to consolidate Hong Kong's niche as an unmatched international financial hub for years to come (Yam 2010: 3).

Yam's proposition, however, was not well-received. While the central financial officials recognized the financial grounds for routing the offshore renminbi to the mainland, they were deterred by the lack of a specific market mechanism that would bridge the offshore and onshore markets. The PBOC and SAFE simply saw China as unready to introduce any kind of offshore business. The country's financial reforms at the time attended to significant domestic agendas, including SOEs and the state-owned commercial bank restructuring in the run-up to WTO accession. These issues dwarfed Hong Kong's initiative and it did not appear to constitute an important part of the country's policy roadmap.[6] With the lack of technical readiness and the drastically different policy priorities of central government, Hong Kong's liberalizing call tanked. It could not shape the central policy agenda or find any support from central bureaucratic parties. The quest, however, went on and resulted in some breakthroughs in the early 2000s.

Like Shanghai's linking of red-chip homecoming with the pursuit of an international board, Hong Kong's initiative gained traction after it was embedded into a separate policy of a distinctive nature. As negotiations on the Closer Economic Partnership Arrangement (CEPA) about cross-border trade and investment facilitation progressed, both China and Hong Kong found that the easing of individual uses and access to the renminbi offshore would not be possible without the PBOC's support. This reintroduced the offshore renminbi agenda into larger negotiations between the two economies and turned it into an integral part of the CEPA agreement concluded in June 2003 (Ba and Yunzhao 2008: 299). Soon, Hong Kong's financial officials and financiers proclaimed the policy success of becoming China's offshore renminbi center.[7] Such optimism, however, turned out to be grossly unfounded as the PBOC and others in the financial bureaucracy fought shy of backing the offshore aspirations, and onshore local and financial industry interests challenged Hong Kong's ambitions. This complicated deliberations and the implementation of the opening initiative pursued by the offshore opening advocates.

Individual renminbi businesses to break ground

As Hong Kong appeared to gain first-mover advantage as China's first offshore renminbi hub, domestic financial centers and their financial interests pushed back. Among them, Shanghai's strong opposition successfully elicited reservations at the central level and thwarted the quest of the offshore community.[8]

Local and bureaucratic dissent

The most vocal opposition came from Shanghai's officials and financiers. To undercut the offshore agenda, senior local officials disputed Hong Kong's edge in offshore renminbi finance and argued that Shanghai was much better-positioned to become China's renminbi hub because foreign companies based in the city would eventually drive strong demand for the renminbi and local enterprise would commit to renminbi investment offshore as the domestic economy further liberalized.[9] Together with Shanghai-based banks and the wider local financial community, they lobbied central financial officials to halt Hong Kong's initiative.

Shanghai-based banks saw very little business opportunity in offshore finance and resisted giving the offshore banks an unfair advantage over their mainland counterparts.[10] The Shanghai securities industry and exchange also challenged Hong Kong's proposal. Fang Xinghai, Vice President of the Shanghai Stock Exchange at the time, argued that Hong Kong's initiative would not only disadvantage Shanghai's financial development, but would also pose considerable systemic risks to China. In his view, Hong Kong's wish to develop an offshore market was simply a "heedless" idea founded on undue expectations of renminbi appreciation. If there was a reversal of the renminbi's strengthening trend, the offshore center would lose its market appeal. Further, Fang warned that an offshore renminbi market was inherently risk-prone to the onshore market because its interest and exchange rates differed from those of the mainland's. Without proper safeguards, this might encourage speculation that would compromise Beijing's monetary policies and destabilize the domestic financial system.[11]

Such a menacing message apparently alarmed the central bureaucracy. Central officials became cautious of Hong Kong's enthusiasm and became sensitized to the potential policy risk implications. For example, members of China's monetary policy committee questioned the viability of an offshore market and the CBRC Chair Liu Mingkang considered the policy discussion premature. From Beijing's perspective, creating an offshore renminbi currency would entail risks that might affect not only the onshore financial system but also that of Hong Kong because the renminbi's depreciation would certainty prompt sell-offs of the currency and the city would experience a capital reversal that would disturb the offshore market.[12] These concerns were equally relevant to keeping the onshore market healthy, as it was politically important to demonstrate China's success in perpetuating the financial stability of the former British colony. Complicated by dissenting local and financial interests, the risk concerns of bureaucratic actors further consolidated their reservations toward Hong Kong's opening initiative.

Indeed, facing strong financial industry opposition at home, both the CBRC and PBOC reacted coolly to the lobbying of an offshore community to start renminbi clearing.[13] Worse still, the financial rationale that underlay Hong Kong's liberalizing initiative—creating a returning circuit for offshore renminbi funds—was thrown into question by the dissenting parties. An official estimate suggested that, while there was a roughly 70 billion yuan flow offshore, only two billion was in stocks. With a tiny market scale, the launching of an offshore renminbi business was simply unwarranted.[14]

Reframing and downscaling the initiative

The offshore community met a setback in the face of strong dissent from the mainland. Henry Tang, Hong Kong's Financial Secretary, conceded that the financial community was probably too "excited" in pursuing the offshore renminbi business.[15] But this did not extinguish all possibility of introducing offshore renminbi business, since some form of cross-border renminbi transactions and services would be necessary under the CEPA framework to promote cross-border investment and trade. However, the opening advocates had to moderate their ambitions to win bureaucratic support and quieten the dissenting parties onshore.

To assuage the reservations of onshore interests, the Hong Kong government and financiers came to realize that any offshore renminbi business should be subject to Beijing's tight control and be officially detached from China's financial opening agenda. As a PBOC official outlined, any offshore activities should be viewed as complementary to the CEPA's goals of facilitating economic transactions between the two economies at both personal and corporate levels, and would have little relevance to promoting renminbi internationalization.[16] So, to allay the PBOC's concerns, the Hong Kong government proposed that an intermediary party should be in place to segregate the onshore and offshore markets and help minimize the risks of renminbi-related activities borne by the central bank. Such a role was to be fulfilled by Hong Kong's neighbor, Shenzhen.

In sharp contrast to Shanghai's opposition, Shenzhen had been keen on establishing a niche between Hong Kong and the mainland, using its financial services office—founded in September 2003—to promote cross-border financial collaboration between banks.[17] This presented the PBOC and SAFE, both sympathetic to Hong Kong's initiative, with some policy leeway in reaching an agreement over ways to bring about renminbi business on a restricted basis. To mitigate any financial risk associated with cross-border renminbi flows, the two agencies proposed that the Shenzhen branch of the PBOC would first accept renminbi funds from deposit-taking banks offshore and then, in turn, perform settlement services and serve as an intermediary for interbank lending on the mainland.[18]

Such arrangements not only allayed bureaucratic concerns about speculative flows by restricting the effective control of capital flow and onshore interbank rates, it also appealed to the different local authorities: While Shenzhen succeeded in taking its first steps toward wider collaboration with Hong Kong on renminbi business, the interests of Shanghai and its financiers were unaffected since they could be reassured by Beijing's commitment to restricting the off-shore activities to individual and business needs.

While the offshore community might have appeared to fail to obtain what it had initially striven for, the concessions had galvanized the debut of renminbi business in Hong Kong—especially in view of the strong opposition immediately after the city declared its intention to become an offshore currency center. Through redefining the opening pursuit into a proposal that carried with it almost no infringement of the interests of Shanghai, onshore financiers or concerned central actors, and making concessions over the opening scope and pace, Hong Kong was able to solicit and consolidate support from both Shenzhen and the sympathetic PBOC and SAFE. Despite their restricted scope, offshore individual renminbi businesses were rolled out after the PBOC and HKMA settled on the regulatory basis of offshore renminbi business in November 2003—a small yet critical milestone in renminbi internationalization.

Banks in Hong Kong were allowed to offer personal renminbi services on a limited and trial basis and credit services to individuals from 2004, including deposit, remittance, and exchange. Just as the PBOC and SAFE had contemplated, the Bank of China (Hong Kong) (BOCHK) was designated as the sole clearing bank (a monopoly it continues to enjoy to date), whereas Shenzhen's PBOC branch would maintain settlement accounts for the BOCHK, paying interest on deposits and channeling funds to the mainland market (PBOC 2003). Soon, seven industries with extensive cross-border activities, including retail, beverages, and transport, were allowed to set up renminbi deposit accounts. Hong Kong residents could also open renminbi check accounts by 2006.

Although the restricted range of renminbi activities serving individuals and companies offshore might have appeared insignificant, they laid the foundation for the dramatic growth of offshore currency markets after the mid-2000s. In just a few years, Hong Kong's renminbi businesses had proliferated thanks to the strengthening of a pro-opening coalition made up of the offshore community and central bureaucratic actors and buttressed by a strong political and technical consensus. Two major areas that saw notable breakthroughs after the PBOC emerged as a leading advocate of renminbi internationalization within the financial bureaucracy in the mid-2000s were offshore renminbi bond issuance and a trade settlements initiative.[19] Respectively, they represented important tests of the suitability of the renminbi as a medium of international reserve and trade—two important facets of an international currency.

Indeed, in 2006 the PBOC was among the first agencies within government to examine the benefits of pursuing renminbi internationalization, and concluded that such a pursuit would enhance China's international status and competitiveness as well as its influence in the global economy (PBOC Study Group 2006).[20] Despite the PBOC's backing and leverage, however, the two offshore initiatives did not come into being as smoothly as many had anticipated. As in the case of individual renminbi businesses, the PBOC's support of the offshore community did little to overcome resistance during policy deliberation. The liberalizing initiatives flourished only after successful concessionary offers by the Hong Kong and PBOC-led coalition to dissenting local, financial industry, and bureaucratic parties.

Dim sum bonds: a litmus test of the renminbi's investment value

Shortly after personal renminbi businesses were introduced in late 2003, the offshore community wasted no time pursuing its next targets—bond issuance and trade settlement. Although the pro-opening coalition could introduce its agenda and bring the PBOC and SAFE on side, it failed to solicit support from beyond the two agencies or to re-define the way offshore renminbi activities were understood in the financial bureaucracy as an extension of CEPA's policy support. The lack of political and technical consensus, and the dissent from other bureaucratic actors, stalled the offshore bond initiative.

The offshore quest and concessions within

Hong Kong's financial community expected that renminbi bonds would stimulate the growth of the local fixed income market that had been dwarfed by the predominance of equity financing and bank loans (taking up 70% and 23%, respectively, of the city's capital market in 2003). The HKMA reasoned that, with the advent of the ADB-pioneered regional bond market initiatives, Hong Kong should spearhead the renminbi bond market before China was ready for foreign investors and issuances. Accordingly, the HKMA saw the agenda as one of the top three policy priorities of 2004, together with a renminbi trade settlement and financial products.[21]

The offshore financiers similarly anticipated enormous opportunities for business, because they thought of bonds as a low risk investment of offshore renminbi funds that had little use besides individual or business purposes, and they considered that the offshore bond market would attract multinationals with Chinese operations to raise renminbi funds.[22] These rationales were promptly acknowledged by the PBOC and SAFE, which had been frustrated by the lengthy negotiations between foreign issuers and mainland regulatory authorities over compliance with the Chinese financial standards discussed in Chapter 4. SAFE officials even suggested that the offshore renminbi bond issuance could start in early 2005 as an alternative to the panda bond and serve as a pilot for fostering fixed income markets in the local currency before China was ready.[23]

This support, however, did not catalyze policy breakthrough until 2007. At the central level, the NDRC, MOF and CBRC were opposed to the offshore bond initiative. First, the MOF and NDRC were wary of losing their influence over the domestic bond market. As the two panda bond issuances by the ADB and IFC were scheduled for 2005, to demonstrate China's commitment to developing regional fixed income markets, the MOF and NDRC were made uneasy by the offshore initiative that might weaken the market appeal of the onshore products. With domestic market development topping the policy agenda, Hong Kong's call was rejected.

Second, the NDRC and MOF were deterred by technical challenges underlying offshore renminbi bond issuance that were far more complicated than the panda bond. At the time, there was a lack of any regulations governing the remittance of bond proceeds, and that posed considerable political risks which might adversely affect the two agencies. Indeed, they were increasingly warned that systemic risk implications might arise if the offshore products disturbed mainland pricing and interest rates, as well as about possible illicit capital outflows. The top decision-making elites were evidently alarmed by these concerns. Premier Wen Jiabo cautioned that the offshore renminbi bond market must not lead to "the loss of state-owned assets." Worse still to the offshore community, the scale of the offshore market appeared questionable, since domestic enterprises had little need to raise capital on Hong Kong's bond market and offshore renminbi deposits at the time were barely large enough to absorb any large issuances.[24]

Accordingly, despite the PBOC and SAFE's sympathetic gestures, Hong Kong's initiative was rejected by the central authorities and did little to entice the interest of onshore financiers. Policy stasis was maintained. But, to signal its continuing political support and placate the offshore community, the central bank eased the controls on personal and business uses of offshore renminbi in late 2005, a move it could accomplish solely under its own authority.[25]

The quest for an offshore bond market did not die out, however. As in the deliberations around individual renminbi businesses, the local parties and the central patron of the pro-opening coalition made concessionary efforts to address the concerns of opposing parties, especially the regulatory challenges and policy risk implications that had unsettled the top elites. The opening advocates also found fresh support from the onshore financial industry and bureaucracy thanks to their changing assessments of the distributional and risk implications of offshore renminbi bond issuance.

To allay concerns that the offshore bond market might affect the mainland's financial parameters, the HKMA agreed that offshore renminbi bonds should be priced with reference to the domestic benchmark yield, the Shanghai Interbank Offered Rate (SHIBOR), that was first trialed from 2006 and officially introduced to the market in January 2007. This not only promoted wider use of the rate beyond the onshore market, it also appealed to mainland financial industry interests (especially banks), since they would retain their influence over the rate as contributor banks. Shanghai found the arrangement palatable because it had been sponsoring the SHIBOR development for years and was home to its principal architect, the National Interbank Funding Center.[26]

On the technical front, the HKMA developed a renminbi real time gross settlement system that ran parallel to those of other hard currencies to make possible multi-currency transactions by issuers and investors. This complemented the PBOC's efforts to develop the procedures governing the remittance of bond proceeds to the mainland. More importantly, within the pro-opening coalition, the PBOC and offshore community agreed to the NDRC defining the eligibility of issuers and the scale of issuances—a move that would not only maintain NDRC's stake over bond market development but also help boost its regulatory reach into the offshore market. With this concessionary move, the coalition hoped to obtain at least the acquiescence of the NDRC.[27]

The leverage of the pro-opening coalition was also strengthened by onshore financiers who pressed their bureaucratic patrons to change position. Initially skeptical about the financial value of issuing renminbi bonds offshore, domestic policy banks that had relied almost exclusively on debt financing were eager to expand their capital source beyond the onshore market.[28] With top credit ratings and the state's guarantee, they would be able to raise funds offshore with ease. Led by politically well-connected governors, they lobbied the top state and party elites and brought the pro-opening coalition staunch support.[29]

This catalyzed the policy breakthrough of January 2007, when the State Council sanctioned renminbi bond issuances by mainland financial institutions with high credit ratings. Both the PBOC and NDRC reviewed the applications of the interested institutions, but the NDRC retained the final say on the scale of the issuance (PBOC 2007). This paved the way for the first offshore renminbi bond issuance in July 2007 by the China Development Bank, the largest policy bank of China. This was followed by ten issuances by policy and commercial banks in 2008 that were oversubscribed by offshore investors with virtually no other investment opportunities. From that point, the dim sum bond market burgeoned and outgrew the scale of onshore panda bond issuances.[30]

Let the market blossom!

Growth and scope, notably the eligibility requirements of the dim sum bond market, remained restricted during the early years largely because the NDRC was vetting each issuance. The bond market pilot, however, blossomed after the agency loosened the regulations, catalyzing a dramatic growth in the market over the next few years.

This was contributed to by several developments in the NDRC's favor. Most importantly, the central elites realized that a mature offshore bond market would provide valuable information about the offshore expectations of China's exchange and interest rate movements, as well as corporate and government creditworthiness—all being important to policymaking in the light of much macroeconomic uncertainty in the post-crisis era. Further, the MOF and NDRC found it hard to challenge the offshore bond market after their panda bond failure. Other than the issuances of the ADB and IFC in 2005, the onshore market was still in its infancy with only one company approved since then. Other foreign institutions were deterred by the lengthy review process and prospect of extensive restrictions after originating the bonds.[31]

On the other hand, leading domestic banks were interested in issuing their dim sum bonds as coupon rates reversed in the two renminbi markets, lowering the financing costs in the offshore venue.[32] State-owned banks with Hong Kong subsidiaries were particularly eager to be book-runners or become part of the syndicate. These financiers lobbied the CBRC and NDRC to expand the scope and pace of offshore bond issuance. This strengthened the pro-opening coalition and stimulated market demand. The PBOC was also committed to expanding the scale of the dim sum bond market because it provided the much-anticipated investment channels for offshore renminbi holders, especially for foreign financial institutions and central banks seeking to diversify their reserve holdings, thus further increasing the renminbi's appeal as an investment and reserve currency in the long term.

The MOF issued the first offshore sovereign bond with times-to-maturity of two, three, and five years in September 2009, followed by another bond sale with short and medium (ten years) maturities a year later. This helped complete the benchmark yield curve important to developing offshore renminbi instruments of varying maturities. The 2010 offering was also unprecedented, since it was tendered through the Central Money Markets Unit (CMU), the HKMA clearing and settlement facility that operated on a Dutch auction with high levels of transparency and efficiency. This signaled Beijing's willingness to follow international bond market practice, and pointed to increasing agreement between the MOF and offshore community over financial technicalities. More importantly, it represented a "vote of confidence" in Hong Kong's financial architecture surrounding the development of the offshore renminbi market.[33]

In 2010, the NDRC lowered the dim sum bond market entry requirements and welcomed the entry of foreign companies that had been attracted by the regulatory simplicity of the offshore market, where international accounting and credit-rating standards were endorsed. Soon, multinationals like McDonald's, Caterpillar, and Citibank issued their dim sum bonds, breaking the dominance of local and mainland issuers. Bond proceeds could be used freely outside China and were only subject to SAFE's approval if they were to be remitted onshore. From 2012, mainland non-financial companies were allowed to raise debts offshore as the NDRC sought ways of helping firms to go beyond the stretched domestic financing channels.[34] The MOF also regularly auctioned sovereign bonds offshore to sate investors' demand.[35]

These deregulatory measures were evidence of the increasing stakes of NDRC and MOF in offshore bond market development. They had found a quick remedy to the financing challenges of domestic firms and the lack of offerings of stable investments in offshore renminbi funds. Their postures consolidated the political support of the opening advocates. Accordingly, the dim sum bond market grew exponentially in just a few years, with outstanding volumes of issuance and bonds reaching 533 and 711.7 billion yuan in 2014, and Chinese banks and their foreign counterparts dividing the bond issuance business between them (See Figure 5.2 showing the bond market growth).

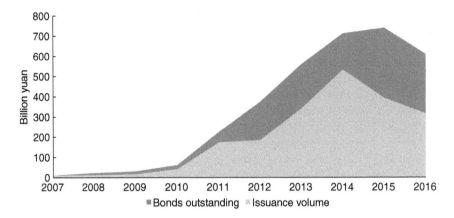

Figure 5.2 Dim sum bond market growth.

Data source: HSBC Global Research

Renminbi trade settlement: the big leap

The other critical area of offshore renminbi market development that witnessed exponential growth concerned international trade and centered on the use of the renminbi in China's trade settlements. As with the offshore bond market, it began as part of Hong Kong's liberalizing initiatives in the mid-2000s and constituted a leap in policy. Phenomenal market growth followed successful concessionary politics between the pro-opening coalition and dissenting parties.

Fast-tracking after crisis

Following the first dim sum bond sale in 2007, the offshore community turned to renminbi trade settlement as its next opening agenda that might further consolidate Hong Kong's market niche. Besides being seen as a better way of handling currency risk and easing payments in foreign trade, the offshore banks hoped to spur the offshore renminbi loan market and expected a better return from renminbi funds in trade financing than from simply investing in bonds or clearing the funds to Shenzhen in a way that earned minuscule interest.

Local lobbying met with little success except friendly gestures from the PBOC. As the subprime crisis loomed, the offshore community was simply unable to shape the central policy agenda and amass any political backing just as the Through Train and international board had failed to do.[36] In the face of systemic risks, measures that might ease capital mobility, even on a pilot scale, were halted or rolled back. The crisis, however, presented a juncture of policy breakthrough galvanized by a shifting calculus among central policymakers when renminbi trade settlement came to be seen as a plausible response to larger economic issues that topped the decision makers' agenda in the aftermath of the crisis.

While the mainland banking system was not severely affected by the crisis, an export slowdown challenged the growth of the real sector. In addition to the currency risk borne by domestic exporters invoicing in US dollars, the financial bureaucracy was alarmed by the heightening risk of the bankruptcy of thousands of SMEs in the vicinity of Shanghai and southern China. The companies had met with considerable difficulties obtaining trade credits from foreign banks. In the assessment of the Ministry of Commerce and the PBOC, should the renminbi be adopted as the settlement currency, then the domestic banks and their offshore subsidiaries could readily provide trade credit to exporters, shortening the settlement period, as firms would no longer need to amass US dollars, and lowering the currency volatility exporters might experience.[37]

This echoed the rationales put forward by the offshore community and brought considerable political support to their initiative. More importantly, deliberations around trade settlement were linked to dim sum bond market growth. Despite strong market interest, the market scale was limited by the offshore renminbi funds available. With the renminbi being used in trade settlement, the offshore community and the PBOC expected that a large pool of funds offshore would be generated for investors, driving a demand for renminbi bonds.[38]

Hong Kong's agenda was also boosted by leading state-owned banks that had established their offshore footprints in the 2000s. In addition to the Bank of China handling renminbi clearing, other domestic banks welcomed renminbi settlement since it created an expectation of enormous growth potential for their businesses, represented an important internationalizing opportunity to streamline their cross-border clearing and settlement infrastructure, and promised to expand their overseas branch networks (Development Research Center 2011: 4–6). The strong interest from the domestic banks successfully elicited the support of the CBRC, which had been eager to strengthen the international competitiveness of Chinese banks, especially after their successful IPOs in the offshore market before the crisis.

Set against these merits, the renminbi trade settlement program was widely favored within the financial bureaucracy. The NDRC, MOF, the Ministry of Commerce, the CBRC, China Customs, and the State Administration of Taxation brought significant leverage to the Hong Kong and PBOC-led coalition, and led to the endorsement of the State Council in late December 2008. In early 2009, the PBOC and HKMA concluded a swap agreement of a maximum of 200 billion yuan to meet the liquidity needs of offshore financial institutions in trade settlement. However, as all this unfolded, Hong Kong's monopoly was challenged.

While Hong Kong found no rival to the launch of the offshore bond market, its quest for trade settlement business was complicated by the dissenting local interests from Shanghai—despite the extensive support the coalition had lined up. Soon after Shanghai was named China's future international financial center in March 2009, it announced its aspiration to introduce trade settlement facilities simultaneously with Hong Kong, and to handle trade not only with neighboring economies like Hong Kong, but also transactions with Taiwan, ASEAN, and the former Soviet states. Such a scope was far more ambitious than what the PBOC had in mind and, if approved, would be representative of Shanghai's elevated status in international renminbi uses.[39]

Though the PBOC and CBRC were initially reluctant to adjust the regulation that would allow trade-related payments onshore, this did not put an end to Shanghai's quest. The city revised its proposal, indicating that the scheme would be eligible only to foreign firms headquartered in Shanghai, in an attempt to obtain the center's blessing. This triggered concerns among the Hong Kong financial community that their project would be derailed by the opposition. To prevent this from happening, and to ensure that the strong central political commitment stayed intact, Hong Kong's officials raised no explicit objection to Shanghai's scheme, instead agreeing to expand the scale of the trade settlement regime in response to onshore local interests. This concession brought Shanghai onside and maintained the political consensus. Accordingly, the renminbi trade settlement regime was rolled out in July 2009 and structured to accommodate the interests of both the financial hubs.

Offshore, cross-border trade between Shanghai, the four cities in Guangdong province, Hong Kong, Macau and ASEAN states would be handled in a renminbi settlement scheme that benefited 365 designated enterprises in the area of import and export payments.[40] A parallel onshore arrangement was created that allowed for "direct" settlement between foreign firms and mainland "correspondent banks," many of which had a significant presence in Shanghai. Besides offering additional market conduits for firms, this also served to balance different local interests with the same policy. Since the scheme's inception, however, a large part of trade settlement had taken place through BOCHK, the offshore clearing bank. This showed how political considerations outweighed actual market demand in deliberations surrounding the implementation specifics of renminbi trade settlement after the opening advocates and interested local parties had reached a compromise.[41]

The restricted scope in the early phase, however, had barred many interested firms from settling trade in renminbi. To boost the program's appeal after a lukewarm first year, the PBOC dramatically expanded its geographic reach in 2010 to 20 provinces and municipalities in China and all countries and regions overseas. Eligibility was extended to all potential importers and services businesses despite some restrictions being maintained on exporters of goods. This increased the number of eligible enterprises to 67,359 by the end of 2010, and led to an 874% growth in renminbi trade settlement between October 2010 and June 2011, which was about 10% of China's total trade in the year (SWIFT 2011 September). In August 2011, the geographic restrictions on domestic firms were rescinded, and all domestic enterprises with foreign business became eligible; all mainland exporters were also allowed to participate in renminbi trade settlement without any prior approval from regulatory authorities from March 2012 (see Figure 5.3 on the market growth of renminbi settlement in the city).

The exponential jump in the levels of renminbi trade settlement did not only benefit the offshore financiers (and to some extent Shanghai); onshore banks

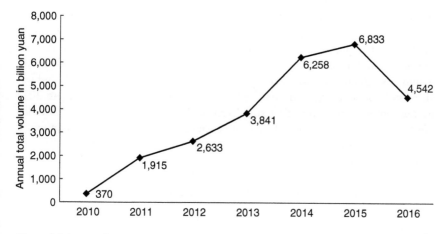

Figure 5.3 Renminbi trade settlement in Hong Kong.
Data source: HKMA

and their subsidiaries also took advantage of disproportionate business opportunities. The BOC's share of trade settlement jumped 457% between 2010 and 2011, 92% of which occurred offshore. Others also recorded significant growth in the period (Lam and Ho 2012: 17). Politically, this consolidated Hong Kong's niche in the offshore renminbi business, and strengthened the support of the financial industry as it reaped enormous material gains. Central bureaucratic actors like the PBOC, NDRC and CBRC backing the venture also had their interests served and promoted. The PBOC drew particular acclaim both at home and abroad as the principal architect of renminbi internationalization and the agency that had ushered into reality both renminbi bond issuance and trade settlement in just a few years (Bell and Feng 2013).

Concessions in implementation

Although the trade settlement program yielded much success, there were repercussions in early 2011 when an increasing number of mainland companies and their offshore subsidiaries began to take advantage of the program's loopholes and engaged in currency speculation and the evasion of China's capital controls by falsely reporting exports and imports. The practice enabled them to earn interest and benefit from exchange rate differentials across the two renminbi markets. Others capitalized on the system as a legal way of moving assets out of the country through mis-invoicing and fraudulent reporting. Although this activity did not constitute a sizable fraction of settlement activities, the central authorities were surprised by the dramatic growth in trade settlement volume passing through Hong Kong in such a short period.

To preempt the opposition from others within the financial bureaucracy that would likely surface if the speculative activities continued to spin out of control, the Hong Kong and PBOC-led coalition tightened their regulations. The PBOC and SAFE introduced additional monitoring of trade settlement transactions to lower the escalating risk from currency speculation on the mainland market, and required all foreign banks to impose regulatory requirements on offshore renminbi transactions in June 2011 such that all financial institutions would have to ensure that currency trading was backed by actual goods and services trade or by business needs.[42] SAFE also surprised the market in late 2011 by tightening capital rules that stipulated banks must maintain long US dollar positions at the end of each day, a move that forced the banks to retain excess US deposits onshore and limited their ability to hoard renminbi. Although SAFE defended its move as an attempt to slow down the buildup of foreign reserves (the largest monthly gains of US$100 and US$112 billion inflow were recorded in September and October 2010), the new regulation was widely believed to target companies unloading capital to China by mis-invoicing in the renminbi trade settlement scheme (Peng et al. 2011: 6).

In the offshore market, the HKMA (2010c) enacted similar rules that curbed the long-dated transactions that currency speculation would always involve. Local banks could no longer square their offshore renminbi forwards over three months with the BOCHK, the clearing bank, and could only do so if it involved trade proceeds; net renminbi positions were capped at 10% of their renminbi assets or liabilities. Almost immediately, this disrupted trading on both the onshore and offshore forward markets and shook confidence in China's commitment to giving a free hand to Hong Kong in the development of the offshore market. The offshore community, however, regarded these regulatory moves as an imperative, even though they would inevitably unsettle the CNH market. To ensure the center's backing of the successful trade settlement program, Hong Kong could not entirely count on the PBOC's support, nor could the latter pursue the opening initiative without considering the changing dynamics onshore.

Constituents of the pro-opening coalition had to manage dissent through concessionary moves, or face dissenting parties intervening and attempting to halt the opening initiative. In this case, both the PBOC and offshore community responded to the abuse of the trade settlement program before other bureaucratic actors and top decision makers acted. Their preemptive acts arguably succeeded in allaying the concerns of the NDRC, which was initially nervous of the mounting policy risks of the trade settlement scheme but stopped short of calling for a pause or reversal. This enabled the renminbi trade settlement to stay on course and, together with offshore bond issuance, continue to represent the most internationalized aspect of renminbi internationalization.

However, as renminbi funds skyrocketed due to trade settlements, offshore financiers found a lack of diverse investment opportunities apart from fixed income products, and repeatedly called for the creation of a swap agreement with the HKMA that would allow them to sell renminbi and acquire US or Hong Kong dollars (see Figure 5.4 for the trend since 2004). The authority rejected the proposal since it was the banks' responsibility to carry out asset

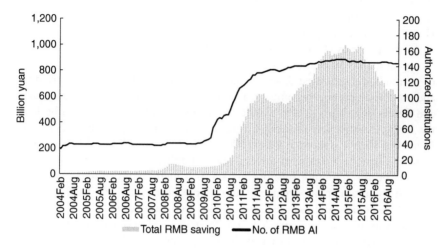

Figure 5.4 Offshore renminbi saving and number of authorized institutions (AI).
Data source: HKMA

allocation and portfolio management duties,[43] even though this stunted the development and innovation of offshore renminbi financial products, including equity and derivatives. Nonetheless, as Hong Kong and its central patrons were painstakingly reacting to the policy risks arising from the trade settlement program at the time, their concerns to push beyond fixed income products was understandable. Offshore market development was also complicated by competing and mixed local interests on the mainland, together with the lack of technical consensus amongst the pro-opening coalition.

Subnational pushes for offshore renminbi business

As the offshore community succeeded in making breakthroughs in bond issuance and trade settlement, Hong Kong's pursuits beyond these two areas encountered competing demands from local authorities. Whereas Shanghai's bid to undermine Hong Kong's role as the primary renminbi hub forced concessions from the opening advocates, Shenzhen and Tianjin, two minor domestic financial centers, intended to foster a partnership with the offshore players. Their quests gave a new definition and framing to the offshore opening agenda and provided additional political leverage that Hong Kong could count on.

Lingering challenges from Shanghai

The success of the dim sum bond market and trade settlement consolidated Hong Kong's prominence in renminbi business and invited stronger support from Beijing. The Twelfth Five-Year Plan (2011–2015), for example, affirmed Hong Kong's role as the primary offshore renminbi hub, and highlighted the city's niche as the global hub of renminbi and foreign asset management (PBOC et al. 2012). All this, however, did not entirely settle the jockeying between Hong Kong and Shanghai.

As the previous chapter examined, Shanghai had aspired to internationalize its capital market since the mid-2000s. It sought to lead the trading and pricing of renminbi-denominated assets, including equity, bonds, futures, derivatives, and commodities, and become an onshore hub of renminbi asset management and fundraising. The city also planned to inaugurate offshore renminbi business for foreign companies, financial institutions, and sovereign entities (Shanghai Municipal Party Committee 2010; NDRC 2011b). Fang Xinghai (2011), Director of Shanghai's Financial Service Office, publicly challenged Hong Kong's wish to be the renminbi offshore market as a mere "self-declared goal," and stressed the ultimate importance of an onshore host underlying Beijing's drive toward renminbi internationalization. He even argued that Hong Kong's success was ultimately dependent on "a faster development of Shanghai's onshore RMB market" and that, while Hong Kong's renminbi business flourished with Beijing's policy support, it could and should be working more closely with Shanghai.

Shanghai's ambition, however, was not strongly backed by many in the central financial bureaucracy, including the PBOC and financial regulators who still viewed Hong Kong as the most suitable pilot site for offshore renminbi business within the Chinese political economic orbit. It was not until January 2012 that the NDRC endorsed Shanghai's ambition to become China's largest onshore financial hub and the global center for "yuan trading, clearing and pricing over the next three years." The state- (and Shanghai-) backed SHIBOR would also be adopted as the benchmark for all renminbi-denominated credits, to enhance the pricing power of the onshore currency market (NDRC 2011b).

Nevertheless, the NDRC's backing was little more than rhetoric and an expression of goodwill designed to placate Shanghai after its setback in launching an international board. For the most part, the central agency simply restated earlier policy objectives advocated by Shanghai and there was no mention of any offshore role the city would assume.[44] With the policy imprimatur, however, Shanghai could at least seek predominance over the onshore market.

This also provided some room for offshore development by making political side-payments. In acknowledging Shanghai's renminbi quests, the central authorities helped maintain Shanghai's acquiescence to Hong Kong's niche in offshore renminbi business and ensured existing initiatives stayed on course. Yet, as Shanghai voiced its dissent over Hong Kong's plans to originate renminbi financial products beyond fixed income instruments (in which area Shanghai had no edge at all), both the PBOC and NDRC refrained from backing the quests of the offshore community. This invariably constrained the offshore pursuit and hampered market development in a way latter sections will examine in depth.

Goodwill from Tianjin and Shenzhen

Unlike Shanghai's reservations to the offshore market growth, Tianjin and Shenzhen had no explicit intent (nor could they) to challenge Hong Kong's market niche. They embedded their offshore renminbi agendas into local developmental agendas sanctioned by the central elites, and sought collaboration with the offshore hub. This expanded the base of political support that Hong Kong could enjoy, and offered some leverage in countering Shanghai's dissent and attempt to impede offshore development.

Tianjin's venture into offshore renminbi business was integral to the city's transformation of the Binhai New District into the "National Hub of Financial Innovation" in 2006 and 2007 that was endorsed by Beijing. The northern city saw working with Hong Kong as a shortcut to internationalizing its financial footprint through offering mainland enterprises and financial firms offshore currency services. After a brief fanfare, the initiative lost momentum after the departure of the mayor, Dai Xianglong, in 2008. Without his connections with the PBOC and SAFE, Tianjin could no longer effectively advance its agenda at the central level. The Binhai project was also seen as immature and having little readiness to pioneer innovative financial services and products by onshore and offshore financiers. Its quest to act as a financial bridge to Hong Kong also met with skepticism due to its small market scale and the absolute dominance of Beijing, which was populated by top state-owned banks and financial institutions that would certainty generate a sufficiently large demand for offshore renminbi services.[45] In such a context, Tianjin's policy failed to gain traction.

By contrast, Shenzhen was in a much better position given its track record of channeling foreign capital and market practices to China from the early reform years. However, because the Shenzhen SEZ lost its advantage when most domestic economic domains were liberalized, the city's officials began to carve new niches in cross-border finance after the late 2000s. To strengthen its pursuits, Shenzhen capitalized on its position as a transit point for offshore renminbi funds to the onshore market from the point when individual renminbi businesses were launched, and as one the five earliest designated trade settlement cities.[46] Like Tianjin's Binhai project, Shenzhen designated a certain area within its jurisdiction as a policy experimentation site. Following Beijing's approval in 2009, the Qianhai district, previously an untapped area, was slated to be the "special zone within the SEZ" that would collaborate with Hong Kong in cross-border renminbi finance. With cutting-edge market expertise from Hong Kong, Shenzhen envisioned playing an active part in offshore renminbi business and China's financial opening, instead of being a mere intermediary connecting the CNY and CNH markets.[47]

In addition to unsuccessful attempts to revive the Through Train scheme and introduce the cross-listing of securities between exchanges as discussed in Chapters 3 and 4, the Shenzhen government and financiers proposed the development of a two-way renminbi loan facility that would allow renminbi onshore to be provided to offshore entities and vice versa, and to issue renminbi bonds for mainland SMEs.[48] These initiatives were well-received by the financial bureau-cracy and Guangdong provincial leadership, who continued to see Shenzhen as the forerunner of China's reforms. This catalyzed the two-way loan facilities of early 2013, when 15 offshore banks made loans to 26 companies in the Qianhai area at negotiated rates of interest, instead of adhering to official ones (Wei 2016: 364). This not only eased mainland interest rates control, it also increased the use of offshore renminbi funds and boosted the permeability of the two ren-minbi markets. Encouraged by this development, the local financiers also cham-pioned new renminbi financial products together with offshore financial institutions that had established footholds in the area, and called for the piloting of QDII2 and QDII3 examined in Chapter 3 (FSDC 2013).

Despite the mixed success of these initiatives, Shenzhen's advances in off-shore renminbi activities in effect integrated Hong Kong's development with center-sponsored local reform experiments, and added to the leverage of the Hong Kong and PBOC-led coalition. The partnership between the two southern cities, however, did little to overcome the unresolved technical matters critical to the introduction of renminbi financial instruments that had been ham-pered by deliberations within the pro-opening coalition, and between the opening advocates and dissenting parties. Discord over financial standards also delayed the offshore product development and launch.

Fragile consensus within the pro-opening coalition

As the subnational dynamics unraveled and complicated the offshore market growth, emerging disagreements between the offshore community, the PBOC, and other financial policymakers supportive of the dim sum bonds and trade set-tlement schemes weakened consensus within the pro-opening coalition. Notably, the Hong Kong government and financiers were at odds with their central patrons over the scope, pace, and technical aspects of offshore market development. This resulted in a stagnation of growth of the offshore renminbi derivatives market and little product innovation. Only after concessions to the financial bureaucracy on market scope and pace were some sporadic initiatives made possible.

How far and how fast can local innovation go?

The offshore community had planned to introduce renminbi derivative products as early as late 2006 after the technical issues over bond issuance offshore with PBOC were resolved. Even short of Beijing's regulatory approval, the HKEx was about to phase in non-deliverable renminbi futures for better exchange risk management because the product would pose few risk concerns to the onshore financial system. Its transaction would not entail cross-border capital flow and would be traded, cleared, and settled through the HKEx in Hong Kong dollars. This promised investors a more transparent risk management tool than the OTC-traded NDF (HKEx 2007b: 5).

The proposal was shelved after the mainland regulatory authorities stepped in, however. The PBOC and CSRC challenged the imperative of developing exchange-traded derivatives while the offshore renminbi bond market was still in its infancy. This deterred the HKEx from any further pursuit without Beijing's sanction. The exchange was counting on Beijing's approval of the listing of mainland firms in Hong Kong, and was anticipating the forthcoming Through Train scheme at the time (Webb 2012). Therefore, the HKEx withdrew its initiative and suggested that further research into the product's feasibility was warranted. From late 2007, the product disappeared entirely from the HKEx agenda, and the exchange shied away from publicly venturing into renminbi-linked derivatives (HKEx 2007c, 2007d).

After that, the HKEx (2011) turned to strengthening its niche in China-related options, futures, and ETFs with underlying equity denominated in Hong Kong dollars. It was not until 2010 that the central authorities reversed their stance over renminbi-denominated financial product development, in response to the explosive growth of the offshore bond market and renminbi trade settlement, which elevated the political status of the pro-opening PBOC and SAFE. Hong Kong's success in avoiding a clash with Shanghai's ambitions, by being supportive of the city's role as China's leading international financial center and by withholding criticism during the international board episode, also went in its favor.

Shanghai financiers were also reassured by their offshore counterparts that they would not hinder Shanghai's pursuit of an international board and that offshore market development would not come at the expense of onshore interests. With the PBOC's endorsement, the HKMA (HKMA 2010a) elucidated new supervisory principles for the operational management of cross-border renminbi flows and businesses. Most restrictions on banks regarding renminbi use would be relaxed as long as the funds were not remitted back to the onshore market. Offshore institutions would also be free to deploy any renminbi funds at hand for international purposes like making loans and developing new financial products. Over the summer, interbank transfers of renminbi funds and those between individual and business accounts were permitted; any overseas companies and financial institutions could open renminbi accounts and exchange as many funds as they wished with banks in Hong Kong (HKMA 2010b).

The PBOC piloted a scheme that allowed the renminbi clearing bank and other eligible financial institutions offshore to invest in the mainland interbank bond market. This appealed greatly to foreign entities holding renminbi offshore and stimulated the growth of renminbi deposits in Hong Kong. For the offshore community, the move also generated a strong impetus for financial product development that went beyond fixed income instruments, expanding the channels for offshore funds returning to the onshore market as renminbi holders demanded a variety of asset classes other than those available offshore.

Considering the deregulatory trends, the HKEx (2010) revived its shelved derivatives plan and positioned itself as the "exchange of choice" for offshore renminbi species, including securities and derivatives that were critical to any further advance of renminbi internationalization. As the offshore interbank market liberalized, deliverable forwards and interest rate swaps of offshore renminbi, as well as non-deliverable swaps and interest-rate swaps, were rolled out on a small scale (Wang 2010). Several CNH and foreign currency futures and options were developed by the HKEx from late 2012, with the CNH/US$ pair marking the first deliverable renminbi futures quoted, margined, and settled in renminbi in the global capital market.[49]

However, the increased latitude over the use of renminbi funds was not translated into unremitting support from the PBOC. Although the HKMA and HKEx had desired to originate more diverse and sophisticated renminbi derivatives for years, the PBOC and SAFE remained cautious of the scope and pace of the offshore market, and were concerned that "excessive" innovation might spur onshore demand for similar products in the nascent mainland derivatives market. Perhaps more importantly, the offshore community was yet to reach consensus with the PBOC and its regulatory peers on financial standards crucial to the pricing and risk assessment of derivatives, posing risk implications to the financial bureaucracy and the larger onshore market.[50]

Discord over financial technicalities

The development of offshore renminbi derivatives was also hampered by the lack of agreement over technicalities like the benchmark yield and trading terms between parties. The Hong Kong authorities and financiers were reluctant to compromise with the PBOC and other onshore stakeholders as this might impinge on the offshore edge in derivatives markets and erode Hong Kong's reputation as an international financial hub. The intransigent position, however, weakened the consensus within the pro-opening coalition, and undermined the commitment of the central patrons.

Major rifts within the coalition manifested themselves in the financial standards for product pricing and the appraising of financial risks. In June 2011, as Beijing was relinquishing control of the offshore market, the Treasury Market Association (TMA), a financial industry body with HKMA representatives as chairperson and board members, published the offshore renminbi fixing rate that would serve as a pricing benchmark for offshore renminbi products (Wang 2011).[51] The TMA expected this to stimulate derivative product development and to address the lack of fixing references that had forced offshore participants to adopt SHIBOR.[52] From January 2012, the TMA released interbank offered rates for offshore renminbi loans with various maturities of up to a year with the hope of promoting offshore renminbi-SHIBOR fixing and making Hong Kong's interbank rates the benchmark for all offshore market products in a similar way to the global role of the London Interbank Offered Rate (LIBOR).[53]

However, Hong Kong's moves provoked Shanghai's financial officials and community, who quickly disputed the importance of the offshore market and were vocal about their ambition to jostle for the pricing power of renminbi products (Fang 2011). To the disappointment of the offshore community, the PBOC and NDRC took an apparently neutral position, even though they had reservations about Shanghai's ambition. Instead of imposing a uniform reference rate across the CNY and CNH markets, the two central agencies allowed for the choices of market participants, and even endorsed SHIBOR as the onshore benchmark rate in late 2011 (NDRC 2011b). Although this was deemed a necessary exchange of favors, designed to prevent Shanghai from competing head-on with Hong Kong, the offshore financiers cast doubt on the PBOC's support, as central bankers repeatedly encouraged the adoption of SHIBOR as the benchmark rate in financial product innovation (Yi 2008). The HKMA was also concerned that the existence of different benchmarks would confuse investors and stunt Hong Kong's renminbi market growth.

The more pronounced discord within the pro-opening coalition arose from the trading terms between counterparts in the derivatives market. Instead of adopting the Master Agreement of the International Swaps and Derivatives Association (ISDA), which governed the clear majority of the global derivatives trade, the PBOC intended to impose a domestic standard it had originated in the offshore market. Offshore financiers were expected to follow the framework of the National Association of Financial Market Institutional Investors (NAFMII), a PBOC-sponsored interbank association, as this would represent the very first step of internationalizing China's domestic financial standards and would also make the NAFMII a more respected body on the mainland.

Unsurprisingly, this invited strong resistance from offshore financiers who had for years adhered to the prevailing global market practice. Despite the similarities between the ISDA and NAFMII frameworks, the Chinese variant was not devised to handle cross-border transactions but only domestic trade, and did not fully cover transactions of forex or credit default swaps. Therefore, offshore adoption of the NAFMII framework would have created a two-tier system of un-harmonized rules, placed additional demands for collateral, and made netting arrangements difficult for offshore derivative trading. More worryingly, if the NAFMII framework was adopted, all renminbi-denominated derivatives would be governed by Chinese legal documentation and, by extension, the mainland authorities. The Hong Kong financiers, including the offshore subsidiaries of domestic banks, held very negative views about the development and were seriously concerned that the domestic standard would significantly erode market confidence and stunt the introduction of offshore renminbi derivatives (Thompson 2010).[54]

Nonetheless, the NAFMII insisted even without securing the agreement of the offshore financiers. Its Secretary General, Shi Wenchao, planned to announce NAFMII's scheme during a visit to Hong Kong in June 2011. As a banker remarked, "we use NAFMII's agreement in China because we have to, but no one is interested in using it where we don't have to."[55] Financial industry resistance, however, presented Hong Kong officials with a dilemma since they had been counting on the PBOC's support over offshore market development. As the city was putting in place the OTC regulations and preparing to launch a clearinghouse in 2013 to compete with regional peers like Singapore (Lau 2011), any gesture that might provoke the PBOC might risk delaying the launch of OTC renminbi products.[56]

So, although the local regulators shared and were sympathetic to the financiers' concerns, they hesitated to voice their position to the PBOC lest it should cause it to hold back support for Hong Kong's renminbi market. In light of the financiers' strong dissent and the prospect of the financiers relocating their trade to other markets, the PBOC reconsidered and eventually paused NAFMII's plan to promote the domestic standard in the offshore market. Still, market participants were disturbed. As a Hong Kong financial official described it, if NAFMII's plan were to get approval, "all it takes is one local Chinese bank to say it's going to use it, then you'll have every local bank using it."[57]

Hong Kong's apparently submissive posture did succeed in sustaining the PBOC's backing for local OTC market development. The HKEx-affiliated clearinghouse, OTC Clear, started clearing services for interest rate swaps and NDFs using renminbi, alongside other foreign currencies, from November 2013 (ISDA 2017). It quickly expanded into the renminbi-linked derivatives clearing business and made several breakthroughs, including its clearing service for cross-currency swaps, which it launched in 2016 (Vaghela 2015). Nonetheless, the 2011 arguments over the offshore benchmark rate and the financial standards for derivatives challenged the pro-opening coalition from within. The offshore community found a half-hearted PBOC occasionally siding with onshore interests and advancing its own policy agenda of promoting the offshore adoption of domestic financial standards.

Headway amid shaky central political commitment

Despite the hiccups in establishing Hong Kong's renminbi derivatives markets, there were some advances in other capital market segments. The CNY and CNH markets were increasingly connected with the launch of several circulation channels in 2011 and 2012. These endeavors, however, were somewhat delayed by dissenting parties that attempted to undermine the renminbi internationalization agenda and the wavering policy commitment of the PBOC and other central agencies supportive of Hong Kong.

Capital market advances and cross-market connections

Capital market advances that promoted Hong Kong's status as a leading offshore renminbi center included renminbi stock issuances that broadened the range of available financial products and the development of renminbi fund products that could channel offshore renminbi to the onshore stock market. In both instances, the offshore community advanced its policy initiatives and lobbied the CSRC but gathered little support.

The offshore community then turned to the PBOC for help in its pursuit of renminbi stock issuance and presented the initiative as an outgrowth of renminbi internationalization, instead of one that might rival Shanghai's quest for an international board (see Chapter 4). This demonstrated to the PBOC that Hong Kong could serve as a plausible and failsafe venue for testing the market appeal of foreign forms issuing renminbi stocks, especially after Shanghai's quest for an international board fell off the central agenda in mid-2011. Subsequent pushes for mainland enterprises to float H-share issuance in renminbi, however, were strongly resisted by both Shanghai interests and the CSRC, as they thought it would undermine the onshore hub's niche serving domestic firms. Following a small-scale IPO in 2011, the HKEx welcomed the world's dual-currency stock in late 2012.

In seeking support for the initiatives that might bridge the CNY and CNH markets, such as the overseas ETFs analyzed in Chapter 3 and renminbi QFII (RQFII), the offshore community engaged in concessionary politics and succeeded. Akin to the QFII of 2002, RQFII would allow foreign institutional investors to invest in China's financial market using their renminbi holdings and to originate fund products available to investors outside China, enriching product diversity beyond the fixed income species. As in the launch of overseas ETFs, the CSRC displayed some interest in the offshore RQFII proposal as early as 2009 but stopped short of taking further action due to disagreements over its scope and pace, notably eligibility requirements between the CSRC and the offshore community.[58]

Whereas Hong Kong-based foreign financiers expected a level playing field with onshore counterparts under RQFII, the CSRC envisioned that the domestic securities and fund management companies which had been developing their offshore foothold since the late 2000s would take the lead in the program's early phase.[59] Through RQFII and overseas ETFs, the mainland brokerages would acquire the market experience of engaging in international retail and institutional sales and product distribution, aspects in which they had previously been inferior to global firms, boosting their market competitiveness. The liberalizing initiatives would also stimulate the development of A-share ETFs on the onshore exchanges, which would be investible by the RQFII funds.[60] For this reason, the Shanghai authorities and financiers backed RQFII, since it would considerably increase onshore market turnover. The lack of compromise by the Hong Kong community, however, meant that both RQFII and overseas ETFs were tabled. The CSRC was also deterred by the overheating equity market at the time and postponed its approval until mid-2011, when the offshore community finally agreed to have the onshore financial industry take the lead (Ulrich et al. 2012: 8–10).

This catalyzed the official promulgation of overseas ETFs and RQFII in August 2011, when the then Vice Premier Li Keqiang visited Hong Kong. Circulation mechanisms aside, the PBOC and MOF promised more regular auctions of government bonds.[61]

The offshore agenda called into question

Despite the support of the top elites, the implementation of liberalizing initiatives that would bring closer ties between the CNY and CNH markets was complicated by dissenting voices from within the financial bureaucracy. Bureaucratic actors once supportive of the pro-opening coalition also became cautious of renminbi internationalization.

Notwithstanding "preemptive" moves by the Hong Kong and PBOC-led coalition to rein in abuse of the renminbi trade settlement regime, regulatory evasion and extensive misuse continued. Fears of hot money inflows intensified, and the renminbi experienced more volatility throughout 2011. In fact, as renminbi trade settlement expanded in scale, investors and major trading partners of China often hoarded renminbi offshore through sanctioned channels before paying with the US dollar in subsequent transactions. This, in effect, provided a legally sanctioned channel for investors betting on renminbi appreciation, and caused the financial bureaucracy to level accusations of "speculative funds" triggering onshore market disturbance.[62]

The NDRC, MOF, and State-owned Assets Supervision and Administration Commission were inclined to slow down or pause the offshore market initiatives even though they had sided with the pro-opening coalition over offshore bond issuance and trade settlement. Some PBOC officials also held this view because they were concerned that the escalating policy risks coming from the offshore renminbi market might affect domestic financial stability. They cautioned in private that the opening agenda accelerated in 2011 would impose an "unnecessary" regulatory burden on domestic authorities, and warned that it would be a mistake to repeat Japan's untoward yen internationalization strategy that had poorly managed associated capital flows in a period of rapid yen appreciation after the 1985 Plaza Accord and eventually led to the painful bursting of asset bubble in the early 1990s.[63] Short of completing reforms such as interest rate liberalization at home, it was said, renminbi internationalization should be put on hold, even though Beijing appeared committed and formally incorporated the agenda into the official five-year planning documents (NDRC 2011a).

Aside from trumpeting the risk implications, dissenting parties also cast doubt on the overall benefit of renminbi internationalization as championed by the pro-opening coalition. Yu Yong-ding (2012), a former PBOC monetary policy committee member, asserted that offshore financiers had been the primary beneficiary at the expense of China, as the country was losing wealth to offshore parties who exchanged low-yield offshore US and Hong Kong dollar assets for high-yield renminbi through a variety of offshore market channels (Chinese Academy of Social Sciences 2012).[64] Therefore, he argued, progress in the offshore renminbi market should be slowed down and capital control should be tightened.

The split within the financial bureaucracy went public during the December 2011 Central Economic Work Conference, a meeting of the top party and state leadership, when the policy priorities and definitions shifted in favor of the dissenting agencies. Domestic financial reforms, including interest rate liberalization and financing the SOEs and SMEs, took precedence over exchange rate decontrol and currency internationalization that were seen as "very dangerous" to China's financial stability.[65]

This clashed with the stance of the pro-opening coalition. The pro-opening camp within the PBOC, notably the in-house Statistics and Analysis Department, retorted that renminbi internationalization could catalyze future capital decontrol, and financial reforms such as interest and exchange rate liberalization should not be seen as requisite to the expansion of the renminbi footprint overseas. The offshore community also disagreed that capital account liberalization had bleak prospects, since Beijing was in a far better position to manage cross-border capital flows.[66] The HKEx Chief Executive, for example, argued that short-term market volatility and irregularities should not stop the longer term development of the offshore market, just as the lack of a high standard of living should not stop a baby's birth (Li 2012).

In the face of loud dissent, the PBOC paused the RQFII scheme until late 2011, when inflows of hot money appeared to moderate. Jointly regulated by the PBOC, SAFE, and CSRC, the early phase of RQFII capped the investment scale at 20 billion yuan to be shared among 20 offshore arms of domestic securities firms and asset management companies; 80% of offshore renminbi funds would be invested in domestic bond markets and the rest in stocks.[67]

Grand opening with great caution

The RQFII and related initiatives, however, were accelerated after mid-2012 when the Chinese economy confronted different market conditions that appeared to help weaken bureaucratic resistance. Instead of being overwhelmed by speculative funds flowing into the onshore market to profit from the renminbi's appreciation, the first and second quarter of 2012 recorded notable capital outflows that had been unseen for several years.

Although this raised concerns among central financial policymakers about an economic slowdown, and the PBOC had to ease liquidity provision to the domestic financial system as capital left China, the central bank also recognized the circumstance as providing an important opportunity to press ahead with offshore renminbi liberalizing initiatives.[68] This would alleviate fund outflows and, if successful, prove to the dissenters within the government that the PBOC's agenda did not necessarily compromise China's financial stability.[69] In concert with the CSRC and SAFE, the PBOC expanded the RQFII quota to 70 billion yuan in April 2012, and funds were allowed to invest in onshore stocks for developing HKEx-listed ETFs. This liberalizing move greatly eased the access of offshore renminbi to the onshore stock market and encouraged financial product development. It also promised substantial material interest to domestic securities and fund industries, onshore exchanges, and the Hong Kong financial community.

The once debilitated pro-opening coalition regained strength. Even China's capital outflows worsened, reaching as much as US$326 billion in 2012, according to a SAFE estimate, while the PBOC and other pro-opening financial policy-makers appeared more committed to easing access to offshore renminbi funds for the onshore market. The central bank's quest was also in part motivated by its bid to include the renminbi in the IMF Special Drawing Right composition after 2010.[70] This contributed to another big leap forward for RQFII, when its aggregate quota was increased to 270 billion yuan in late 2012. A few months later, the regulatory authorities invited subsidiaries of mainland commercial banks and insurers, as well as all Hong Kong-based financial institutions, to take part in the scheme. Investment ratio restrictions were rescinded, enabling greater asset allocation flexibility for investors.[71] In a related move, the CSRC relaxed QFII rules by substantially lowering the eligibility requirements of foreign institutions and expanding the investment scope. QDII's aggregate quota also increased from US$30 billion to 80 billion in 2012, and again to US$150 billion in July 2013 (CSRC 2012, 2013). The PBOC widened the interbank bond market to Hong Kong, Taiwan, and Singapore insurance companies in 2012, and followed this with an invitation to QFII holders in 2013.

These drastic opening moves generated considerable market interest in Hong Kong's market, and boosted the status of the PBOC and SAFE (and to some extent the CSRC) as the leading bureaucratic advocates of capital market liberalization. As offshore renminbi activities gained solid footholds in Hong Kong, the city's officials and financial industry also became important allies to the PBOC in promoting its agenda of expanding the renminbi's reach beyond the region. Leading financial executives in Hong Kong, for example, were instrumental in lining up their London counterparts on transnational platforms such as the HKMA-led Hong Kong–London Forum that contributed to the takeoff of renminbi business in the UK in late 2013 (Green and Gruin 2017). Furthermore, as offshore subsidiaries of mainland financial institutions profited from the expanding range of offshore renminbi business, they leveraged their connections in the mainland, sometimes lobbying on behalf of the Hong Kong authorities as they sought to keep the opening momentum on track and press for new business opportunities (Robertson 2015).

This helped Hong Kong's renminbi market survive the dramatic reversal of domestic economic conditions after 2014 that witnessed the outflow of at least a quarter of China's four trillion US dollar foreign reserve.[72] Despite a litany of strong measures from Beijing designed to crack down on and stem capital flight, the offshore renminbi market was not seriously disrupted, except for a shrinking of renminbi transactions in trade settlement and bond origination. Rather than rolling back liberalizing measures, central financial policymakers had grown more sophisticated in managing the policy risks according to the nature of the liberalizing moves concerned. This was best evidenced in the "asymmetrical" degree of opening that differentiated between inbound and outbound renminbi traffic and enabled better capital flow management (Chen 2017; Habermeier et al. 2017).

Whereas inbound investment was loosened to attract foreign capital and dampen the renminbi's depreciation pressure, outbound capital traffic was mostly halted. This led to the failure of endeavors like QDII2, which was halted even before its inception, as well as RQDII/RQDII2, which would have allowed mainland investors to use onshore renminbi funds for outbound investment but was soon restricted by the PBOC and CSRC. Further, Stock Connects, which involved individual investors, were structured with closed-ends to minimize systemic risks arising from capital flight (see Chapter 3).

On the other hand, the PBOC unleashed liberalizing initiatives that targeted medium and long-term inbound investment by institutional investors. For instance, Beijing considerably liberalized its interbank bond market in July 2015, when the PBOC exempted foreign central banks, international financial institutions, and sovereign wealth funds from the prior approval they had previously needed to invest in China's interbank bond market without any limit. Early 2016 saw another easing that welcomed nearly all financial institutions worldwide for as long as they were recognized as having a medium or long-term investment orientation (Deutsche Bank 2016). In July 2017, a Bond Connect scheme, which operated in a similar fashion to the Stock Connects, was launched via the HKEx. Only northbound traffic was allowed, however, to avoid capital evasion from onshore investors (Linklaters 2017).

These contributed to Hong Kong's status as the leading offshore renminbi center even amid market uncertainties onshore and potential competition from other renminbi hubs.[73] Hong Kong handled 71% of global renminbi payments in 2015 and was the fourth largest currency center in 2016, thanks to a 59% turnover increase in renminbi transactions. The city took the largest share of the 1.5 trillion yuan RQFII quota among the 17 jurisdictions with which the PBOC had concluded such an arrangement (KPMG 2017). This remarkable market status would not have been possible without the careful political maneuvering of opening advocates who navigated the "deep water zone" of the economic and financial reforms.

Conclusion

This chapter analyzed the policy trajectory of renminbi internationalization that centered on the maturation of Hong Kong as an offshore renminbi center. It disaggregated the development into multiple but related aspects, and traced how underlying political economic dynamics cutting across the subnational, financial industry, and bureaucracy contributed to a gradual and punctuated opening after the mid-2000s. This analysis challenges accounts which attribute the origin of renminbi internationalization to the central authorities and pay little attention to the dynamics beyond the central financial bureaucracy.

Motivated by prospective material interests (and to some extent financial grounds), the offshore community called for the introduction of some *de jure* offshore facilities in the early 2000s to handle the growing quantities of offshore renminbi. The initiative failed to take off due to conflicting policy priorities, the lack of technical readiness, and loud dissent from onshore constituents, notably Shanghai-based interests and the financial regulators. It was not until the conclusion of the Closer Economic Partnership Arrangement between China and Hong Kong that offshore renminbi business reappeared on the agenda. To achieve a breakthrough, the offshore community reframed and scaled down its quest. Instead of conceiving it as one that might compromise China's capital control, the initiative was re-defined in isolation from the larger financial opening agenda, and introduced only as a supplementary measure that facilitated individual and business needs under CEPA. The offshore community also agreed to involve Shenzhen as an intermediary that connected the CNY and CNH markets to assuage onshore dissenters wary of financial risks. This paid off when the PBOC and SAFE became patrons of the offshore constituents. Individual renminbi businesses were rolled out in 2004.

Though this appeared to be minor progress, the formative years were crucial to bringing together offshore local and financial industry constituents with the PBOC into a pro-opening coalition that laid the political foundation of later advances, and they revealed the imperative of policy re-framing and concessionary politics to any successful liberalizing pursuit. The offshore pursuits for renminbi bond issuance and trade settlement met with different dynamics during deliberations. The former encountered dissent from the MOF and NDRC as the initiative conflicted with their stakes in onshore bond market development and entailed high financial risks. The constituents of the pro-opening coalition successfully managed these concerns through adopting SHIBOR as a benchmark rate and upgrading the trading system, and deferred to the NDRC over the scale of issuance. This led to the debut of renminbi bond issuance in 2007 that met increasing demand from onshore and offshore firms and experienced strong growth as the regulations were loosened and dissenting agencies found a strong interest in offshore bond issuance.

The trade settlement scheme gained wide support within the financial bureaucracy after the subprime credit crisis since it reduced exchange rate risk and relieved the financing stress of domestic SMEs, and promised internationalizing opportunities to domestic banks. As Shanghai set in and was eager to take part, the Hong Kong and PBOC-led coalition did not object to expanding the scheme's scale so that the offshore development would not be derailed. Both Hong Kong and Shanghai operated parallel mechanisms and witnessed exponential growth of renminbi trade settlement volume in the late 2000s. To preempt dissent arising from abuses of the system, and to ensure that the initiative stayed on course, the pro-opening coalition tinkered with the regulations during implementation.

Notwithstanding these policy successes, further advances were complicated by the subnational dynamics and discord between the offshore community and its central patrons within the pro-opening coalition. Shanghai's ambition to foster offshore renminbi business inevitably challenged Hong Kong, and prompted gestures from the NDRC and PBOC to endorse Shanghai's ambition to be a leading onshore center in order to obtain the city's acquiescence. Goodwill from Tianjin and Shenzhen, by contrast, provided additional leverage to the Hong Kong and PBOC-led pro-opening coalition by linking the offshore agenda with local developmental projects blessed by Beijing. However, within the coalition, the offshore constituents were sometimes at odds with the PBOC over derivative product development. Continuing disagreements and an unwillingness to compromise about financial technicalities, notably the benchmark rate and derivatives trading framework, undermined the consensus within the coalition. This put most of the local initiatives on hold until the offshore market was granted more discretion in deploying the use of renminbi funds.

Nonetheless, the equity market saw some progress that increased both renminbi product diversity and connections between the offshore and onshore markets. With the PBOC's support, and framed as an outgrowth of offshore financial market development, renminbi-denominated equities were made available in Hong Kong in 2011 without unsettling Shanghai. Further, through concessionary offers that granted the onshore brokerages the lead in product development and market sales, overseas ETFs and RQFII funds were phased in with the CSRC's support. These breakthroughs were overshadowed by a thinning political commitment within the financial bureaucracy as speculative funds appeared to misuse the offshore renminbi hub for their own benefit. This led to reservations about the viability of renminbi internationalization

A changing economic situation after 2012, however, proved to be a critical juncture that allowed the Hong Kong and PBOC-led coalition to advance its agenda. As concerns over capital outflows intensified, the PBOC took the opportunity to press ahead with initiatives that had previously been slowed to facilitate renminbi inflows from the offshore market. The scale was expanded drastically to meet the interests of not just the offshore community, but also onshore financiers and financial hubs who helped sustain the opening tendency—even in 2014 and 2015, when the Chinese economy experienced strong downward pressures and witnessed a massive exodus of funds. At the same time that the authorities were clamping down on capital flight, Beijing became more discerning about easing the capital mobility associated with the Hong Kong renminbi market. Whereas outbound traffic witnessed either blockage or extensive restrictions, the inbound regime was loosened for medium and long-term investments. Proceeding with great caution, grand openings took place in the interbank bond market, and were marked by the Stock and Bond Connects between Hong Kong and the mainland.

These findings suggest that renminbi internationalization has been a differentiated process presenting uneven and imbalanced progress along various fronts, and shaped by political interplays unfolding not only within the financial bureaucracy and industry but also among the different financial hubs in the onshore and offshore markets. The offshore authorities, however, were not just another set of policymaking actors with little leverage. They generated the liberalizing initiatives, partnered with financiers and bureaucratic actors, and sought their support. Together they constituted the pro-opening coalition and engaged in give-and-take throughout the deliberation and implementation that engendered the openings.

This implies that successful renminbi internationalization initiatives are often phased in with the intention of advancing domestic interests and this necessitates accommodations that give rise to politically viable arrangements. The underlying political economic dynamics that both promote and undermine the process, along with the interplay between constituents that cuts across different levels of analysis, complement and echo recent studies that reveal the constraints which China's political economy has placed on making the renminbi a successfully international-ized currency (Cohen 2015; Otero-Iglesias and Vermeiren 2015; Germain and Schwartz 2017).

Notes

1 Spatially confined enclaves, for example, have been in place in developing economies while the selective introduction of foreign capital and technologies has taken place. Similarly, some offshore financial centers are situated as segregated parts of larger economies. On international applications, see Palan (2006).
2 This subsection title was the brainchild of Hui and Bunning (2010).
3 "Zhaoshang yinhang lian yewu chong xian shengji" (Offshore business of China Merchants Bank revived), *Shanghai Securities News*, June 4, 2003.
4 Zhong, Wei, "500 yi renminbi zai Xianggang nengfou chengwei lian jinrong zhongxin" (Would the 50 billion renminbi in Hong Kong make an offshore currency center), *Global Times*, September 15, 2002.
5 Banks hoarding renminbi funds could only provide currency exchange services, but were not allowed to offer deposit services or loans to individual or corporate clients.
6 "Zhongguo duanqi nei jiang bu zai Xianggang sheli renminbi lian zhongxin" (China would not turn Hong Kong into an offshore renminbi center in the short term), *China News Services*, November 13, 2002.
7 "Dong Jianhua: Xianggang jiang you jingying renminbi lian zhongxin youxian quan" (Tung Chee-wah: Hong Kong enjoys the first-mover advantage of offshore renminbi center), *Guangdong-Hong Kong Information Daily*, July 29, 2003.
8 Richard McGregor and Victor Mallet, "China alters tack on HK's plan for renminbi," *Financial Times*, August 17, 2003.
9 Yang, Xianyue, "Shanghai ji xu fazhan lian jinrong shicang" (Shanghai should develop the offshore financial center), *International Financial News*, June 24, 2002.
10 Interview with Shanghai state-owned commercial bank manager, February 2012.
11 Fang, Xinghai, "Renminbi lian zhongxin: yige caolu de zhuyi" (RMB offshore center: a heedless idea), *Shanghai Securities News*, August 20, 2003.
12 McGregor and Mallet, "China alters tack on HK's plan for renminbi."
13 Gu, Yao, "Renminbi zai Gang liudong cuisheng bianju, Gang zi yinhang an zhan neidi yewu" (Forthcoming changes on offshore renminbi business, Hong Kong-based banks jockeying in China market), *Jiefang Daily*, August 26, 2003.
14 "Li Yang: Zai Gang sheli lian zhongxin buru qingsuan tixi" (Li Yang: Better to have a settlement mechanism than an offshore center in Hong Kong), *China Business Times*, September 16, 2003.
15 Wei, Rongzhi, "Tang Yingnian shenyan lian zhongxin" (Henry Tang reserved about [setting up a] renminbi center), *International Finance News*, November 27, 2003.
16 "Yanghang: Xianggang bushi renminbi lian zhongxin" (Central bank: Hong Kong is not the offshore center), *People's Daily*, November 21, 2003. The other plausible rationale for the CEPA preferential economic policies was to mollify Hong Kong's increasing discontent against Tung Chee-wah's administration fraught with governance challenges at the time, and win the hearts and minds of the Hong Kong public.
17 Jia, Yubao, "Si da liliang zhu tui Shen-Gang hezuo" (Four major forces help push ahead Shenzhen–Hong Kong collaboration), *21st century Business Herald*, September 18, 2003.

18 Xiong, Junhui, "Renminbi huiliu fangan puguang" (Returning arrangement of off-shore renminbi fund became public), *Wenweipo*, August 21, 2003.

19 These two aside, individual/retail level renminbi businesses also saw new developments. For example, renminbi insurance policies, wealth management products, and treasury management services proliferated after the mid-2000s.

20 Although the report was not an official publication, it was authored by the PBOC's renminbi internationalization study group, together with three other articles on renminbi regionalization, settlement and pricing, and the economic foundation of currency internationalization.

21 "Jinguanju san celue kuo renminbi yewu" (Three strategies of HKMA to expand renminbi businesses), *Hong Kong Economic Journal*, September 9, 2004.

22 "Gang zhengqu fa renminbi zhaiquan" (Hong Kong striving to issue renminbi bond), *Mingpao*, August 24, 2004.

23 Liu, Debin, "Zhou Xiaochuan ting Gang fa renminbi zhai" (Zhou Xiaochuan supported Hong Kong issuing renminbi bond), *Hong Kong Economic Times*, June 4, 2005.

24 Feng, Chengzhang, "Zai kaifang renminbi yewu Wen zong you baoliu" (Premier Wen reserved about further expansion of renminbi business), *Mingpao*, January 16, 2006. "Faxing jingwai renminbi zhaiquan burong you shi" (No margin of error in offshore renminbi bond issuance), *Hong Kong Economic Journal*, July 4, 2006.

25 "Ren Zhigang: neidi buwei dui Gang fa renminbi zhai cun yiyi" (Joseph Yam: mainland bureaucracy has dissenting view on renminbi bond issuance in Hong Kong), *Mingpao*, November 3, 2005.

26 The interbank body also serves as the China Foreign Exchange Trade System, handling forex, bond, and derivative trading in both renminbi and foreign currencies. "Fengxian jiandi renminbi zhaiquan faxing jie shiji" (Reduced risk makes favorable timing for issuance of renminbi bond), *Hong Kong Economic Journal*, January 16, 2007.

27 "Gang fa renminbi zhai jiaoshou xitong jiuxu" (Trading and settlement system of renminbi bond ready in Hong Kong), *Hong Kong Economic Times*, February 27, 2007.

28 The policy banks include the Agricultural Development Bank of China, the China Development Bank, and the Export-Import Bank of China—all founded in 1994 after the banking sector reforms that separated policy-oriented investments and financing activities from the state-owned commercial banks. See Pei (1998).

29 Yu, Mu, "Gang fa renminbi zhaiquan Hu-Wen zen pansuan" (How President Hu and Premier Wen assess renminbi bond issuance in Hong Kong), *Hong Kong Economic Times*, January 11, 2007.

30 The term "dim sum bond" originated from a Standard Chartered report in October 2010, a few years after the first issuance in 2007. See Shettigar et al. (2010).

31 Henry Sanderson, " 'Panda' Bond Sellers Authorized to Send Money Home by China Government," *Bloomberg News*, September 30, 2010, www.bloomberg.com/news/2010–09–30/-panda-bond-sellers-authorized-to-send-money-home-by-china-government.html.

32 Since 2009, for example, most bonds offer coupon rates between 1.5% and 2.0%, 210 basis points (2.1%) lower than the average of the onshore market.

33 Nethelie Wong and Clare Jim, "China launches offshore yield curve as HK yuan market takes off," *Reuters*, November 30, 2010.

34 "NDRC promotes 'dim sum' bonds," *FT China Confidential*, January 11, 2012.

35 Wang, Duan and Liu Wei, "Xianggang shouhuo 'jinrong libao'" (Hong Kong received a 'financial red packet'), *Century Weekly*, no. 33, August 22, 2011.

36 "Ren zong yu Gang tu renminbi jiesuan" (Joseph Yam called for renminbi trade settlement), *Hong Kong Commercial Daily*, November 26, 2008.

37 Fu, Tingting and Yu Zhanhao, "Gang renminbi maoyi jiesuan haoshi jin" (Renminbi trade settlement is getting close), *Hong Kong Economic Times*, December 9, 2008.

38 "Renminbi moyi jiesuan zhu yinhang kuo xicha" (Renminbi trade settlement helps bank widen interest margin), *Hong Kong Economic Times*, December 18, 2008.

39 Deng, Zongjian, "Hu Gang jinsai 'kua jing' jiesuan cang xuanji" (Calculus behind Shanghai and Hong Kong's quest for cross-border settlement), *Hong Kong Economic Times*, April 10, 2009.

40 The four cities are Guangzhou, Dongguan, Shenzhen and Zhuhai.

41 Fu, Tingting, "Renminbi jieusn shuanggui bingxing" (Dual track arrangement in renminbi trade settlement), *Hong Kong Economic Times*, July 3, 2009.

42 Saikat Chatterjee, "CNH Tracker: Plodding toward internationalising the yuan," *Reuters*, June 23, 2011.

43 "Yinhang ren bi guosheng, jinguanju ju huhuan" (Banks hold excess renminbi, the HKMA refuses to offer swap arrangement), *Mingpao*, September 29, 2011.

44 Interview with Chinese Academy of Social Sciences researcher, Beijing, February 2012.

45 Lee, Wun-yip, "Tianjin jinrong daji huopi" (Tianjin's financial development plan approved), *Mingpao*, November 2, 2009.

46 "Shen chang hezuo dajian Ganggu zhitong che" (Shenzhen called for collaboration to build Through Train).

47 Yang, Tao, "Qianhai jinrong gaige you he butong" (How Qianhai financial reform differs), *Century Weekly*, no. 29, July 23, 2012.

48 "Qianhai fazhan kuajing daikuan Gang renbi chulu zeng" (Qianhai to develop cross-border loan, offshore renminbi has expanded channels), *Hong Kong Economic Journal*, April 13, 2012.

49 For more details, see HKEx, "RMB Currency Products," www.hkex.com.hk/eng/prod/drprod/rmb/rmbfut.htm.

50 Interview with PBOC Research Bureau researcher, Beijing, February 2012.

51 Calculated by pooling the rates provided by 15 local and international banks, the fixing gives the exchange rate between the US dollar and offshore renminbi, and the differentials between the CNY and CNH markets.

52 Fiona Law, "Hong Kong to Set Up Yuan Fixing Rate," *The Wall Street Journal*, May 14, 2011.

53 Katrina Nicholas, "Hong Kong's TMA Starts Publishing Dim Sum Loan Rates from Banks," *Bloomberg News*, January 4, 2012, www.bloomberg.com/news/2012–01–04/hong-kong-s-tma-starts-publishing-dim-sum-loan-rates-from-banks.html.

54 Jiang, Kaini, "Tui neidi changwai jiaoyi, gang jintui weigu" (Hong Kong caught in a dilemma in promoting OTC derivative trade), *Hong Kong Economic Journal*, November 21, 2011

55 Saikat Chatterjee and Rachel Armstrong, "China quietly tightening grip on offshore yuan market," *Reuters*, June 20, 2011.

56 "Changwai yansheng gonggu jiesuansuo, zui chi mingnian chengli" (OTC derivatives clearing house to be in operation next year at the latest), *Mingpao*, January 4, 2011.

57 Daniel O. Leary, "PBOC Queries NAFMII Int'l Doc Push," *Derivatives Week* 20, no. 47, November 28, 2011, pp. 1 and 12.

58 Cai, Zongqi, "Yao Gang: shishi tuichu xiao QFII shidian" (Yao Gang: Pilots of Mini-QFII introduced in appropriate time), *China Securities Journal*, December 2n 2010.

59 Interview with mainland securities professional, Beijing, February 2012; Wu, Xiaojing, "Xiao QFII huzhiyuchu zhupao jijin gongsi guoji hua buiju" (Mini-QFII is forthcoming, helps the internationalizing strategy of mainland fund companies), *Shanghai Securities News*, July 12, 2010.

60 Hannah Kuchler, "'Mini-QFII' to give Chinese brokers another advantage," *Financial Times Tilt*, July 6, 2011.

61 Wang and Liu, "Xianggang shouhuo 'jinrong libao'"

62 Zhou, Zixun, "Lilu shichang hua gaige de zuida zuli zai nail" (Where the biggest obstacles lie for interest rate liberalization), *Shanghai Securities News*, January 9, 2012.

63 Wang Lijuan, "Xinjiapo tanlu renminbi" (Singapore probing its way to renminbi), *Economy and Nations Weekly*, May 2, 2011. For a discussion of these historical precedents, see Frankel (2012).

64 Yu, Yong-ding, "Zangfou renminbi guojihua" (Appraising renminbi internationalization), *Century Weekly*, no. 1, January 2, 2012.

65 Zhou, Zixun, "Lilu shichang hua gaige shizai bixing" (Interest rate liberalization must come first), *Securities Times*, January 20, 2012.

66 Research Team of Statistics and Analysis Department, People's Bank of China, "Wo guo jiakuai ziben zhanghu kaifang tiaojian jiben chengshu" (China met basic conditions of accelerating capital account liberalization), *China Securities Journal*, February 23, 2012.

67 "RQFII chuqi shidian 200 yi yuan edu quanbu xifa" (20 billion of initial RQFII quota all approved), *Shanghai Securities News*, January 30, 2012.

68 Interview with PBOC Monetary Policy Department II official, Beijing, July 2015.

69 Yu, Mu, "Reqian liuchu Zhongguo qizhi chongji renminbi" (Hot money leaving China weakens not only renminbi), *Hong Kong Economic Times*, May 25, 2012.

70 China missed the IMF review in 2010 and passed the assessment in November 2015. For details, see Prasad (2016), pp. 141–9.

71 Yu, Mu, "Zou zi 2 wan yi, Waiguanju yuyan youzhi" (SAFE hesitated to acknowledge a two trillion capital flight), *Hong Kong Economic Times*, March 2, 2013.

72 Saikat Chatterjee, "Hong Kong cracks down on illegal money flows from China trade," *Reuters*, May 4, 2016.

73 Following Hong Kong, Macau was made the second offshore renminbi clearing center in 2004. The true internationalizing moment, however, came between 2012 and 2014, when Taipei, Singapore, London, Frankfurt, Seoul, Toronto and other foreign financial centers concluded agreements with the PBOC and started handling renminbi transactions.

6   Conclusion

This study advances a coalitional politics explanatory framework for the puzzling policy trajectory surrounding three cases of China's financial opening after the end of the twentieth century. It reveals how opening advocates—pro-opening local governments, financial industry interests, and central bureaucratic actors—acted at different stages of policymaking, including when shaping policy tendencies and opening outcomes. This chapter summarizes the major findings and highlights the work's contribution to, and implications for, the understanding of Chinese political economy and IPE, before turning to a discussion of the possibilities for future research.

Major findings of the three episodes

The book demonstrates that the policymaking process of China's financial opening has been far less "elitist" or "centralist" than the previous literature has described. A diverse set of actors has been involved, each playing parts in different policymaking stages. Notably, local authorities and financial industry interests have been important actors originating and promoting liberalizing initiatives in policy formation, and then partnering with central bureaucratic actors in the deliberation and implementation of policy. Together, the opening advocates have constituted pro-opening policy coalitions that have advanced liberalizing agendas and engaged in leverage and concessionary politics. Variation in these political dynamics has engendered different policy tendencies and opening outcomes.

Outbound equity investment regime

The evolution of the outbound equity investment regime was subject to alternating policy tendencies and outcomes. Stasis in the early 2000s was broken by the QDII program, an institutional investment channel, and by the hurriedly timetabled departure of the Through Train. The scheme, however, was canceled within months and left investors with only QDII until late 2011, when overseas ETFs underwritten with Hong Kong equities were introduced to the mainland bourses. The Stock Connects scheme, which made possible two-way capital traffic between onshore and offshore bourses in a contained system, was introduced in late 2014. To date, however, direct and unimpeded access to offshore equity investment via QDII2 or a Through Train-like scheme remains impossible for normal Chinese investors.

Hong Kong-based interests were at the center of all the different liberalizing initiatives, but not all were successful. By themselves, the sound financial grounds and concessionary offers of the pro-opening coalition did not result in QDII, since it aroused dissent onshore due to conflicting policy priorities and political ends. It was not until the mid-2000s, when the offshore community reframed the initiative as a means of addressing pressing domestic economic challenges, that QDII gained support from the PBOC and financial regulators. It was subsequently launched in 2006.

For similar reasons the Through Train scheme, championed by the offshore community, was initially endorsed by NDRC, PBOC and SAFE in 2007. This group constituted a strong pro-opening coalition, catalyzed by the convergence of multiple parties. The bureaucratic actors sought the quick relief of economic overheating and saw in Hong Kong's quest a policy remedy. They were joined by Tianjin and the Bank of China, who were viewed as prospective onshore hosts in the Through Train's early stages. Concessionary moves designed to assuage other localities and banks and seek their support, however, were thwarted by opposition from financiers, the bureaucracy, and interventions from top party state decision makers alarmed by the systemic risks the Chinese economy confronted. This stopped the Through Train and reversed the opening quest; QDII remained the only *de jure* channel for outbound equity investment.

After the financial crisis, multiple local initiatives for Through Train-like schemes failed to elicit bureaucratic support. This illustrated the limit of local governments' lobbying, and showed that endeavors must be backed by financial industry interests and bureaucratic patrons to succeed. Hong Kong's interests then turned to overseas ETFs as an alternative to the Through Train, and it was hoped that the scheme would offer indirect exposure to overseas equities products for mainland bourses without the need to ease cross-border capital flows. Although this did not interest the securities regulator, which did not see the capital market as ready for the new species and was concerned about the potential risks, the offshore community found patronage from the PBOC thanks to its efforts to define the initiative as an outgrowth of the offshore renminbi market. To obtain the CSRC's support, the opening advocates agreed to eligibility restrictions which provided for the exclusive participation of onshore brokers and barred their offshore counterparts despite their financial expertise.

Although this catalyzed the debut of overseas ETFs in 2011, it demonstrated that viable policy initiatives serving the interests of investors do not necessarily survive the policy process. This was evident again in the CSRC and PBOC's attempt to launch QDII2 after 2013. Despite strong market expectations, onshore local interests competing to spearhead the initiative complicated implementation. Worse still, heightening policy risks in 2015 due to the domestic economic slowdown forced the shelving of QDII2. However, as QDII2 was stalled, there was a breakthrough in access to offshore equity thanks to the offshore community's endeavors to pioneer mutual market access that made possible two-way equity investment flows between offshore and onshore exchanges.

The Stock Connect proposal gained broad support from Shanghai- and Shenzhen-based interests, and won the backing of the CSRC and PBOC due to the anticipated material and political gains. The PBOC particularly welcomed the scheme because it promoted the renminbi's international investment uses without increasing the associated policy risks. This catalyzed the launch of the Shanghai– and Shenzhen–Hong Kong Stock Connects in November 2014 and December 2016, respectively.

Internationalizing China's stock market

The Shanghai authorities, bourse and onshore securities industry were the primary constituents of a pro-opening coalition that called for the internationalizing of China's domestic stock market after the turn of the century. Early calls for a red-chip homecoming were followed by a fanfare announcing the coming of an international board that stoked expectations and these were further heightened by the ostensible political support of the central and local authorities. Hopes were dashed, though, when that support was withdrawn.

Motivated by hopes of boosting the city's status as China's leading financial hub, the Shanghai-led interests called for the secondary listing of Hong Kong's red-chip firms on their local exchange. The initiative was endorsed by the CSRC, which was eager to elevate Shanghai's bourse to the status of the country's main board in the early 2000s. The opening call, however, was complicated by technical concerns as well as by the failure of the opening advocates to broker consensus when they found it hard to compromise with dissenting parties.

The initiative did not miscarry completely at that point, however, because Shanghai made red-chip homecoming an integral part of its new pursuit for an international board in the mid-2000s. This generated even stronger interest from the securities regulator despite divergent views on the appropriate regulatory standards for the listing of foreign firms in China. Central elites weighed in after the subprime credit crisis, and came to view the international board as an important symbol of capital market internationalization that might make Shanghai China's international financial center. This showed how local authorities and financiers could manipulate issue linkages in their favor: through re-linking the red-chip homecoming to local capital market development and subsequently the pursuit of internationalization, Shanghai's initiatives had received the blessing of top decision makers and been accelerated.

To garner broader support, the Shanghai-based interests and the CSRC geared themselves to working out particulars and leveraging foreign financiers to actualize their agenda. Continuing rhetoric hinting at the imminent launch of the board after 2011 stoked wider market anticipation, but this did little to resolve the lingering challenges from Shenzhen and Hong Kong that weakened

Shanghai's pursuit, or the disagreements over important technical matters like the method of listing, accounting standards and the pricing currency of shares.

The unyielding stance of the Shanghai and CSRC-led coalition over these issues wasted opportunities to solicit wider political support within the financial bureaucracy. As a result, the apparent consensus maintained by the pro-opening coalition broke down. Furthermore, the push for the international board was complicated by the unready state of regulation and the weakening political commitment of the PBOC and SAFE. This highlighted the importance of concessionary offers by pro-opening coalitions: although they did not guarantee success in every case, the failure to extend concessions over technical and implementation specifics invariably bred stronger dissent and opposition.

The opening advocates also saw their agenda called into question after late 2011, when the domestic economy appeared to be heading toward a crisis. The international board and the red-chip homecoming began to be considered untimely and an aggravating risk to the domestic financial system. This eventually rolled back Shanghai's entire liberalizing venture and it no longer found any place in central or local discussions. Its reversal also pointed to the limits of relying on the top decision-making elites to bring about the opening advocates' desires. Their endorsement had not guaranteed a smoother, less contested policy deliberation or a transition to implementation.

The endeavors of recent years to resurrect the international board also failed to make headway. The Shanghai–Hong Kong Stock Connect, launched in late 2014, represented a de facto substitute for the international board, as it provided mainland investors with access to shares of non-local companies and red-chip firms with little easing of Beijing's regulatory parameters. The decade-long quest for the internationalizing of the Shanghai stock market finally came to an end.

The offshore renminbi market in Hong Kong

The Hong Kong authorities and financiers were indispensable opening advocates for the world's first offshore renminbi center after the turn of the century. They forged crucial aspects of renminbi internationalization and made dramatic advances in the second half of the first decade. Unlike the two episodes of equity market liberalization, they witnessed a punctuated policy trajectory—early individual renminbi businesses were rolled out slowly followed by exponential growth in offshore bond and trade settlement schemes and then uneven but gradual advances in the equity and derivatives markets and increasing connections between the offshore and onshore renminbi markets.

The offshore community constituted the pro-opening coalition that was instrumental in advancing the liberalizing initiatives. Its endeavors in the early part of the century, motivated by prospective financial gains, failed to obtain any central support. It was not until the discussion of economic agreement between the mainland and Hong Kong—CEPA—that the idea of creating an offshore renminbi center resurfaced. Resistance from onshore parties, notably Shanghai-based interests concerned about their market status being compromised and bureaucratic actors wary of the policy risk entailed, sidetracked the initiative.

In response, the offshore community scaled down its ambitions and redefined the initiative as a set of supporting measures essential to CEPA, instead of as advances in the offshore renminbi center per se. With the backing of the PBOC and SAFE, individual renminbi businesses were introduced. Although the re-framing of the quest resulted in a suboptimal outcome for the offshore community, it did help kick-start renminbi business and maintain Hong Kong's first-mover advantage.

The offshore opening advocates went on to immediately press for renminbi bond issuance but encountered conflicting policy priorities at the finance ministry and NDRC, which had higher regard for the onshore fixed income market and were also deterred by the absence of related regulation. To address these concerns, the Hong Kong and PBOC-led coalition made several important concessions, including giving the NDRC the authority to determine the scale of issuance, and it gathered support from China's policy-oriented banks that were interested in the initiative. This galvanized the birth of the offshore bond market in 2007 and was followed by the gradual lifting of restrictions in the post-crisis years as the initially dissenting bureaucratic parties became supportive of offshore bond market growth. Hong Kong's leading position originating and trading offshore renminbi bonds remained unmatched.

As China weathered the global crisis, Hong Kong's call for renminbi trade settlement found almost unanimous favor within the central financial bureaucracy. Despite Shanghai's challenge to Hong Kong, the offshore initiative stayed on course as the pro-opening coalition agreed to Shanghai serving as a parallel hub. This paved the way for the scheme's launch in July 2009. However, multiple tightening moves followed to preempt the potential dissent that might be caused by abuses of the program and malpractice among market participants. This underscored the imperative of concessionary politics among opening advocates, even though it sometimes necessitated a sharing of the rewards of the liberalizing quests with potential competitors. In fact, Hong Kong's acquiescence to Shanghai's pursuit of renminbi trade settlements did not end up weakening its niche; over the years, market forces reinforced its leading status.

Advances that went beyond fixed income products and trade settlements were complicated by subnational and intra-coalition dynamics. Whereas the spectacular growth of offshore renminbi business unsettled Shanghai and prompted the PBOC and NDRC to issue rhetorical support for the city, Tianjin and Shenzhen authorities and financiers actively supported the offshore opening advocates and pro-opening coalition, and embedded the offshore renminbi pursuit within local developmental agendas.

However, this did not do away with discord coming from within the Hong Kong and PBOC-led coalition. The offshore community and its central patrons disagreed on the pace of innovation beyond fixed income products, and technical matters like benchmark rates and the trading terms of derivatives. This undermined the political consensus and stasis ensued. Advances in equity markets, like overseas ETFs and renminbi-denominated stocks, were made possible in 2011 when the offshore parties agreed to largely confine involvement to onshore financiers, securing the CSRC's support.

Notwithstanding some doubts on the virtue of the larger renminbi internationalization agenda, the PBOC and offshore community succeeded in fostering connections between the offshore and onshore renminbi markets by way of careful capital flow management and liberalizing initiatives that facilitated inflow capital traffic. This enabled the offshore renminbi market to survive the domestic economic downturn after 2014 and Hong Kong continued to be the leading renminbi hub outside the mainland.

Policy mechanisms revisited

The three liberalizing episodes give us strong evidence for the three policy change mechanisms set out in Chapter 2. Although in reality they intertwined, their effects were quite discernible as each assumed a salience that varied during different policymaking stages. It is worth generalizing some observations and suggesting extensions.

Agenda-setting politics

Agenda setting was crucial to the formation of policy initiatives across the three cases. Consistent with Wang (2008) and Mertha (2009), actors outside the central authorities played the part of policy advocates. Although financial liberalization had been at the top of China's reform agenda since accession to the WTO, financial services opening apart, policy agendas and priorities regarding financial opening had rarely been pre-defined or managed to reach any consensus. This left ample leeway for domestic constituents to push ahead with varying aspects of financial opening and shape the policy agenda of the central authorities.

These endeavors rarely generated wider support unless they were defined or framed with an appealing "story plot" for the bureaucratic actors they were pitched to. The stances of those actors often depended on whether the policy initiatives might foster their political interests or help address their policy problems and associated policy risk. Bureaucratic actors tended to favor initiatives compatible with their policy priorities and agendas, and those that helped address the pressing challenges they were responsible for. Accordingly, Hong Kong's policy innovations were not always well-received, even when they were based on sound financial grounds. Those that thrived often did so when they were framed to have relevance for potential central patrons.

Similarly, local and financial pro-opening constituents could link opening initiatives to other policy issues of importance and interest to other policy actors; or de-link the schemes from concerns that might likely prompt dissent and opposition. The former is best exemplified by Shanghai's success in linking its pursuit of an international board with the intent of China's top leaders to promote stock market internationalization. For the latter, Hong Kong's man-euvers to disconnect its quest for individual renminbi business from the larger financial opening agenda allayed onshore dissent and obtained backing from the PBOC in the early 2000s.

Whereas agenda setting and framing were critical to the quests of opening advocates and coalitions, dissenting parties also resorted to these strategies when trying to undermine the liberalizing initiatives. The international board was derailed and fell from the central agenda when the NDRC and other agencies capitalized on the changing economic conditions and presented rival policy agendas. The offshore renminbi center faced uncertainties in 2011 when dis-senting parties portrayed a different outlook for renminbi internationalization that carried the implicit risk of compromising domestic financial stability, rather than promoting domestic reform. Dissenting bureaucratic actors also success-fully disputed the ability of the Through Train to handle economic overheating and used the enormous capital outflow following its announcement to undercut support for the initiative.

Leverage politics

In addition to agenda setting, leverage politics reinforced the political support that opening advocates might obtain when promoting their liberalizing agendas. This was indispensable for local and financial industry pro-opening interests within the three episodes: some went for institutional connections, while others counted on informal or previously existing ties. These coexisted and should not be seen in exclusive terms. Hong Kong's push for outbound equity investment conduits and offshore renminbi business, and Shanghai's international board ambitions, traveled through established channels of finan-cial bureaucracy. However, this does not discount the relevance of the informal connections among the constituents. The connections between Shanghai and CSRC officials undoubtedly boosted the appeal of the local initiative at the central level. The same factor also enabled the big leap in off-shore renminbi market development driven by Hong Kong and mainland monetary officials (Wang 2009; Cheung 2011).

Although it has not been possible to entirely disentangle the formal and informal threads underlying the connections between opening advocates, the importance of informal ties is best demonstrated by Tianjin's role as the first and leading onshore host of the Through Train scheme. This was largely due to the mayor's connections with the bureaucracy and top elites. Similarly, the lobbying of the policy banks for offshore renminbi bonds was led by politically well-connected executives and this helped elicit the backing of the top elites.

By contrast, the absence of a central patron invariably meant an opening quest was doomed. The failure of local advocates to revive the Through Train after its reversal and the multiple bourses that called for overseas ETFs are exem-plars of such cases. ETFs only gained traction after Hong Kong secured the PBOC's support. On the other hand, Shenzhen's abortive rally for a secondary international board exemplified the interdependent nature of local and financial industry interests. A financier-led initiative could hardly even gain a foothold on the policy agenda if it lacked a local sponsor.

As was the case with agenda-setting politics, dissenting parties also leveraged their connections to undercut opening initiatives. Across the three cases, onshore financiers capitalized on their connections with regulators to undercut the liberalizing attempts championed by the pro-opening coalition. This was most evident in the Through Train turnabout, where the leading banking, securities and asset management firms petitioned against the scheme. Dissenting bureaucratic actors also tapped their connections with top elites to strengthen their attempts to challenge liberalizing agendas, especially when scenarios of systemic risk were envisaged. This helps explain the demise of the Through Train and Shanghai's international board, as well as the slowdown of offshore market growth

Concessionary politics

To allay dissent, opening advocates engage in concessionary politics during policy deliberation and implementation. As China specialists adhering to the fragmented authoritarian perspective affirm, concessionary moves are essential to the buildup of consensus among policy actors because they represent the cost of obtaining support from other parties during the bargaining process (Halpern 1992; Lampton 1992; Shirk 1992). This study finds that concessionary politics played a ubiquitous part in the three cases, and took two major forms: the adjustment of implementation specifics like scope, pace, location, and the technical particulars; and the political side-payments that made use of linkage between policy issues.

The former was frequently employed and often involved the scaling down of the liberalizing pursuit in response to dissenting voices whose support (or acquiescence at the very least) was critical to sustaining the agenda the opening advocates championed. Examples include the concessions offered by the offshore community regarding the eligibility requirements of the Through Train and overseas ETFs, as well as the scope of offshore renminbi business in the early years. Concessionary offers that might expand the liberalizing scale usually targeted interested localities and financiers, not only to preempt dissent, but also to obtain wider support. This was illustrated in the promise of the Through Train coalition to expand the scheme to other interested onshore financial hubs and banks. Hong Kong's acquiescence to Shanghai operating a parallel renminbi trade settlement route and the mutual market access roadmap underpinning the Stock Connects are two examples of successfully expanding the win-set of financial opening.

Concessions over regulatory and technical standards were equally important for opening advocates hoping to obtain support or deflect dissent from inside and outside the pro-opening coalitions. The success of Hong Kong in adopting SHIBOR as the pricing benchmark and deferring to the NDRC the authority to define the scale of the dim sum bond issuance made possible its takeoff. By contrast, Shanghai's insistence on technical particulars like the method of listing and accounting standards for foreign firms in the latter phase of the international board deliberations only engendered stronger resistance.

Political side-payments that involved exchanges of support on several issues were occasionally employed as a concessionary strategy. Notably, Shanghai and Hong Kong engaged in such a *quid pro quo* exercise as part of their respective liberalizing pursuits. While the offshore community was unsettled by the accelerating momentum of the international board in the late 2000s, it acquiesced to Shanghai's quest in exchange for support for offshore market development. Although it is unclear why the strategy was relatively under-utilized, a plausible reason could be that policy actors found it difficult to link up two (or more) issues that might promise a similar, if not equal, exchange of political support.

Although concessionary offers could not ward off all disagreement, failure to make them invariably resulted in stronger dissent—as illustrated by the fall of the international board. The case also highlights the importance of the intra-coalition dynamics in concessionary politics. Before extending any offers, constituents of the pro-opening coalition at least had to agree on the extent of accommodation with dissenting parties. Preemptive regulatory moves to tighten the renminbi trade settlement scheme represented one successful case; Shanghai's reluctance to adjust its preferred technicalities and the resultant alienation of bureaucratic actors during the deliberations surrounding the international board are at the other extreme.

Lastly, the three cases reveal how differentiating the ingredients underlying the consensus building process helps us to understand the shifting stances of actors during deliberations. While the convergence of policy outlook among policy actors was important, this did not take precedence over the pursuit of shared interest or agreed policy priorities (and technical matters). In fact, the lack or weakening of these often weakened the consensus originating from shared policy outlooks. The political commitment of the PBOC and top elites to the international board, for example, was eroded by conflicting policy priorities in late 2011. This was also the case during renminbi internationalization when the NDRC, MOF, and some within the PBOC became reserved.

Indeed, technical issues were equally, if not more, important to political concerns. Their importance, however, has often been underappreciated. Since agreements over financial standards and regulatory issues were rarely in place, concessions within the coalition and with other policy actors were essential to driving the liberalizing initiatives. The lack or weakening of technical consensus also "spilled over" to undermine political consensus. This was exemplified during both the pursuit of an international board, and the attempts to advance beyond fixed income products in the offshore renminbi market that caused the unraveling of central political commitments.

Contributions to and implications for Chinese political economy

This study contributes in several ways to the literature on Chinese political economy. It reveals the pluralistic nature of the financial policymaking process, sheds light on the importance of formal institutional setups and party apparatus, and provides an analytical basis for understanding the seemingly peculiar trajectory of China's financial opening.

Although China's financial policymaking is always seen as a process in which the central bureaucracy and top party state elites assume a decision-making preponderance, the roles of local governments and financial industries in the different policymaking stages deserve more attention. Their involvement in advancing liberalizing initiatives, seeking political support and engaging in concessionary moves suggests that analyses attending to the financial industry and, more importantly, underappreciated local dimensions might yield more explanatory leverage. This can already be seen in the emerging body of literature surrounding China's exchange rates politics and renminbi internationalization that attempts to shed some light on the domestic black box (Helleiner and Malkin 2012; Steinberg and Shih 2012).

Instead of focusing on a specific policy actor, the coalition politics perspective considers the different domestic constituents and illustrates their interplay and relevance to policy formation, deliberation, and implementation. Motivated by shared interests, the policy actors coalesced into issue-based coalitions that drove policy changes by way of shaking up policy agendas and problem definitions, building support through formal and informal connections, and offering concessions at different policymaking stages.

Even though central bureaucratic actors are assumed to have been of great importance in nearly all studies of China's politics of finance, this study qualifies such views and presents a more nuanced understanding of the role of the financial bureaucracy throughout the policymaking process. Such actors do not monopolize the process, but they are open to the initiatives of local and financial interests in policy formation. Even in the deliberation and implementation phases, they partner with local and financial industry constituents to work out implementation specifics and, more importantly, any leeway to be used as accommodations during concessionary politics inside and outside the pro-opening coalition in the knowledge that policy change is not possible without successfully addressing the concerns of dissenting parties during policy deliberation.

Nonetheless, the policy preferences and positions of central bureaucratic actors are not pre-determined, as the customary analytical schema presumes. Distributional implications and policy risk concerns are found to shape central policymakers' preferences and no agency fits neatly under the "reformer" or "conservative" label. Although these labels provide a general contour to China's financial bureaucracy, they only account for a little of the changing positions of central actors during varying aspects of financial opening. One only needs to consider the dramatic departures from the policy status quo in the three cases considered, where so-called conservative agents such as the NDRC strongly backed and pioneered their own liberalizing initiatives.

Regarding China's financial industry interests, this study affirms their influence over the promotion of financial opening, but it goes beyond the literature's usual focus on the banking industry. It finds that active roles were played by the securities industry and local exchanges whose influence not only maintained clientelist ties with the regulators, but was boosted by local government support and policy initiatives. The analysis of financiers' interests and their connections with bureaucratic actors also points to the need to consider the intra-financial industry dynamics, in which competition between the different financial industries was often more intense than that between foreign and domestic financiers during China's opening (Hsueh 2011).

More importantly, the book demonstrates that the local authorities of financial hubs were indispensable to driving China's financial opening, often even featuring in discussions of FDI promotion and in the "race for the money" narratives of their wishes to become financial centers (Yang 1997; Zweig 2002; Jarvis 2011). The subnational authorities initiated liberalizing agendas, worked with financiers and central bureaucratic patrons, and managed dissenting views through political maneuvers. This challenges the top-down paradigm of China's central and local relations that often assumes the central authorities to be the primary originator of policy initiative and the local interests to be merely the implementation agents of central government mandates. As Heilmann (2009: 458) remarks: "it is precisely the dialectical interplay between dispersed local initiative and central policymaking—maximum tinkering under the shadow of hierarchy—that has made China's economic governance so adaptive and innovative."

The book also raises questions about the importance of formal bureaucratic arrangements and reveals how policy changes were introduced by coalitions and their constituents. Often financial opening initiatives, successful or not, did not travel through or adhere to formal institutional conduits between local financiers and central authorities. Although formal institutions certainly constitute an important locus of policymaking driven by the pro-opening coalitions and constituents, shifts of policy tendencies, especially drastic changes, can hardly be made sense of with only reference to them.

In most cases, the formal bureaucratic setups defined the scope of the political and policy activities of central bureaucratic actors during policymaking, and provided readily available channels for local and financial industry interests to advance their own agendas and seek support. But these were by no means the only possibilities for bottom-up liberalizing initiatives. While Hong Kong and Shanghai went through the relatively "established" conduits in their pursuit of offshore currency business and the international board, these were always supplemented by informal political connections between the central elites, bureaucratic patrons, and local and financial industry interests. This did not just help the pro-opening local and financial constituents secure central support, it also enabled the central agency to demonstrate its liberalizing intent with a readily available partner for policy deliberation and implementation.

In contrast, Hong Kong's early quest to create an outbound equity investment channel went through the defined channels and reached the securities regulator but did not generate any opening momentum. It was only the interest of the central bank that galvanized its eventual launch in the mid-2000s. Similarly, overseas ETFs and Stock Connects gained traction due to the backing of the PBOC, which saw these initiatives as complementary to its renminbi internationalization agenda. This suggests that the formal division between central bureaucratic actors does not restrict the scope of their endeavors as "policy producers." As the Through Train episode reveals, even though the NDRC was not vested with any officially defined portfolio of securities market development, it sidetracked the regulator introducing the scheme.

The emphasis of the state's apparatus, however, does not negate the importance of China's party machinery. The three opening episodes provide some suggestive evidence that indicates how the top party elites shaped policy trajectories by providing general guidance on policy orientation or endorsing decisions made by bureaucratic actors. They assumed a more active, if not interventionist, role when the country faced heightened policy risks during financial opening, catalyzing the reversal of any liberalizing momentum.

Finally, the book demonstrates that China's financial opening defies a simplistic (and essentialist) characterization with such labels as "gradualist" and "experimentalist," which imply a certain "policy style" of the country, if there ever was one. Although such labels continue to find some place in the discussions of officials, they appear to be a stereotype that is used to reinforce government rhetoric surrounding implementation, rather than a true depiction of reality. The typology of policy tendencies—opening, reversal and stasis—which this study advances goes beyond the tendency to see these possibilities in isolation, and enables a systematic examination of the political economic conditions by which the status quo and capital restriction are maintained and how opening might be made possible.

Contributions to and implications for IPE

In addition to implications for Chinese political economy, this study contributes to the IPE literature in several ways. First, it offers a systemic exposition of China's experience of financial opening, an area of inquiry that is curiously sparse. Apart from the entry of foreign firms after WTO accession and, recently, the global implications of renminbi internationalization, the larger development of other aspects of the financial market seems to have evaded the attention of most IPE researchers. Analyses of the policy initiatives that attempted to open up outbound equity investment channels and promote stock market internationalization as presented in Chapters 3 and 4 go some way to filling the empirical void.

Second, the involvement of domestic constituents beyond the central bureaucracy and the dynamics of changing policy tendencies shed light on the enduring questions of the domestic-international nexus in IPE and have a bearing on several segments of the IPE literature. The "inside-out" coalitional politics account of this study suggests that external actors like foreign financial institutions and governments have little independent or direct effect on shaping the policy trajectory of China's financial opening, and the three cases represent activity driven largely by endogenous forces. This, however, does not mean domestic actors were completely insulated from the influence of foreign actors or the international context. Rather, they intertwined with the domestic unfolding indirectly by way of pro-opening constituents within China, especially those based offshore in Hong Kong, and they catalyzed changes through the shaping of the calculus of policy actors at critical junctures like external crises.

While some of the early liberalizing proposals were the brainchild of foreign financiers based offshore, they had to find appeal among onshore constituents before becoming part of the policy agenda. The lobbying of foreign financiers in concert with local authorities and financiers did not add much weight to forces that aimed to change the policy outcome—as exemplified in the push for the international board. This lends support to studies assessing the relevance of foreign actors at work in China's financial development and runs counter to the structural perspectives that place great emphasis on the effect of market forces and the leverage of IFIs and powerful states (Bottelier 2007; Schlichting 2008).

Moreover, the three cases show that external crises exerted varying effects on opening initiatives. Endeavors to bring about outbound equity investment experienced reversal due to the subprime credit crunch, whereas the momentum of inbound securities issuance and renminbi internationalization actually accelerated in the post-crisis setting, when the central bureaucratic actors and elites changed their perceptions and assessments of the opening initiatives. This supports studies that see external financial crises as stimuli for policy adjustments and change in China (Wang 1999; Yang 2011, 2015; Breslin 2012). Even though crisis events did not break down political obstacles completely, they shaped decision makers' preferences and the political priorities of financial opening and therefore helped speed up the process (Haggard and Maxfield 1996; MacIntyre, Pempel, and Ravenhill 2008; Martinez-Diaz 2009).

This also calls into question the state-level explanations of the state's selective opening. Although determinants like China's strong economic fundamentals might account for the "residual controls" of the domestic financial system, they fail to capture the uneven liberalizing tendencies in financial opening (Lukauskas and Minushkin 2000). Analyses based on policy sequencing and sectoral characteristics similarly miss the variation of levels of openness within the financial sector and underlying policy shifts (Thurbon 2001; Ploberger 2009; Hsueh 2011). This necessitates investigation at the domestic level that goes beyond the unitary state assumption and brings together the multiplicity of local and financial industry interests as drivers (and dissenters) of financial opening.

Third, this study affirms the relevance of an interest-based analysis in the domestic approach of IPE and suggests that the preferences of domestic actors in China need not be specified (and pre-determined) entirely with reference to country-specific factors like political orientation and standings peculiar to the

Chinese setting. Across the three cases, central level, pro-opening Chinese officials were motivated by their self-serving concerns in a similar manner to the experiences of other "interventionist" states. They promoted opening for their private ends and responded to the demands of their constituents (Loriaux et al. 1997; Perez 1997).

Yet, unlike the customary understanding in the literature that seldom disputes the primacy of officials in decision making, their leverage as "change agents" was far from constant or uniform throughout the policy process. Even though they might have been crucial in the deliberation phase, much in policy formation and implementation involved and depended upon constituents outside the financial bureaucracy. This shows that existing assessments of Chinese bureaucratic interplay and the connections with financial outreach are at best incomplete and have overlooked equally important stakeholders.

The coalition perspective addresses this shortfall and expands the analytical coverage to the financial industry and, more importantly, local dimensions. It also explores how the different domestic actors interacted and took part in collective pursuits of financial opening. The initiatives of the securities firms and local bourses featured across the three cases demonstrate the promise of financial industry analysis within IPE scholarship, yet it also points to the imperative of differentiating the different financial industry interest groups—instead of seeing the sector as a homogenous group—that might enable a better understanding of important developments like renminbi internationalization, in which the non-banking financiers have received little attention from researchers (Sobel 1994; Lavelle 2001; Helleiner and Malkin 2012).

Finally, the importance of local authorities as the policy drivers of financial opening puts the "local state" back into the literature and echoes calls to "rescale" the analytical focus of IPE to a subnational dimension. As Verdier (2002) and Paul (2005) show, intergovernmental dynamics are integral to a complete understanding of financial development and internationalization. This study extends their findings and concludes that China is no exception.

Avenues for future research

This section discusses avenues of further enquiry based on the book's implications for the IPE and Chinese political economy literature. The study's findings and analytical framework point to several areas for future research. In addition to examining China's financial opening experience, the framework might illuminate important domestic capital market developments since the 2000s and generate nuanced analyses of domestic financial industry interests that go beyond the banks. The analytical focus on subnational entities and financiers might also make possible comparative exercises that go beyond China.

Relevance to domestic financial liberalization

The three episodes of financial opening illustrated in this study involve attempts to bring about cross-border capital flows and connections between domestic and international markets. Even for "difficult cases" like currency internationalization, subnational and financial interests wielded considerable influence in defining the policy agenda and shaping the ways the opening initiative was configured and implemented. Students of Chinese political economy should therefore extend the analysis to the domestic aspect of financial liberalization.

Indeed, it would be unsurprising to see similar dynamics if analysts turn to developments at home. One only needs to consider the evolution of the domestic equity market to stumble across some suggestive evidence. In the mid-1980s, stock exchanges emerged largely free from the influence of central authorities thanks to the sanctions (and backing) of local governments acting in the interests of the local economy (Walter and Howie 2001, 2006; Green 2004). Though this early history could be discounted in view of the complete absence of a regulatory apparatus at the time, the proliferation of local financing platforms and exchanges in recent years that are beyond the influence of the central authorities appears to be a replay of the episode.

Similarly, the emergence of China's high-tech financing platforms reveals a similar pattern to the three financial opening cases examined here. Shenzhen-based interests pushed the agenda, sought the support of bureaucratic actors, engaged in give-and-take with dissenting parties from the early 2000s, and found success after lengthy deliberations. Initiatives since the late 2000s to create an OTCBB (briefly described in Chapter 4) also involved multiple local and financial industry interests, each trying to shape the central policymaking process. Domestic financial liberalization experiences like these are significant not only in policy terms but also, given their bearing on the development of China's informal and hybrid financial sectors, in terms of providing an empirical basis to better understand the politics of financial development by examining the subnational and financial industry dynamics (Li and Hsu 2009; Allen et al. 2013).

Toward finer analyses of financial industry interests

This study shows the imperative of differentiating financial interests in any future study of China's political economy. The focus on banking institutions is understandable, given their preponderance, but it overlooks emerging classes of financiers, including the securities industries and stock exchanges featured in all three cases examined here.

More specifically, existing studies have tended to see the prevailing influence of the state over domestic financial firms, arguing that the state continues to exercise significant leverage through personnel control (the *nomenklatura* system) and majority shareholdings (Burns 1994; Brødsgaard 2012). This, however, neglects—if not dismisses—the other roles that firms might assume as publicly listed companies with increasing overseas footprints. The fact that they are owned by states does not necessarily translate into a tenable view that preferences within the financial sector are monolithic. Accordingly, perhaps it is more accurate and fruitful to examine varying degrees of tension between these competing "identities"—market player and business agent of the state—as analysts delve into the different financial industries such as banks, securities firms and bourses.

The latter two are particularly interesting cases given their dependence on local authorities. Unlike large state-owned banks with national networks (and stakes), very often brokerages anchor in certain financial hubs and draw business from the firms of certain geographic areas. They also maintain close connections with bourses grounded at a local level. Even those on the mainland are under the "vertical" management of the securities regulator, and over decades they have formed strong and mutualistic ties with local authorities and operated beyond the specified confines granted by the regulator. For an internationally oriented bourse like that of Shanghai, its overseas outreach raises the possibilities of preferences and behaviors beyond those the existing literature has envisaged. In contrast, the offshore bourse in Hong Kong has experienced an increasing tension in its identity— it is a publicly listed entity under the shadow of the Chinese authorities. These multiple dimensions and considerations among financiers highlight the need for a more context-specific assessment when trying to understand political and policy outcomes (Helleiner and Pagliari 2011: 179).

In fact, as Woll (2008) shows, business interests are socially "constructed" and seldom immutable and pre-defined. Often, they confront uncertain environments and have multiple understandings of their beliefs and identities that go beyond the image of revenue maximizers in the market. Hence, IPE and China studies scholarship might find much benefit in an appreciation of the variation of policy beliefs among financiers, and the strategic environments the different industries confront that result in a diversity of preferences and strategies.

Comparative exercises beyond China

Relatedly, a turn to different types of financiers and financial hubs promises comparative exercises across national settings. Despite this study's focus on China's experience, the Chinese experience should not be regarded as unique or seen in essentialist terms. The pluralistic nature of financial policymaking suggests that the motivations of domestic constituents and the way they shape policy process are not as peculiar and "Chinese" as they seem.

Not only were they like the trajectories of other policy domains, they were also part and parcel of other decision contexts. Strategies of defining and framing issues and political side-payments made possible by issue linkages, for instance, have been a common politicking practice in democratic settings. This implies that there is great promise in the disaggregation of China into smaller subnational analytical units. As Kasza (2011: 187) remarks:

> In future one might hope to see more research that compares China to other countries by employing subnational units of comparison. Once the object of study becomes one factory or stock exchange, one city or region, or one foreign-owned enterprise or bank in each of several countries, the range of appropriate cases will expand far beyond countries of similar size.

Along such avenues of research design, local financial hubs and bourses are two plausible examples of underappreciated analytical units (except Lavelle 2001; Paul 2005). A turn to these domestic policy actors might give rise to a more nuanced understanding of policy trajectory and outcomes by centering studies at the local or financial industry level of analysis. For instance, instead of comparing the aggregate Chinese and Indian experience (Sharma 2009; Allen et al. 2010), exploration of the nexus between financial hubs, financiers and stock exchanges in the two national contexts might reveal little-known subnational dynamics. This would not only contribute to IPE scholarship, it would also relate to the largely forgotten tradition among economic historians of considering the interplay between financial centers, industry, and national power (Kindleberger 1974; Cassis 2010; Quennouelle-Corre and Cassis 2011).

China's Integration with the global capital market

This study casts light on a broader issue surrounding China's integration and nexus with the global capital market. Although the country is increasingly integrated with the global capital market and is actively involved in the governance of global finance, this has barely compromised the Chinese state's policy autonomy and agency of domestic constituents.

The significant expansion of foreign footprints in the financial services sector since the 2000s did not galvanize any substantial easing of capital flows. Even though foreign financiers and governments might have hoped to leverage the opportunity to pry open China's capital control regime, such efforts largely turned out to be futile. Chinese officials repeatedly maintained that they conceived of no connection between the financial sector opening and the easing of capital transactions. As a matter of fact, under the International Monetary Fund's (IMF) purview, China faces no *de jure* commitment like that of the WTO accession agreement, nor has it sought use of the Fund's resources since the 1990s as other regional economies have. It is therefore unsurprising that the IFI could do little to mold Beijing's stance except to exercise its surveillance and advisory roles (Helleiner and Momani 2014; Momani 2015).

Indeed, what Jacobson and Oksenberg (1990: 18) depicted regarding China's engagement with the Fund in the 1980s still appears to be true. In their view, Chinese officials tended to "reject *demands* by outside agencies to undertake changes but also … accept outside *advice* when the advice seemed appropriate" because of their "sense of pride, greatness, and self-confidence" (emphasis in original). In the context in which the country now stands as the world's second largest economy, these tendencies have invariably been exaggerated during its dealing with IFIs. More importantly, the changing assessment of capital controls by the IMF in the post-subprime crisis setting has arguably (and ironically) strengthened the Chinese position of adhering to the status quo and pursuing financial opening after its own fashion (Gallagher 2012, 2015).

This, however, is not to deny the influence of foreign actors and changing international contexts. Yet, unlike other aspects like current account and financial services openings, the three cases demonstrate that their effects have been far from imposing. Although foreign financiers sometimes raise specific demands, in no instances have domestic constituents been subjected to binding commitments that compel them to introduce the liberalizing initiatives. Instead, their moves have often been enabled or reinforced by external actors and undergone development in indirect ways.

As reviewed in earlier sections, foreign actors have offered important partnerships to pro-opening domestic constituents and outlined the vision and policy options of what the initiatives would entail. Critical junctures like WTO accession and external crises have been "windows of opportunity," catalyzing changes by altering the preferences of domestic actors and, for opening advocates specifically, providing grounds for defining and framing the opening initiatives in ways that were essential in the quest for wider support. Indeed, domestic actors continue to maintain considerable policy and political autonomy over whether to capitalize on external developments like crises, the relative decline of others, or use of the special niche enjoyed by Hong Kong.

The city occupies a special niche connecting socialist China and the global capital market (Meyer 2000; Chiu and Lui 2009; Donald 2014). It has facilitated the opening initiatives of onshore change agents by proffering policy ideas and financial knowhow to onshore local authorities, financial industry interests, and central financial policymakers since the early 2000s. This, in turn, has shaped the ideational and technical parameters of China's decade of financial opening. Even in the seemingly domestic unfolding of the international board, the offshore financiers indirectly shaped the menu of policy choice available to the onshore actors, informing them of the technical feasibility and political economic constraints of their policy quests.

More importantly to China as a whole, Hong Kong represents a "safety valve" that affords the pro-opening agents room to advance their liberalizing agendas and onshore dissenters the space to find assurance that the liberalizing moves are external (if not completely isolated) from the mainland's political economy. This is best evidenced by the renminbi internationalization championed by the central bank and, to a lesser extent, the Through Train scheme which the NDRC and SAFE sponsored. In this context, Hong Kong serves as a "filter" for policy ideas that gives the pro-opening onshore actors the ability to select and moderate, if not shield against and resist, the external pressures of capital market opening.

China's state and financial power

The Chinese experience of financial opening necessitates further pondering of its prospects as a rising international financial power. As this study demonstrates, the country's outreach to the global market is not driven primarily by market forces, but by state agents and the private interests close to them. Although equity market liberalization and currency internationalization are only two of the many aspects of financial opening, they show that changes are tied to a multitude of domestic constituents and constrained by competing political economic imperatives. Even though renminbi internationalization has raised much alarm in the core economies, the changing policy tendencies and policy outcomes merely reflect its incoherence at home and affirm its role as a "reluctant challenger" (Drezner 2009; Helleiner and Malkin 2012).

Indeed, although financial liberalization is often seen as tantamount to a lifting of the state's control, IPE researchers have shown that, even in economies with a neoliberal outlook, state authorities that fade away from the front stage return in various forms and play roles ranging from the provision of level playing fields to the re-regulation of the market in the interests of domestic constituents (Helleiner 1995; Vogel 1996; Loriaux et al. 1997; Hsueh 2011). For a China that has never donned a neoliberal façade, it is not surprising that the Chinese authorities have assumed significant weight in the pursuit of financial opening. As this study demonstrates, alongside China's "on again off again" approach to its financial opening, the persistence and endurance of the state's authorities have been remarkable; it is they who have painstakingly propelled and remained vigilant to the market developments that might unsettle the political economic interests of their domestic constituents or generate substantial policy risk for the country.

The opening tendency became possible and sustainable not because of the retrenchment of state authorities and the inroads of market forces, but because of the accommodation of opening advocates soliciting support and preempting dissent through concessionary offers. Instead of evolving into an open financial system that might best serve investors' interests, the Chinese opening operates through and is propelled by parochial groups. Although in some cases this generates "goods" available to the public, often it does not because the most financially viable options are always watered down, tabled or delayed. This is illustrated by the many instances where concessionary offers to scale down or place restrictions on liberalizing initiatives came at the expense of market efficiency and financial convenience.

And so, short of presenting another gloomy assessment (or optimistic prediction from within) about China's financial ascent, this study points to the enduring relevance of domestic political interests—both as opportunities for and restrictions upon—China's financial opening. When the vested interests of local cadres and powerful groups resist change, pro-opening agents engage in "spoliatory politics," sharing the political and material dividends of financial opening to sustain liberalizing pursuits (Ngo 2002). The tug-of-war between the agents of change and dissenting elements has resulted in a partial and limited opening of China's capital market despite Beijing's aggressive outreaches in global finance. The scope and success of these actors ultimately hinges on domestic debate and contest. As such, projections of the future international financial power of China will find great benefit in a more holistic understanding of the domestic policymaking dynamics that have often evaded the attention of comparative and international political economy specialists.

Bibliography

Abdelal, Rawi, 2007, *Capital Rules: The Construction of Global Finance*, Cambridge: Harvard University Press.

Ahlers, Anna L., and Gunter Schubert, 2015, "Effective Policy Implementation in China's Local State," *Modern China* 41 (4): 372–405.

Allen, Franklin, Rajesh Chakrabarti, Sankar De, Jun "QJ" Qian and Meijun Qian, 2010, "Law, Institutions, and Finance in China and India," in Barry Eichengreen, Poonam Gupta, and Rajiv Kumar, eds., *Emerging Giants: China and India in the World Economy*, Oxford: Oxford University Press, pp. 125–83.

Allen, Franklin, Jun "QJ" Qian, Chenying Zhang and Mengxin Zhao, 2013, "China's Financial System: Opportunities and Challenges," in Joseph P. H. Fan and Randall Morck, eds., *Capitalizing China*, Chicago: University of Chicago Press, pp. 63–143.

Andrews, David M., 1994, "Capital Mobility and State Autonomy: Toward a Structural Theory of International Monetary Relations," *International Studies Quarterly* 38: 193–218.

Antholis, William, 2014, Inside Out India and China: *Local Politics Goes Global*, Washington: Brookings Institution Press.

ASIFMA, 2016, "Shenzhen-Hong Kong Stock Connect FAQ," December.

Auerbach, Nancy Neiman, 2009, "Financial Liberalization," in Kenneth A. Reinert and Ramkishen S. Rajan, eds., *The Princeton Encyclopedia of the World Economy*, Princeton, NJ: Princeton University Press, pp. 428–30.

Ba, Shusong, 2011, "Guoji ban tuichu de hongguan yu shichang hanyi" (The macro and market implications of the launch of the international board), *Huachuang Securities Research Report*, June 19.

Ba, Shusong and Guo Yunzhao, 2008, *Lian Jinrong Shichang Fazhan Yanjiu: Guoji Qushi yu Zhongguo Lujing* (Research of Offshore Financial Center Development: International Trend and China's Path), Beijing: Beijing daxue chuban she.

Bell, Stephen, and Hui Feng, 2009, "Reforming China's Stock Market: Institutional Change Chinese Style," *Political Studies* 57 (1): 117–40.

Bell, Stephen, and Hui Feng, 2013, *The Rise of the People's Bank of China: the Politics of Institutional Change*, Harvard: Harvard University Press.

Bottelier, Pieter, 2007, "China and the World Bank: How a partnership was built," *Journal of Contemporary China* 16 (51): 239–58.

Bowles, Paul, and Baotai Wang, 2013, "Renminbi Internationalization: A Journey to Where?" *Development and Change* 44 (6): 1363–85.

Branstetter, Lee, 2007, "China's Financial Market: An Overview," in Charles W. Calomiris, ed., *China's Financial Transition at a Crossroads*, New York: Columbia University Press, pp. 23–76.

Breslin, Shaun, 2012, "Paradigm(s) Shifting? Responding to China's Response to the Global Financial Crisis," in Wyn Grant and Graham K. Wilson, eds., *The Consequences of the Global Financial Crisis: the Rhetoric of Reform and Regulation*, Oxford: Oxford University Press, pp. 226–46.

Brødsgaard, Kjeld Erik, 2012, "Politics and Business Group Formation in China: The Party in Control?" *The China Quarterly* 211: 624–48.

Brooks, Sarah M., 2004, "Explaining Capital Account Liberalization in Latin America: A Transitional Cost Approach," *World Politics* 56 (April): 389–430.

Broz, J. Lawrence, 1999, "Origins of the Federal Reserve System: International Incentives and the Domestic Free-rider Problem," *International Organization* 53 (1): 39–70.

Burns, John P., 1994, "Strengthening Central CCP Control of Leadership Selection: The 1990 Nomenklatura," *The China Quarterly* 138 (June): 458–91.

Cairney, Paul, 2012, Understanding Public Policy: Theories and Issues, New York: Palgrave Macmillan.

Calder, Kent E., 1997, "Assault on the Bankers' Kingdom: Politics, Markets, and the Liberalization of Japanese Industrial Finance," in Michael Loriaux, Meredith Woo-Cumings, Kent Calder, Sylvia Maxfield, and Sofia A. Pérez, eds., *Capital Ungoverned: Liberalizing Finance in Interventionist States*, Ithaca, NY: Cornell University Press, pp. 17–56.

Calomiris, Charles W., 2007, ed., *China's Financial Transition at a Crossroads*, New York: Columbia University Press.

Cassis, Youssef, 2010, *Capitals of Capital: the Rise and Fall of International Financial Centres, 1780–2009*, Cambridge: Cambridge University Press.

Central Committee of the Communist Party of China, 2013, "Decision of The Central Committee of The Communist Party of China On Some Major Issues Concerning Comprehensively Deepening The Reform," November 12.

Central Policy Unit, 2007, "Report of the Focus Group on Financial Services, Economic Summit on China's Eleventh Five-Year Plan and the Development of Hong Kong," (January), www.info.gov.hk/info/econ_summit/eng/action.html.

Chan, Anita, and Jonathan Unger, 1999, "China, Corporatism, and the East Asian Model," *The Australian Journal of Chinese Affairs* 33 (January): 29–53.

Chang, Parris Hsu-Cheng, 1969, Patterns and Processes of Policy Making in Communist China 1955–1962: Three Case Studies, Unpublished Doctoral Dissertation, Columbia University.

Chang, Parris H., 1978, *Power and Policy in China*, University Park and London: The Pennsylvania State University Press.

Chen, Daofu, 2007, "Dongnanya jinrong weiji jingyan jiaoxun jiejian" (Lessons learnt from Southeast Asian financial crisis"), Development Research Center, State Council, October 10th, no. 160.

Chen, Weitseng, 2017, "Size Matters? Renminbi Internationalization and the Beijing Consensus," in Weitseng Chen, ed., *The Beijing Consensus: How China has Changed the Western Ideas of Law and Economic Development*, New York: Cambridge University Press, pp. 144–75.

Cheng, T. J., and T. C. Chou, 2000, "Informal Politics in Taiwan," in Lowell Dittmer, Haruhiro Fukui and Peter N. S. Lee, eds., *Informal Politics in East Asia*, Cambridge: Cambridge University Press, pp. 42–65.

Cheung, Peter T. Y., 2011, "Who's Influencing Whom: Exploring the Influence of Hong Kong on Politics and Governance in China," *Asian Survey* 51 (4): 713–38.

Chin, Gregory T., 2013, "Understanding Currency Policy and Central Banking in China," *The Journal of Asian Studies* 72 (3): 519–38.

Chin, Gregory, and Eric Helleiner, 2008, "China as a Creditor: A Rising Financial Power," *Journal of International Affairs* 62 (1): 87–102.

Chinese Academy of Social Sciences, 2012, *World Economy Analysis and Forecast (2012)*, Beijing: Social Sciences Academic Press.

Chiu, Stephen, and Tak-Lok Lui, 2009, *Hong Kong: Becoming a Chinese Global City*, London and New York: Routledge.

Chung, Jae Ho, 2010, "Deputy-Provincial Cities: Embedded yet De facto Players," in Jae Ho Chung and Tao-Chiu Lam, eds., *China's Local Administration: Transition and Changes in the Sub-National Hierarchy*, London and New York: Routledge, pp. 111–26.

Chung, Jae Ho, 2015, "China's Local Governance in Perspective: Instruments of Central Government Control," *The China Journal* 75: 38–60.

Chung, Jae Ho, 2016, *Centrifugal Empire: Central-Local Relations in China*, New York: Columbia University Press.

Chung, Jae Ho, 2017, "Implementation: Changing Norms, Issue-Variance, and Unending Tugs of War" in John A. Donaldson, ed., *Assessing the Balance of Power in Central–Local Relations in China*, London: Routledge, pp. 138–61.

CIRC (China Insurance Regulatory Commission) and PBOC (People's Bank of China), 2004, "Temporary Measures on Overseas Use of Foreign Exchange Insurance Funds," August 9th, www.circ.gov.cn/web/site45/tab2746/info21582.htm.

CIRC, PBOC and SAFE (State Administration of Foreign Exchange), 2007, "Interim Measures for the Administration of Overseas Investment with Insurance Funds," June 28, www.circ.gov.cn/web/site0/tab7758/info3980761.htm

Cohen, Benjamin J., 2012a, "The Benefits and Costs of an International Currency: Getting the Calculus Right," *Open Economies Review* 23 (1): 13–31.

Cohen, Benjamin J., 2012b, "The Yuan Tomorrow? Evaluating China's Currency Internationalisation Strategy," *New Political Economy* 17 (3): 361–71.

Cohen, Benjamin J., 2015, *Currency Power: Understanding Monetary Rivalry*, Princeton, NJ: Princeton University Press.

CSRC (China Securities Regulatory Commission), 2007, "Hege jingnei jigou touzizhe jingwai zhengquan touzi guanli shixing banfa" (Trial Measures for the Administration of Overseas Securities Investment by Qualified Domestic Institutional Investors), June 20th, www.lawinfochina.com/display.aspx?lib=law&id=6128&CGid=.

CSRC (China Securities Regulatory Commission), 2011, "2011 nian quanguo zhengquan qihuo jianguan gongzuo huiyi zai Jine zhaokai" (2011 National Working Conference on Securities and Futures Regulation convened in Beijing), January 14, http://cnfinance.cn/articles/2011-01/15-11492.html

CSRC (China Securities Regulatory Commission), 2012, "RQFII Investment Quota to be Increased by 50 Billion RMB Yuan," April 3, www.csrc.gov.cn/pub/csrc_en/OpeningUp/RelatedPolices/RQFII/201212/t20121210_217806.html.

CSRC (China Securities Regulatory Commission), 2013, "QFII Quota Raised to USD150 Billion and RQFII Pilot Expanded in Singapore and London," July 12, www.csrc.gov.cn/pub/csrc_en/newsfacts/release/201308/t20130815_232696.html.

CSRC and SFC (Securities and Futures Commission), 2014, "Joint Announcement of China Securities Regulatory Commission and Securities and Futures Commission," April 10, www.sfc.hk/edistributionWeb/gateway/EN/news-and-announcements/news/doc?refNo=14PR41.

Demirguc-Kunt, Asli, and Enrica Detragiache, 2001, "Financial Liberalization and Financial Fragility," in Gerard Caprio, Patrick Honohan and Joseph E. Stiglitz, eds., *Financial Liberalization: How Far, How Fast?* Cambridge and New York: Cambridge University Press, pp. 96–124.

Deng, Xiaoping, 1993, *Deng Xiaoping Wen Xuan (Selected Works of Deng Xiaoping)*, *volume 3*, Beijing: Renmin chuban she.

Dery, David, 2000, "Agenda Setting and Problem Definition," *Policy Studies* 21 (1): 37–47.

Deutsche Bank, 2016, *Investing in China's Bond Market*, July.

Development Research Center [of the State Council], 2011, "Kuajing maoyi renminbi jiesuan shidian qingkuang diaoyan baogao" (A research report of the renminbi trade settlement pilot scheme), no. 3795, March 9.

Dittmer, Lowell, 2000, "Informal Politics among the Chinese Communist Party Elite," in Lowell Dittmer, Haruhiro Fukui and Peter N. S. Lee, eds., *Informal Politics in East Asia*, Cambridge: Cambridge University Press, pp. 106–40.

Domes, Jürgen, 1984, "Intra-Elite Group Formation and Conflict in the PRC," in David Goodman, ed., *Groups and Politics in the People's Republic of China*, Cardiff: University College Cardiff Press, pp. 26–39.

Donald, David A., 2014, *A Financial Centre for Two Empires: Hong Kong's Corporate, Securities and Tax Laws in its Transition from Britain to China*, Cambridge: Cambridge University Press.

Drezner, Daniel W., 2009, "Bad Debts: Assessing China's Financial Influence in Great Power Politics," *International Security* 34 (2): 7–45.

Duckett, Jane, 2003, "Bureaucratic Interests and Institutions in the Making of China's Social Policy," *Public Administration Quarterly* 27 (1–2): 210–37.

Falkenheim, Victor C., 1987, ed., Citizens and Groups in Contemporary China, Ann Arbor: Center for Chinese Studies, the University of Michigan.

Fang, Xinghai, 2011, "Great Opportunities for Shanghai and Hong Kong during the Twelfth Five-Year Period," Speech prepared for the Asian Financial Forum, Hong Kong, January 17.

Fewsmith, Joseph, 2001, "The Political and Social Implications of China's Accession to the WTO," *The China Quarterly* 167: 573–91.

Fewsmith, Joseph, 2008, *China since Tiananmen: from Deng Xiaoping to Hu Jintao*, Cambridge and New York: Cambridge University Press.

Feyzioğlu, Tarhan, Nathan Porter and Előd Takáts, 2009, "Interest Rate Liberalization in China," IMF Working Paper WP/09/171 (August), www.imf.org/~/media/Websites/IMF/imported-full-text-pdf/external/pubs/ft/wp/2009/_wp09171.ashx.

Frankel, Jeffrey, 2012, "Internationalization of the RMB and Historical Precedent," *Journal of Economic Integration* 27 (3): 329–65.

Freeman III, Charles, and Wen Jin Yuan, 2012, "The Influence and Illusion of China's New Left," *The Washington Quarterly* 35 (1): 65–82.

Freire, Mila, and John Petersen, 2004, eds., *Subnational Capital Markets in Developing Countries: from Theory to Practice*, Washington: World Bank; New York: Oxford University Press.

Frieden, Jeffry A., 1991, "Invested Interests: the Politics of National Economic Policies in a World of Global Finance," *International Organization* 45 (4): 425–51.

FSDC, 2013, "Proposals to Advance the Development of Hong Kong as an Offshore Renminbi Center," Hong Kong, FSDC Research Paper no. 3 (November).

Gallagher, Kevin P., 2012, "Regaining Control? Capital Controls and the Global Financial Crisis," in Wyn Grant and Graham K. Wilson, eds., *The Consequences of the Global*

Financial Crisis: the Rhetoric of Reform and Regulation, Oxford: Oxford University Press, pp. 109–38.

Gallagher, Kevin P., 2015, *Ruling Capital: Emerging Markets and the Reregulation of Cross-Border Finance*, Ithaca, NY: Cornell University Press.

Gallagher, Mary Elizabeth, 2002, "'Reform and Openness' Why China's Economic Reforms Have Delayed Democracy," *World Politics* 54 (3): 338–72.

Gande, Amar, 1997, "American Depositary Receipts: Overview and Literature Survey," *Financial Markets, Institutions & Instruments* 6 (5): 61–83.

Germain, Randall, and Herman Mark Schwartz, 2017, "The Political Economy of Currency Internationalisation: the Case of the RMB," *Review of International Studies*, doi:10.1017/S0260210517000109.

Goldstein, Steven M., 1995, "China in Transition: The Political Foundations of Incremental Reform," *The China Quarterly* 144 (December): 1105–31.

Goodman, David S. G., 1984, "Group and Political Studies of the PRC: An Introductory Perspective," in David Goodman, ed., *Groups and Politics in the People's Republic of China*, Cardiff: University College Cardiff Press, pp. 1–9.

Goodman, John B., and Louis W. Pauly, 1993, "The Obsolescence of Capital Controls? Economic Management in an Age of Global Markets," *World Politics* 46 (1): 50–82.

Green, Jeremy, and Julian Gruin, 2017, "Hong Kong, London, and the Offshore Renminbi: International Financial Centres and China's Financial Transnationalization," Paper presented at the Hallsworth Conference on China and the Changing Global Order, Manchester, March 23–24.

Green, Stephen, 2004, *The Development of China's Stock Market, 1984–2002: Equity Politics and Market Institutions*, London and New York: RoutledgeCurzon.

Habermeier, Karl, Annamaria Kokenyne Ivanics, Salim M. Darbar, Chikako Baba, Zhu Ling, and Viktoriya Zotova, 2017, "Capital Account Opening and Capital Flow Management," in W. Raphael Lam, Markus Rodlauer, and Alfred Schipke, eds., *Modernizing China*, Washington: IMF, pp. 215–47.

Haggard, Stephan, and Sylvia Maxfield, 1996, "The Political Economy of Financial Internationalization in the Developing World," *International Organization* 50 (1): 35–68.

Halpern, Nina P., 1992, "Information Flows and Policy Coordination in the Chinese Bureaucracy," in Lampton and Lieberthal, eds., *Bureaucracy, Politics, and Decision-Making in Post-Mao China*, Berkeley, CA: University of California Press, pp. 125–48.

Harding, Harry, 1985, "Competing Models of the Chinese Policy Process: Toward a Sorting and Evaluation," in King-yuh Chang, ed., Perspectives on Development in Mainland China, Boulder and London: Westview Press, pp. 61–84.

Heilmann, Sebastian, 2005, "Regulatory Innovation by Leninist Means: Communist Party Supervision in China's Financial Industry," *The China Quarterly* 181 (March): 1–21.

Heilmann, Sebastian, 2008, "Policy Experimentation in China's Economic Rise," *Studies in Comparative International Development* 43: 1–26.

Heilmann, Sebastian, 2009, "Maximum Tinkering under Uncertainty: Unorthodox Lessons from China," *Modern China* 35 (4): 450–62.

Heilmann, Sebastian, 2017a, ed., *China's Political System*, London: Rowman & Litttlefield.

Heilmann, Sebastian, 2017b, *Red Swan: How Unorthodox Policy-Making Facilitated China's Rise*, Hong Kong: Chinese University of Hong Kong Press.

Heilmann, Sebastian, and Elizabeth J. Perry, 2011, "Embracing Uncertainty: Guerrilla Policy Style and Adaptive Governance in China," in Sebastian Heilmann and Elizabeth

J. Perry, eds., *Mao's Invisible Hand: the Political Foundation of Adaptive Governance in China*, Cambridge, MA: Harvard University Asia Center, pp. 1–29.

Helleiner, Eric, 1994, "Freeing Money: Why have States been More Willing to Liberalize Capital Controls than Trade Barriers," *Policy Science* 27: 299–318.

Helleiner, Eric, 1995, "Explaining the Globalization of Financial Markets: Bringing States back in," *Review of International Political Economy* 2 (2): 315–41.

Helleiner, Eric, and Anton Malkin, 2012, "Sectoral Interests and Global Money: Renminbi, Dollars and the Domestic Foundations of International Currency Policy," Open Economies Review 23 (1): 33–55.

Helleiner, Eric, and Bessma Momani, 2014, "The Hidden History of China and the IMF," in Eric Helleiner and Jonathan Kirshner, eds., *The Great Wall of Money: Power and Politics in China's International Monetary Relations*, Ithaca, NY, and London: Cornell University Press, pp. 45–70.

Helleiner, Eric, and Jonathan Kirshner, 2014, eds., *The Great Wall of Money: Power and Politics in China's International Monetary Relations*, Ithaca, NY, and London: Cornell University Press.

Helleiner, Eric, and Stefano Pagliari, 2011, "The End of an Era in International Financial Regulation? A Postcrisis Research Agenda," *International Organization* 65 (Winter): 169–200.

Henning, C. Randall, 1994, *Currencies and Politics in the United States, Germany, and Japan*, Washington: Institute for International Economics.

HKEx, 2007a, *HKEx Fact Book 2007*, www.hkex.com.hk/-/media/HKEX-Market/Market-Data/Statistics/Consolidated-Reports/HKEX-Fact-Book/HKEx-Fact-Book-2007/FB_2007.pdf.

HKEx, 2007b, *Exchange Newsletter*, January, http://sc.hkex.com.hk/TuniS/ips1.hkex/eng/newsconsul/newsltr/2007/exchange_jan07.htm.

HKEx, 2007c, "Status Report on New Product and Market Development Initiative," July 16, Hong Kong.

HKEx, 2007d, "Status Report on New Product and Market Development Initiative," October 15, Hong Kong.

HKEx, 2010, *The HKEx Strategic Plan 2010–2012*, March 4, www.hkexgroup.com/-/media/hkex-group-site/archive/invest/finance/2009/f108_09.

HKEx, 2011, Exchange Newsletter, Hong Kong, October.

HKEx, 2013, The HKEx Strategic Plan 2013–2015, January 15, www.hkexgroup.com/-/media/hkex-group-site/ssd/investor-relations/regulatory-reports/documents/2013/f108_12

HKEx, 2017, *Concept Paper: New Board*, June, www.hkex.com.hk/-/media/HKEX-Market/News/Market-Consultations/Concept-Paper-on-New-Board/cp2017061.pdf

HKMA, 2010a, "Elucidation of Supervisory Principles and Operational Arrangements Regarding Renminbi Business in Hong Kong," February 11, www.hkma.gov.hk/eng/key-information/guidelines-and-circulars/circulars/2010/20100211-1.shtml.

HKMA, 2010b, "Renminbi Business in Hong Kong," July 19, www.hkma.gov.hk/media/eng/doc/key-information/guidelines-and-circular/2010/20100719e1.pdf.

HKMA, 2010c, "Renminbi (RMB) Cross-Border Trade Settlement and Net Open Position," December 23, www.hkma.gov.hk/media/eng/doc/key-information/guidelines- and-circular/2010/20111223e1.pdf.

Hsueh, Roselyn, 2011, *China's Regulatory State: a New Strategy for Globalization*, Ithaca, NY: Cornell University Press.

Huang, Jing, 2000, *Factionalism in Chinese Communist Politics*, Cambridge: Cambridge University Press.

Huang, Yasheng, 2008, Capitalism *with Chinese Characteristics: Entrepreneurship and the State*, Cambridge and New York: Cambridge University Press.

Hui, Daniel, and Dominic Bunning, 2010, "The Offshore Renminbi: A Practical Primer on the CNH Market," *HSBC Global Research*, December 1.

Hung, Ho-fung, 2016, The China Boom: Why China will not rule the World, New York: Columbia University Press.

Hurst, William, 2010, "Cases, Questions, and Comparison in Research on Contemporary Chinese Politics," in Allen Carlson, ed., *Contemporary Chinese Politics: New Sources, Methods, and Field Strategies*, New York: Cambridge University Press, pp. 162–77.

International Monetary Fund, 2016, *Annual Report on Exchange Arrangements and Exchange Restrictions 2016*, Washington: International Monetary Fund.

ISDA, 2017, Asia-Pacific Regulatory Profiles, January, www.isda.org/a/mTEDE/apac-regulatory-profiles-january-2017.pdf

J. P. Morgan, 2005, *Depository Reference Guide*, New York.

Jacobson, Harold K., and Michel Oksenberg, 1990, *China's Participation in the IMF, the World Bank, and GATT: Toward a Global Economic Order*, Ann Arbor: University of Michigan Press.

Jarvis, Darryl S. L., 2011, "Race for the Money: International Financial Centers in Asia," *Journal of International Relations and Development* 14 (1): 60–95.

Jarvis, Darryl S. L., and Martin Griffiths, 2007, "Learning to Fly: the Evolution of Political Risk Analysis," *Global Society* 21 (1): 5–21.

Kaminsky, Graciela Laura, and Sergio L. Schmukler, 2008, "Short-Run Pain, Long-Run Gain: Financial Liberalization and Stock Market Cycles," *Review of Finance* 12 (2): 253–92.

Karolczuk, Stephane, 2017, "QDII, RQDII, QDII2, QDIE, QDLP and Luxembourg Vehicles," Hong Kong: Arendt and Medernach, April.

Kasza, Gregory J., 2011, "Placing China in Comparison: An Outsider's Perspective," in Scott Kennedy, ed., Beyond the Middle Kingdom: Comparative Perspectives on China's Capitalist Transformation, Stanford, CA: Stanford University Press, pp. 181–9.

Kennedy, Scott, 2008, "China's Emerging Credit Rating Industry: The Official Foundations of Private Authority," *The China Quarterly* 193 (March): 65–83.

Kennedy, Scott, 2011, "Overcoming Our Middle Kingdom Complex: Finding China's Place in Comparative Politics," in Scott Kennedy, ed., *Beyond the Middle Kingdom: Comparative Perspectives on China's Capitalist Transformation*, Stanford, CA: Stanford University Press, pp. 3–22.

Khwaja, Asim Ijaz, and Atif Mian, 2011, "Rent Seeking and Corruption in Financial Market," *Annual Review of Economics* 3: 579–600.

Kindleberger, Charles P., 1974, *The Formation of Financial Centers: A Study in Comparative Economic History*, Princeton, NJ: International Finance Section, Princeton University.

Kirshner, Jonathan, 2014, "Regional Hegemony and an Emerging RMB Zone," in Eric Helleiner and Jonathan Kirshner, eds., *The Great Wall of Money: Power and Politics in China's International Monetary Relations*, Ithaca, NY, and London: Cornell University Press, pp. 213–40.

KPMG, 2017, "Going Global: Trends and Implications in the Internationalisation of China's Currency," https://assets.kpmg.com/content/dam/kpmg/cn/pdf/en/2017/01/going-global-chinas-currency.pdf.

Kroeber, Arthur, 2013, *China's Global Currency: Lever for Financial Reform*, Brookings-Tsinghua Center for Public Policy, Monograph Series no. 3, February. www.brookings.edu/wp-content/uploads/2016/06/china-global-currency-financial-reform-kroeber.pdf

Kwon, Eundak, 2004, "Financial Liberalization in South Korea," *Journal of Contemporary Asia* 34 (1): 70–101.

Lai, Karen P. Y., 2012, "Differentiated markets: Shanghai, Beijing and Hong Kong in China's Financial Centre Network," *Urban Studies* 49 (6): 1275–96.

Lam, Gary, and Simon Ho, 2012, "Hong Kong Banks: A Paradigm Shift—Total Hong Kong–China Financing," *Citigroup Global Market Research*, Hong Kong, April 19th.

Lampton, David M., 1992, "A Plum for a Peach: Bargaining, Interest, and Bureaucratic Politics in China," in Lampton and Lieberthal, eds., *Bureaucracy, Politics, and Decision-Making in Post-Mao China*, Berkeley, CA: University of California Press, pp. 33–58.

Lampton, David, and Kenneth Lieberthal, 1992, eds., Bureaucracy, Politics, and Decision-Making in Post-Mao China, Berkeley, CA: University of California Press.

Langlois, Jr., John D., 2001, "The WTO and China's Financial System," *The China Quarterly* 167: 610–29.

Lardy, Nicholas R., 2008, "Financial Repression in China," Peterson Institute for International Economics Policy Brief, no. PB08-8 (September), https://piie.com/sites/default/files/publications/pb/pb08-8.pdf.

Lau, Edmond, 2011, "Over-the-Counter Derivatives Market Reforms in Hong Kong," Keynote Address at the 2011 ISDA Annual Conference: Shaping the Future of Derivatives, Hong Kong, October 25, www.hkma.gov.hk/eng/key-information/speech-speakers/eyplau/20111025.shtml.

Laurence, Henry, 2001, *Money Rules: the New Politics of Finance in Britain and Japan*, Ithaca, NY, and London: Cornell University Press.

Lavelle, Kathryn C., 2001, "Architecture of Equity Markets: the Abidjan Regional Bourse," *International Organization* 55 (3): 717–42.

Li, Charles, 2012, "'Raising Children' and 'Building a Nursery'—Additional Thoughts on the Internationalisation of the RMB," *Charles Li Direct*, January 3rd, www.hkex.com.hk/eng/newsconsul/blog/120103blog.htm.

Li, Charles, 2014, "Shanghai-Hong Kong Stock Connect," April 29, www.hkex.com.hk/eng/newsconsul/hkexnews/2014/Documents/1404293news.pdf.

Li, Charles, 2016, "Putting the Pieces Together for an Ideal Market," *Charles Li Direct*, March 2, www.hkexgroup.com/media-centre/charles-li-direct/2016/putting-the-pieces-together-for-an-ideal-market.

Li, David D., 2001, "Beating the Trap of Financial Repression in China," *CATO Journal* 21 (1): 77–90.

Li, Jianjun, and Sara Hsu, 2009, eds., *Informal Finance in China: American and Chinese Perspectives*, New York: Oxford University Press.

Li, Linda Chelan, 1998, *Centre and Provinces— China 1978–1993: Power as Non-Zero-Sum*, New York: Oxford University Press.

Li, Maosheng, and Yuan Dejun, 2003, *Zhongguo Zhengquan Shichang Wenti Baogao* (A report on problems of the China Securities Market), Beijing: Zhongguo shehui kexue chubanshe.

Li, Shoushuang, Su Longfei and Zhu Rui, 2011, *Zhongguo hongchou shangshi zhinan* (A Guide for Red-chips Listing), Hong Kong: Hong Kong Mobile Financial Publication.

Liang, Wei, 2002, "China's WTO Negotiation Process and its Implications," *Journal of Contemporary China* 11 (3): 683–719.

Lieberthal, Kenneth, and Michel Oksenberg, 1988, *Policy Making in China: Leaders, Structures, and Process*, Princeton, NJ: Princeton University Press.

Linklaters, 2017, "Bond Connect—another major milestone in mutual market access," July 3, https://lpscdn.linklaters.com/-/media/files/linklaters/pdf/mkt/hongkong/170703_bond_connect_client_bulletin.ashx

Lo, Chi, 2010, *China after the Subprime Crisis: Opportunities in the New Economic Landscape*, Houndmills, Basingstoke and New York: Palgrave Macmillan.

Loriaux, Michael, 1997, "Capital, the State, and Uneven Growth in the International Political Economy," in Michael Loriaux, Meredith Woo-Cumings, Kent Calder, Sylvia Maxfield, and Sofia A. Pérez, eds., *Capital Ungoverned: Liberalizing Finance in Interventionist States*, Ithaca, NY: Cornell University Press, pp. 208–30.

Loriaux, Michael, Meredith Woo-Cumings, Kent Calder, Sylvia Maxfield, and Sofia A. Pérez, 1997, eds., *Capital Ungoverned: Liberalizing Finance in Interventionist States*, Ithaca, NY: Cornell University Press.

Lukauskas, Arvid, and Susan Minushkin, 2000, "Explaining Styles of Financial Market Opening in Chile, Mexico, South Korea, and Turkey," *International Studies* Quarterly 44: 695–723.

Ma, Jingyun, Fengming Song and Zhishu Yang, 2010, "The Dual Role of the Government: Securities Market Regulation in China 1980–2007," *Journal of Financial Regulation and Compliance* 18 (2): 168–77.

MacIntyre, Andrew, T. J. Pempel and John Ravenhill, 2008, eds., *Crisis as Catalyst: Asia's Dynamic Political Economy*, Ithaca NY: Cornell University Press.

Mackel, Paul, Daniel Hui, Perry Kojodjojo, and Dominic Bunning, 2011, "Offshore renminbi: an Updated Primer," *HSBC Global Research*, Hong Kong, September 20.

Mallaby, Sabastian, and Olin Wethington, 2012, "The Future of the Yuan," *Foreign Affairs* (January): 135–46.

Martinez-Diaz, Leonardo, 2009, *Globalizing in Hard Times: the Politics of Banking Sector Opening in the Emerging World*, Ithaca, NY: Cornell University Press.

McGuinness, Paul B., and Kevin Keasey, 2010, "The Listing of Chinese State-Owned Banks and their Path to Banking and Ownership Reform," *The China Quarterly* 201 (March): 125–55.

McNally, Christopher A., 2012, "Sino-Capitalism: China's Reemergence and the International Political Economy," *World Politics* 64 (4): 741–76.

McNally, Christopher A., 2015, "The Political Economic Logic of RMB Internationalization: A Study in Sino-Capitalism," *International Politics* 52 (6): 704–23.

McNally, Christopher A., and Julian Gruin, 2017, "A Novel Pathway to Power? Contestation and Adaptation in China's Internationalization of the RMB," *Review of International Political Economy*, doi: 10.1080/09692290.2017.1319400.

Mertha, Andrew, 2008, *China's Water Warriors: Citizen Action and Policy Change*, Ithaca, NY: Cornell University Press.

Mertha, Andrew, 2009, "'Fragmented Authoritarianism 2.0': Political Pluralization in the Chinese Policy Process," *The China Quarterly* 200: 995–1102.

Meyer, David R., 2000, *Hong Kong as a Global Metropolis*, Cambridge and New York: Cambridge University Press.

Miller, Ken, 2010, "Coping With China's Financial Power: Beijing's Financial Foreign Policy," *Foreign Affairs* 89 (4): 96–109.

Milner, *Helen* V., 1999, "The Political Economy of International Trade," *Annual Review of Political Science* 2: 91–114.

Ministry of Foreign Affairs (China), 2009, "UK–China Economic and Financial Dialogue II Policy Outcomes," May 12th, www.fmprc.gov.cn/eng/zxxx/t562279.htm.

Mintrom, Michael, and Phillipa Norman, 2009, "Policy Entrepreneurship and Policy Change," *The Policy Studies Journal* 37 (4): 649–67.

Mityakov, Sergey V., 2011, "Sectoral Interests and Financial Liberalization: the Case of Mexico," *Business and Politics* 23 (1): 1–35.

Momani, Bessma, 2015, "China at the IMF," in Domenico Lombardi and Hongying Wang, eds., *Enter the Dragon: China in the International Financial System*, Waterloo: Centre for International Governance Innovation, pp. 291–318.

Montinola, Gabriella, Yingyi Qian and Barry R. Weingast, 1995, "Federalism, Chinese Style: the Political Basis for Economic Success in China," *World Politics* 48 (1): 50–81.

Mosley, Layna, 2003, *Global Capital and National Governments*, Cambridge and New York: Cambridge University Press.

Mosley, Layna, and David Andrew Singer, 2008, "Taking Stock Seriously: Equity-Market Performance, Government Policy, and Financial Globalization," *International Studies Quarterly* 52: 405–25.

Nathan, Andrew J., and Kellee S. Tsai, 1995, "Factionalism: A New Institutionalist Restatement," *The China Journal* 34 (July): 157–92.

Naughton, Barry, 1999, "China: Domestic Restructuring and a New Role in Asia," in T. J. Pempel, ed., *The Politics of the Asian Economic Crisis*, Ithaca, NY: Cornell University Press, pp. 203–23.

NDRC (National Development and Reform Commission), 2008, "The Outline of the Plan for the Reform and Development of the Pearl River Delta (2008–2020)," Beijing, December.

NDRC (National Development and Reform Commission), 2011a, "Zhonghua Renmin Gongheguo guomin jingji he shehui fazhan di shier ge wu nian guihua gangyao" (The Twelfth Five-Year Plan For National Economic and Social Development of the PRC), Beijing.

NDRC (National Development and Reform Commission), 2011b, "Shierwu shiqi Shanghai guoji jinrong zhongxin jianshe guihua" (Guiding Principles and Development Goals of the Shanghai Financial Center in the Twelfth Five-Year Plan), Beijing.

Nelson, Joan M., 1990, ed., *Economic Crisis and Policy Change: the Politics of Adjustment in the Third World*, Princeton, NJ: Princeton University Press.

Ngo, Tak Wing, 2002, "Development Imperative and Spoliatory Politics: A Comparative Study of Mainland China, Taiwan, and Hong Kong," in Luigi Tomba, ed., *East Asian Capitalism: Conflicts, Growth and Crisis*, Milan: Feltrinelli Editore, pp. 193–220.

Ngo, Tak-Wing, and Yongping Wu, 2009, eds., *Rent Seeking in China*, New York: Routledge.

Odell, John S., 2001, "Case Study Methods in International Political Economy," *International Studies Perspectives* 2: 161–76.

Otero-Iglesias, Miguel, and Mattias Vermeiren, 2015, "China's State-Permeated Market Economy and Its Constraints to the Internationalization of the Renminbi," *International Politics* 52 (6): 684–703.

Overholt, William H., Guonan Ma and Cheung Kwok Law, 2016, *Renminbi Rising: A New Global Monetary System Emerges*, Chichester: John Wiley & Sons.

Palan, Ronen, 2006, *The Offshore World: Sovereign Markets, Virtual Places and Nomad Millionaires*, Ithaca, NY: Cornell University Press.

Paul, Darel E., 2005, *Rescaling International Political Economy: Subnational States and the Regulation of the Global Political Economy*, New York: Routledge.

Pauly, Louis W., 1988, *Opening Financial Markets: Banking Politics on the Pacific Rim*, Ithaca, NY: Cornell University Press.

PBOC, 2003, "People's Bank of China Announcement No. 16 of 2003," Beijing, November 18.

PBOC, 2006, "People's Bank of China Announcement No. 5 of 2006," Beijing, April 13.

PBOC, 2007, "People's Bank of China Announcement No. 3 of 2007," Beijing, January 14.

PBOC Study Group, 2006, "Renminbi Guojihua de shiji, tujing ji qi celue" (The Timing, Path, and Strategies of RMB Internationalization), *China Finance* 5: 12–13.

PBOC, CBRC, CSRC and CIRC, 2008, "Jinrong ye fazhan he gaige Shiyiwu guihua" (Financial Sector Development and Reform in the Eleventh Five-Year Plan Period), Beijing, February 19.

PBOC, CBRC, CSRC, CIRC and SAFE, 2012, "Jinrong ye fazhan he gaige Shierwu guihua" (Financial Sector Development and Reform in the Twelfth Five-Year Plan Period), September 17.

PBOC, 2014, "Notice of the People's Bank of China on Matters concerning the Overseas Securities Investment by RMB Qualified Domestic Institutional Investors," Beijing, November 5.

Pearson, Margaret M., 2005, "The Business of Governing Business in China: Institutions and Norms of the Emerging Regulatory State," *World Politics* 57 (2): 296–322.

Pei, Minxin, 1998, "The Political Economy of Banking Reforms in China, 1993–1997," *Journal of Contemporary China* 7 (18): 321–50.

Pei, Minxin, 2006, *China's Trapped Transition: the Limits of Developmental Autocracy*, Cambridge, MA: Harvard University Press.

Peng, Ken, Adrienne Lui, Minggao Shen and Ben Wei, 2011, "CNH: Short-term Opportunities & Long-term Potential," *China and Hong Kong Macro View* (Citigroup Global Market), January 5.

Peng, Wensheng, Chang Shu and Raymond Yip, 2007, "Renminbi Derivatives: Recent Development and Issues," *China and World Economy* 15 (5): 1–17.

Pepinsky, Thomas B., 2012, "Do Currency Crises Cause Capital Account Liberalization?" *International Studies Quarterly* 56 (3): 544–59.

Perez, Sofia A., 1997, *Banking on Privilege: the Politics of Spanish Financial Reform*, Ithaca, NY: Cornell University Press.

Pettis, Michael, 2012, "The Pace of Financial Sector Reform," *China's Financial Market*, October 29.

Ploberger, Christina, 2009, "China's Integration into a Global Economy: A Case of Natural Economic Development or the Deliberate Outcome of Political Decisions to Re-legitimise the Leading role of the CCP?" in Zhongmin Wu, ed., *Financial Sector Reform and the International Integration of China*, Abingdon and New York: Routledge, pp. 224–42.

Prasad, Eswar S., 2016, *Gaining Currency: The Rise of the Renminbi*, New York: Oxford University Press.

Prasad, Eswar, Kenneth Rogoff and Shang-Jin Wei, 2009, "Financial Globalization: A Reappraisal," *IMF Economic Review* 56 (1): 8–62.

PRC (People's Republic of China) and HKSAR (Hong Kong Special Administrative Region), 2009, "Supplement VI to CEPA," May 9th, www.tid.gov.hk/english/cepa/legaltext/files/sa6_main_e.pdf.

PRC (People's Republic of China) and HKSAR (Hong Kong Special Administrative Region), 2010, "Supplement VII to CEPA," May 27, www.tid.gov.hk/english/cepa/legaltext/files/sa7_main_e.pdf.

PricewaterhouseCoopers, 2011, "Greater China IPO Watch 2010," July, www.pwccn. com/webmedia/doc/634459901933624430_gc_ipo_survey_rpt_jul2011.pdf.

Pye, Lucian W., 1981, *The Dynamics of Chinese Politics*, Cambridge, MA: Oelgeschlager, Gunn and Hain.

Quennouelle-Corre, Laure, and Youssef Cassis, 2011, eds., *Financial Centres and International Capital Flows in the Nineteenth and Twentieth Centuries*, Oxford: Oxford University Press.

Quintyn, Marc G, Bernard J Laurens, Hassanali Mehran, and Tom Nordman, 1996, *Monetary and Exchange System Reform in China: an Experiment in Gradualism*, Washington: International Monetary Fund.

Ramos, Roy, and Gurpreet Singh Sahi, 2010, "Offshore RMB, 2: Mapping the Pools, Flows & Evolving roles; FAQs," *Goldman Sachs Global Investment Research*, New York, August 25.

Ramos, Roy, Enoch Fung and Michael Buchanan, 2010, "RMB Liberalization Forum Takeaways: a Transforming Landscape," *Goldman Sachs Global Investment Research*, New York, August 31st.

Rancière, Romain, Aaron Tornell and Frank Westermann, 2008, "Financial Liberalization," in Steven N. Durlauf and Lawrence E. Blume, eds., *The New Palgrave Dictionary of Economics*, Basingstoke and New York: Palgrave Macmillan.

Reardon, Lawrence C., 2002, *The Reluctant Dragon: Crisis Cycles in Chinese Foreign Economic Policy*, Hong Kong: Hong Kong University Press.

Reny, Marie-Eve, 2011, "Review Essay: What happened to the Study of China in Comparative Politics?" *Journal of East Asian Studies* 11: 105–35.

Riedel, James, Jing Jin and Jian Gao, 2007, *How China Grows: Investment, Finance and Reform*, Princeton, NJ: Princeton University Press.

Robertson, Justin, 2015, *Localizing Global Finance: The Rise of Western-Style Private Equity in China*, London: Palgrave.

Sabatier, Paul A., and Hank C. Jenkins-Smith, 1993, eds., *Policy Change and Learning: An Advocacy Coalition Approach*, Boulder, CO: Westview Press.

SAFE (State Administration of Foreign Exchange), 2007, "Kaizhan jingnei geren zhijie touzi jingwai zhengquan shichang shidian fangan" (Pilot Scheme for Introducing Mainland Individual Direct Investment to Overseas Securities Markets), Beijing, August 20.

Schenk, Catherine, 2011, "The Re-emergence of Hong Kong as an International Financial Centre 1960–78: Contested Internationalisation," in Laure Quennouelle-Corre and Youssef Cassis, eds., *Financial Centres and International Capital Flows in the Nineteenth and Twentieth Centuries*, Oxford: Oxford University Press, pp. 229–53.

Schlichting, Svenja. 2008, *Internationalising China's Financial Markets*, New York: Palgrave Macmillan.

Shanghai Head Office, PBOC, 2009, "2008 nian Guoji Jinrong Shichang Baogao" (International Financial Market Report 2008), Shanghai, March.

Shanghai Municipal Party Committee, 2010, "Zhonggong Shanghai shiwei guanyu zhiding Shanghai shi guomin jingji he shehui fazhan di shier ge wu nian guihua de jianyi" (Recommendations of the Shanghai Party Committee on the Making of Shanghai's Twelfth Five-Year Plan for the Economy and Social Development), Shanghai, November 9.

Shanghai People's Government, 2006, "Shanghai Guoji Jinrong Zhongxin Jianshe Shiyi wu Guihua" (Eleventh Five-Year Plan for Building an International Financial Center in Shanghai), Shanghai, November 23.

Sharma, Shalendra D., 2009, *China and India in the Age of Globalization*, New York: Cambridge University Press.

Shettigar, Bharat, Vijay Chander and Kaushik Rudra, 2010, "Adding Dim Sum to the Menu," *The Credit Edge* (Standard Chartered Research), London, September 22.

Shih, Victor, 2004, "Factions Matter: Personal Networks and the Distribution of Bank Loans in China," *Journal of Contemporary China* 13 (38): 3–19.

Shih, Victor, 2005, "Elite Decision-Making in China's Financial Sector: A Quasi-Market Analysis," Presentation at the Centre d'Etudes Prospectives et d'Informations Internationales (CEPII) "System Financier Chinois" Conference, Paris, France, September 19.

Shih, Victor, 2007, "Partial Reform Equilibrium, Chinese Style: Political Incentives and Reform Stagnation in Chinese Financial Policies," *Comparative Political Studies* 40 (10): 1238–62.

Shih, Victor, 2008, *Factions and Finance in China: Elite Conflicts and Inflation*, Cambridge: Cambridge University Press.

Shirk, Susan, 1992, "The Chinese Political System and the Political Strategy of Economic Reform," in Lampton and Lieberthal, eds., *Bureaucracy, Politics, and Decision-Making in Post-Mao China*, Berkeley, CA: University of California Press, pp. 59–91.

Shirk, Susan, 1993, *The Political Logic of Economic Reform*, Berkeley, CA: University of California Press.

Singer, David Andrew, 2007, *Regulating Capital: Setting Standards for the International Financial System*, Ithaca, NY: Cornell University Press.

Sobel, Andrew C., 1994, *Domestic Choices, International Markets: Dismantling National Barriers and Liberalizing Securities Markets*, Ann Arbor, MI: University of Michigan Press.

SSE (Shanghai Stock Exchange), 2010, "Shanghai Stock Exchange Strategic Plan (2011–2020)," Shanghai, December 12.

SSE Innovation Laboratory, 2007, "Shanghai Zhengquan Jiaoyi Suo Shichang Zhiliang Baogao 2007" (Shanghai Stock Exchange Market Quality Report 2007), Shanghai, March.

State Council of China, 2009, "Guowuyuan guanyu tuijin Shanghai jiakuai fazhan xiandai fuwu ye he xianjin zhizao ye jian she guoji jinrong zhongxin he guoji hangyun zhongxin de yijian" (Opinion on Promoting the Accelerated Development of the Modern Service Industries and Advanced Manufacturing to Establish Shanghai as an International Financial Center and International Shipping Center), Beijing, April 29.

State Council of China, 2010, "Guowuyuan guanyu jinyi bu zuo hao liyong waizi gongzuo de ruogan yijian" (Opinion on works to better utilize foreign capital), April 6.

State Council of China, 2011, "Guowu Yuan pizhuan Fazhan Gaige Wei guanyu 2011 nian shenhua jingji tizhi gaige chongdian gongzuo yijian de tongzhi" (Note on State Council's approval of the NDRC's opinion on the leading issues of consolidating economic reforms in 2011), Beijing, May 28.

Steinberg, David, 2015, *Demanding Devaluation: Exchange Rate Politics in the Developing World*, Ithaca, NY: Cornell University Press.

Steinberg, David A., and Victor C. Shih, 2012, "Interest Group Influence in Authoritarian States: the Political Determinants of Chinese Exchange Rate Policy," *Comparative Political Studies* 45 (11): 1405–34.

Steinfeld, Edward, 2008, "The Capitalist Embrace: China Ten years after the Asian Financial Crisis," in MacIntyre, Pempel, and Ravenhill, eds., *Crisis as Catalyst: Asia's Dynamic Political Economy*, Ithaca NY: Cornell University Press, pp. 183–205.

Subacchi, Paola, 2016, *The People's Money: How China Is Building a Global Currency*, New York: Columbia University Press.

Subramanian, Arvind, 2011a, *Eclipse: Living in the Shadow of China's Economic Dominance*, Washington: Peterson Institute for International Economics.

Subramanian, Arvind, 2011b, "The Inevitable Superpower: Why China's Dominance Is a Sure Thing," *Foreign Affairs* 90 (5): 66–78.

SWIFT, 2011, "RMB Internationalisation: Implications for the Global Financial Industry," La Hulpe, Belgium, September.

SZSE (Shenzhen Stock Exchange), 2010, *Shenzhen Stock Exchange Factbook 2010*, Shenzhen.

SZSE (Shenzhen Stock Exchange), 2016, "Shenjiaosuo ganggutong yewu jieshao" (SZSE's Introduction of Hong Kong Stock Connect Business), Shenzhen, August 31.

Thogersen, Stig, 2006, "Approaching the Field through Written Sources," in Maria Heimer and Stig Thogersen, eds., *Doing Fieldwork in China*, Honolulu: University of Hawaii Press, pp. 189–208.

Thompson, Harry, 2010, "China beefing up derivatives master agreements; possible Isda friction?" *Asia Risk*, September.

Thornton, Alistair, 2012, "Anemic Ascent: Why China's Currency is far from Going Global," Lowy Institute for International Policy (August), www.lowyinstitute.org/publications/anaemic-ascent-why-chinas-currency-far-going-global.

Thurbon, Elizabeth, 2001, "Two Paths to Financial Liberalization: South Korea and Taiwan," *The Pacific Review* 14 (2): 241–67.

Tobin, Daimen, and Laixiang Sun, 2009, "International Listing as a Means to Mobilize the Benefits of Financial Globalization: Micro-level Evidence from China," *World Development* 37 (4): 825–38.

Toksoz, Mina, 2014, *Guide to Country Risk*, London: Economist Books.

Trusted Sources, 2010, "The Shanghai International Board: Challenges and Opportunities," A report prepared for the City of London Corporation, London, June.

Tsai, Kellee S., 2002, *Back-Alley Banking: Private Entrepreneurs in China*, Ithaca, NY: Cornell University Press.

Tsui, Kai-yuen, and Youqiang Wang, 1994, "Between Separate Stoves and a Single Menu: Fiscal Decentralization in China," *The China Quarterly* 177: 71–90.

Ulrich, Jing, Amir Hoosain, Ling Zou, and Henry Kerins, 2012, "RMB Internationalization: Evolution of the Offshore Market," *J. P. Morgan's Hands-on China Report*, New York, March 28.

Unger, Jonathan, 2002, ed., *The Nature of Chinese Politics: From Mao to Jiang*, Armonk, NY: M. E. Sharpe.

Vaghela, Viren, 2015, "Hong Kong CCP to be first to clear cross-currency swaps," *Asia Risk*, May 22.

Verdier, Daniel, 2002, *Moving Money: Banking and Finance in the Industrialized World*, New York: Cambridge University Press.

Vogel, Ezra, F., 2011, *Deng Xiaoping and the Transformation of China*, Cambridge, MA: Belknap Press of Harvard University Press.

Vogel, Steven K., 1996, *Freer Markets, More Rules: Regulatory Reform in Advanced Industrial Countries*, Ithaca, NY: Cornell University Press.

Walter, Andrew, 2008, *Governing Finance: East Asia's Adoption of International Standards*, Ithaca, NY: Cornell University Press.

Walter, Carl E., and Fraser J. T. Howie, 2001, *"To Get Rich is Glorious!": China's Stock Markets in the '80s and '90s*, New York: Palgrave.

Walter, Carl E., and Fraser J. T. Howie, 2006, *Privatizing China: the Stock Markets and their Role in Corporate Reform*, 2nd edition, Singapore: John Wiley & Sons (Asia).

Walter, Carl E., and Fraser J. T. Howie, 2011, *Red Capitalism: The Fragile Financial Foundation of China's Extraordinary Rise*, Singapore: John Wiley & Sons (Asia).

Wang, Hongying, 1999, "The Asian Financial Crisis and Financial Reforms in China," *The Pacific Review* 12 (4): 537–56.

Wang, Jiang-yu, 2009, "Regulatory Competition and Cooperation between Securities Markets in Hong Kong and Mainland China," *Capital Market Law Journal* 4 (3): 383–404.

Wang, Kathy, 2010, "RMB-denominated OTC derivatives poised to take off in Hong Kong," *Asia Risk*, September.

Wang, Kathy, 2011, "Hong Kong moves to set 'fixing' rates for offshore renminbi deals," *Asia Risk*, July.

Wang, Ming, Jerome Yen and Kin Keung Lai, 2014, *China's Financial Markets: Issues and Opportunities*, Abingdon: Routledge.

Wang, Shaoguang, 2008, "Changing Models of China's Policy Agenda Setting," *Modern China* 34 (1): 56–87.

Webb, David, 2012, "HKEx's Yuan-denominated Gaffes," January 20th, http://webb-site.com/articles/gaffe120120.asp.

Wei, Shen, 2016, *Shadow Banking in China: Risk, Regulation and Policy*, Cheltenham: Edward Elgar.

Weible, Christopher M., Paul A. Sabatier and Kelly McQueen, 2009, "Themes and Variations: Taking Stock of the Advocacy Coalition Framework," *The Policy Studies Journal* 37 (1): 121–40.

Winters, Jeffrey, 1996, *Power in Motion: Capital Mobility and the Indonesian State*, Ithaca, NY: Cornell University Press.

Woll, Cornelia, 2008, *Firm Interests: How Governments Shape Business Lobbying in Global Trade*, Ithaca, NY: Cornell University Press.

Woo-Cumings, Meredith, 1997, "Slouching toward the Market: The Politics of Financial Liberalization in South Korea," in Michael Loriaux, Meredith Woo-Cumings, kent Calder, Sylvia Maxfield, and Sofia A. Pérez,., eds., *Capital Ungoverned: Liberalizing Finance in Interventionist States*, Ithaca, NY: Cornell University Press, pp. 56–91.

Woods, Ngaire, 2006, *The Globalizers: The IMF, the World Bank and their Borrowers*, Ithaca, NY, and London: Cornell University Press.

Xia, Bin, and Chen Daofu, 2011, "Shier wu shiqi Zhongguo de jinrong gaige yu fazhan" (Financial Reform and Development in China's Twelfth Five-Year Plan), China Development Research Foundation, Beijing, June.

Xu, Chenggang, 2009, "Discussion on 'China's Financial System: Opportunities and Challenges'," Paper presented at the National Bureau of Economic Research Conference, December 15–16, www.nber.org/chapters/c12464.pdf.

Yam, Joseph, 2006, "Market expectation of renminbi exchange rate movements," *HKMA Viewpoint*, October 6, www.hkma.gov.hk/eng/publications-and-research/reference-materials/viewpoint/20061005.shtml.

Yam, Joseph, 2007a, "Pilot scheme for Mainland individuals to invest directly in Hong Kong securities," *HKMA Viewpoint*, August 23rd, www.hkma.gov.hk/eng/publications-and-research/reference-materials/viewpoint/20070823.shtml.

Yam, Joseph, 2007b, "The 'Through Train' Scheme," *HKMA Viewpoint*, September 20th, www.hkma.gov.hk/eng/publications-and-research/reference-materials/viewpoint/20070920.shtml.

Yam, Joseph, 2010, "Off-shore Renminbi Market," Institute of Global Economics and Finance, The Chinese University of Hong Kong, Working Paper no. 2, July.

Yang, Dali, 1997, *Beyond Beijing: Liberalization and Regions in China*, London: Routledge.

Yang, Jiang, 2011, "Rethinking the Beijing Consensus: How China responds to crises," *The Pacific Review* 24 (3): 337–56.

Yang, Jiang, 2014, "The Limits of China's Monetary Diplomacy," in Eric Helleiner and Jonathan Kirshner, eds., *The Great Wall of Money: Power and Politics in China's International Monetary Relations*, Ithaca, NY, and London: Cornell University Press, pp. 156–83.

Yang, Jiang, 2015, "Vulgarisation of Keynesianism in China's Response to the Global Financial Crisis," *Review of International Political Economy* 22: 360–90.

Yeung, Benjamin, 2008, "China in the Era of Globalization: The Emergence of the Discourse on Economic Security," *Pacific Review* 21 (5): 635–60.

Yi, Gang (Deputy PBOC Governor), 2008, *"The* Development of SHIBOR as a Market Benchmark," Speech at the 2008 SHIBOR Work Conference, Beijing, January 11.

Yu, Yong-ding, 2012, "Revisiting the Internationalization of Yuan," Asian Development Bank Working Paper, no. 366, July, www.adb.org/publications/revisiting-internationalization-yuan.

Zhang, Cinder Xinde, and Tao-Hsien Dolly King, 2010, "The Decision to List Abroad: The Case of ADRs and Foreign IPOs by Chinese Companies," *Journal of Multinational Financial Management* 20 (1): 71–92.

Zhang, Jianjun (Deputy Governor of PBOC Shenzhen Branch), 2008, "Zhongguo xianjin guanli de zhidu yanjiu: Shenzhen anli" (A study of cash management system of China: The case of Shenzhen), *Shenzhen Finance* 8.

Zhao, Simon X. B., 2003, "Spatial Restructuring of Financial Centers in Mainland China and Hong Kong: A Geography of Finance Perspective," *Urban Affairs Review* 38: 535–71.

Zhao, Suisheng, 1993, "Deng Xiaoping's Southern Tour: Elite Politics in Post-Tiananmen China," *Asian Survey* 33 (8): 739–56.

Zhao, Suisheng, 1995, "The Structure of Authority and Decision-Making: A Theoretical Framework," in Carol Lee Hamrin and Suisheng Zhao, eds., *Decision-Making in Deng's China*, New York: M. E. Sharpe Press, pp. 233–45.

Zhu, Yapeng, 2012, "Policy Entrepreneurs, Civil Engagement and Local Policy Innovation in China: Housing Monetarisation Reform in Guizhou Province," *The Australian Journal of Public Administration* 71 (2): 191–200.

Zhu, Yue, Timothy Moe, Christopher Eoyang, Hanfeng Wang, and Ben Bei, 2011, "Next Station Shanghai," *Goldman Sachs Global Economics, Commodities and Strategy Research*, New York, May 30.

Zweig, David, 2001, "China's Stalled 'Fifth Wave': Zhu Rongji's Reform Package of 1998–2000," *Asian Survey* 41 (2): 231–47.

Zweig, David, 2002, *Internationalizing China: Domestic Interests and Global Linkages*, Ithaca, NY: Cornell University Press.

Index

Page numbers in **bold** denote figures, those in *italics* denote tables.

European Union (EU) 106
exchange rates: politics 167
Exchange Trade Funds (ETF) 16, 31, 48,
  50, 53, 69, 147, 153; as alternative to
  Through Train scheme 69–71; and
  cross-border investment 70; domestic
  equity-linked 70; Hong Kong-linked
  71, 73, 75, 149, 158; market growth of
  70; pricing of 71; product development
  for overseas markets 71; T + 1 and T +
  2 trade settlement arrangement 71

Fang, Xinghai 56, 98, 111, 127, 140
finance, China's politics of 167
financial bureaucracy 1, 13, 44, 56, 62,
  114, 121, 122, 148, 152, 171;
  assessments of the international board
  111; central bureaucratic actors 32–3; at
  central government level 32; channels of
  164; deliberations over listing methods
  88; fast tracking of Through Train
  initiative 60–1; financial opening,
  impact of 36; intra-elite competition in
  32; opposition from within 63–5;
  political commitment within 153; on
  renminbi trade settlement 162; on risk
  of the bankruptcy 135; role in
  policymaking process 167; technical and
  regulatory issues 64
financial cooperation, cross-border 56
financial globalization 3
financial innovation 5, 9, 60, 69, 141
financial interests: analyses of 172–3; and
  China's political economy 172
financial liberalization, in China 2–3, 5,
  24, 176; after WTO accession 53;
  ancillary risks of 37; attempts at 14–15;
  beneficiaries of 35; control of short-term
  capital flows during 65; endogenous 6;
  genesis of 11–12; initiatives in equity
  markets for 6; interest rate 14; IPE
  scholarship of 7; outcomes of 11; policy
  reversal and 12–13; reform agenda 163;
  social costs of 37; stagnant domestic
  13–14
financial opening, in China 3; agenda-
  setting politics 17; attempts at 14–15;
  basic style of 4; bureaucratic actors and
  financial interests in 6–7; central
  bureaucratic actors in 32–3; changing
  policy tendencies of 24–5; concessionary
  politics in 17; decision making of
  10–11; distributional implications of
  34–6; domestic actors in 29–33;

domestic financial reforms 4; dynamics
  of policy changes in 9–11; entry and
  ownership restrictions 14; external
  leverages for 4; financial industry
  interests in 30–1; financial repression
  and selective opening 5–6; impact on
  financial bureaucracy 36; internal
  opening 14; local authorities of financial
  centers 29–30; mechanisms of policy
  change for 39–46; policy risk of 36–9;
  political origins of 3–11, 28; regulatory
  approach to 6; role of state authorities
  in 4; state as analytical focus in 4–5;
  styles of 4, 46, 169; subnational
  governments and 7–9; three episodes of
  15–16, 30, 171; two determinants of
  actors' positions on 33–9
financial product development 70–1, 93,
  122, 153
financial reforms, in China 6, 9, 65, 121;
  domestic 149; "Trojan horse" strategy
  for 121
financial safety net 65
financial security 3, 5, 13, 65
Financial Service Development Council
  (FSDC) 74, 142
financial services: evolution of 17; foreign
  financiers 174; internationalization of
  2–3; policy agendas and priorities 163;
  state's responses to foreign entry into 6
financial stability, of China 63, 149;
  Through Train scheme, impact of 64
financial transactions, cross-border 67–8
Five-Year Plan: eleventh (2006–2010)
  59–60, 95; twelfth (2011–15) 69, 112,
  139
foreign asset management *see* asset
  management
foreign currency holdings 56, 59;
  investment opportunities using 61
foreign direct investment (FDI) 13, 56,
  87, 99, 168
foreign exchange: management of 108;
  reserves in China 57
foreign firms, valuation of 105–7
foreign institutional investors 56, 147
foreign reserve accumulation 61
foreign securities *see* securities issuances, by
  foreign firms
foreign-owned enterprise 173
"fragmented authoritarianism" model, for
  economic reform 10, 25, 28, 40, 42
Free Trade Zone (FTZ) 74, 77, 112, 114
FTSE100, 70

For Product Safety Concerns and Information please contact our EU
representative GPSR@taylorandfrancis.com
Taylor & Francis Verlag GmbH, Kaufingerstraße 24, 80331 München, Germany

www.ingramcontent.com/pod-product-compliance
Ingram Content Group UK Ltd.
Pitfield, Milton Keynes, MK11 3LW, UK
UKHW021612240425
457818UK00018B/512